From

VINES *to* WINES

THE COMPLETE GUIDE
to Growing Grapes & Making Your Own Wine

5th edition

Jeff Cox

Foreword by Tim Mondavi

Storey Publishing

The mission of Storey Publishing is to serve our customers by publishing practical information that encourages personal independence in harmony with the environment.

Edited by Carleen Madigan and Nancy Ringer
Cover design by Alethea Morrison
Book design by Jeff Stiefel
Index by Christine R. Lindemer, Boston Road Communications
Cover photography by © Brzozowska/iStockphoto.com (back), Mars Vilaubi (bottom front), and © Purestock/Getty Images (top front and spine)
Illustrations by Alison Kolesar, except pages 82 and 116 by the author

Storey Publishing
210 MASS MoCA Way
North Adams, MA 01247
www.storey.com

Printed in United States by Sheridan Books, Inc.
10 9 8 7 6 5 4

Library of Congress Cataloging-in-Publication Data

Cox, Jeff, 1940–
  From vines to wines : the complete guide to growing grapes and making your own wine /
      by Jeff Cox. — 5th edition.
    pages cm
  Includes index.
  ISBN 978-1-61212-438-4 (pbk. : alk. paper)
  ISBN 978-1-61212-439-1 (ebook) 1. Viticulture. 2. Wine and wine making. 3. Viticulture—
      United States. I. Title.
SB389.C69 2015
634.8—dc23

                              2014033708

CONTENTS

List of Tables   v

Acknowledgments   vi

Foreword by Tim Mondavi   vii

Preface   viii

Introduction: Making Wine   1

Part 1: Selecting the Vines

The Secrets of Good Wine   11

The Origin of Classic Wine Grapes   12

A Self-Education in Wine   15

Vinifera in the United States   19

Identifying Wine-Growing Areas   21

Part 2: Growing the Grapes

Parts of the Grapevine   36

How Much Wine to Make   37

Finding a Favorable Site   41

Grape Trellises   50

Constructing a Trellis   56

Ordering and Planting Grapestock   60

Managing Vineyard Rows and Aisles   64

Irrigation   68

Pruning in the First Two Years   69

Establishing a Training System   75

Pruning Mature Vines   77

Cluster Thinning   93

Training Systems Illustrated   96

Pest Control Strategies   102

Fertilization   105

Tending Grape Crops   108

Determining Ripeness   108

Harvesting Botrytized Grapes   117

Weather as a Harvest Factor   117

Harvesting   118

Part 3: Making the Wine

Crush Immediately after Picking 120

Decisions of the First Few Days 123

The Primary Fermentation 146

The Secondary Fermentation 153

The First Racking 157

Cold Stabilization 159

Using Barrels 160

Further Racking and Aging 168

Wine Disorders 170

Filtering 172

Fining 172

Blending 173

Final Measurements before Bottling 175

Bottling 176

Corking 179

Labeling 180

Making Sparkling Wine 182

Cellaring the Wine 202

Wine Accoutrements 204

Sensory Evaluation of Wine 207

Appendix 1. The Home Winemaker's Record Book 212

Appendix 2. For More Information 214

Appendix 3. Sources of Supplies 218

Appendix 4. Sources for Grapevines 221

Appendix 5. Grape Pests and Diseases 222

Index

243

Tables

1. An Overview of the Major Steps　　　　6

2. Recommended Wine Grapes for U.S. Regions　　　　26

3. Heat Summations at Various Towns and Cities
   in California by Climatic Regions　　　　30

4. Vinifera in California — Habits and Regional Suitability　　　　33

5. Superior Wine Grapes for California's Hot Regions　　　　34

6. A Guide to Vine Spacing　　　　40

7. Index of Sunlight Received by Various Slopes (45° North Latitude)　　　　42

8. Index of Sunlight Received at Various Latitudes (15° Slope)　　　　43

9. Soil Types in Wine Regions of France　　　　44

10. Growing Seasons　　　　52

11. Trellising Systems　　　　56

12. Cane-Length Pruning Recommendations for Eastern Regions　　　　82

13. Balanced Pruning for Mature Vines in Mid-Atlantic
    and Northern-Tier Regions　　　　83

14. Leaf Deficiency Symptoms of Four Trace Elements
    Important to Quality Grape Production　　　　107

15. Hydrometer Readings/Brix Equivalents　　　　111

16. Correcting Hydrometer Readings Based on Temperature　　　　111

17. pH Effect on Sulfite Additions　　　　133

18. Figuring Sugar Adjustment　　　　136

19. Using Washing Soda to Leach a New Barrel　　　　164

20. Sanitizing a Barrel for Storage　　　　166

21. Optimum Serving Temperatures　　　　210

FOR SUSANNA

ACKNOWLEDGMENTS

The role of the author of a book like this one is to be a synthesizer and coordinator of knowledge — most of it developed or discovered by other people. I would like to thank the following people personally:

Jack Hudders, for getting me interested in wine. Bob Teufel and Mike Michaelson, for fomenting that interest over the years. Tom Jacobsen and Tim White, who kindly offered to read the manuscript with their experts' eyes.

Friends in the Napa Valley who took me in: Gary Wu of Beaulieu Vineyards; the Kresge family; Peter Forni; the Triglia family; Arnold Tudal; and Theo Rosenbrand of Sterling Vineyards. Also Tobey of Wine & The People in Berkeley; Tom Cottrell and Bob Pool of the New York State Agricultural Experiment Station in Geneva; Dr. Konstantin Frank; all the folks at Sakonnet Vineyards in Rhode Island; and Dr. John McGrew of the USDA.

Most special thanks to Joe Swan, Randall Grahm, Darrell Corti, Tom Dehlinger, Forrest Tancer, and Bernard Portet, who have taught me so much about wine and winemaking.

And a special thanks to Tom Tiburzi, who heads up winemaking at Domaine Chandon.

— J. C.

FOREWORD

I congratulate Jeff on this important book. Having a good understanding of the basics of wine gives rise to a better appreciation of those subtle nuances one discovers when enjoying it. Myriad details and much hard work ultimately unite to make wine the most delicious and pleasurable of beverages. *From Vines to Wines* helps provide you with the knowledge you need to become a winegrower in the best sense of the word.

I have always used the term *winegrower* rather than *winemaker* because it better expresses my belief that the personality of great wine is a manifestation of its terroir — the distinct soil, climate, and people involved in the process. The love of wine is inextricably linked to a respect for the land and what it brings us. Wine is grown, and we meticulously cultivate our vineyards to ensure that eventually there is a clear sense of place in the glass. The terroir provides the character potential for the wine, the vintage provides a unique personality, and we then interpret those distinctions in our own style.

I have always been a great believer of research, so that we can continue to gain valuable insight into farming practices that help us produce wines of concentration, elegance, and rich varietal character. For example, we have learned volumes from preserving our old vines, many of which are still producing exceptional wines of great depth and complexity. We have learned that high-density planting produces richer, more flavorful wines. We carefully match clones and rootstocks to specific soils and climates. We know that gentle handling throughout the entire process is vitally important. Finally, our belief in sustainable farming affects everything we do — as we are committed to being stewards of the land so that it remains rich and healthy for many generations to come.

The intrigue of wine is unlimited. As a winegrower, I have the great pleasure to observe the varied moods of a single wine in its lifetime — on the vine, in the fermenter, during its aging in barrel and in bottle, and in a glass throughout the course of a meal. With frequent tastings, we can see through these changes in the wine's mood (as well as our own) and understand its exciting potential.

This is the joy of wine. May it continue to bring grace to your table and zest to your life.

— Tim Mondavi,
winegrower and co-owner,
Continuum Estate Winery

PREFACE

Fresh grapes and wine are perhaps the most luscious foods we mortals encounter during our sojourn here. That's a big part of the unique affinity between grapevines and humankind. That's how the vine has tempted us to take it down from the wild trees, to protect it and work with it, so we can have its fruit at will.

The vine repays our care with lavish benefits. For three days after drinking a bottle of 1969 Chambertin, the sun and blood of Burgundy drenched my aura. The memory of the taste lingered.

Vines splurge on flavor in those very climates that are most hospitable to humans — northern California and southern France, for two outstanding examples. They seem to be luring us, coaxing us to stay and care for them, suggesting how good life can be in those places.

Not every climate ripens the most flavorful grape varieties so slowly and perfectly. But every place has its potential: in the colder regions east of Paris the vignerons take their high-acid, low-sugar underripe grapes and transmute them into Champagne. In Austria, where hard freezes hit clusters still hanging on the vine, they make *eiswein*.

In the United States, we've hardly begun to explore our viticultural potential. Who knows what vinous treasures could flow from the south-facing shale and slate hills of eastern Pennsylvania or from the fertile, stony soils of the Ozarks? Our Lafites and Romanée-Contis are undiscovered beneath forests and fences. Or, possibly, they're waiting for us in our backyards.

In wine-growing areas you see the vines stretched on their trellises, their arms wide open in welcome, or, in a different light, resembling rows of the crucified. In winter, there are the bones: black and dead-looking trunks waiting to be reborn in new green flesh. The new growth creates the grapes, develops them over a summer, and finishes its work with sugar and perfume. The ripe grapes can be transformed into wine (a totally transcendent change that couldn't be predicted from knowledge of grape juice alone), but only with the intervention of man or woman to perform the practical rituals of winemaking. Wine is truly a collaboration of vine and human, and the consummation of their affinity.

Winemaking meshes a person into some of the cycles of the vine. But to also grow the vines and control all aspects of the process that leads to wine enmeshes one completely. And once so enmeshed, the grower reattaches to the earth. Thank goodness one doesn't have to sit in *zazen* on Mount Shasta to achieve this state. It can be as simple as having a relationship with a bunch of grapes.

The relationship, however, requires the sensitivity and affection that characterize a human affair. Whether man or woman, you are the husband of the grapes. You have to understand your partner's needs and fulfill them. If you've chosen a variety suited to your soil and climate, your taste and temperament, the result can express both your property and yourself in subtly telling ways for those who can appreciate the expression. A bottle of homemade wine speaks of your industry before it's opened and the quality of your taste after it's opened.

I'm writing this introduction on a hillside overlooking the Napa Valley above St. Helena. Below me are thousands of acres of vines, just showing the new shoots of spring. Here's a whole valley exploring this relationship, a whole society devoted to perfecting the wine.

Good wine flows freely here. The people are friendly and open. Is it possible to be this close to nature in its grandest forms, both cultivated and natural, and not be that way?

Flowers, especially roses, go with wine, and as I walked the neighborhood streets in St. Helena this morning, roses toppled in bushels from treetops and hedges. Before lunch, I hiked a trail into the mountains. This is Napa at its most verdant. Columbine, iris, wild geranium, and so many other flowers cultivated with such care in America's flower gardens grow wild here, in little patches in the woods, or showing among the wild oats. A single iris by the trail, delft blue and bone white. A group of carmine columbines scattered down a slope of lichen-covered dead wood.

Because of the quality of the wines made here, people pay attention to their food. I know of no other small town in America that has as many world-class restaurants as Yountville, just south of St. Helena.

There's something wonderfully human and concise about this town's dedication to flowers, wine, and food. The community makes its own wines and profits from it. There's a *reason* for this place. It's where the good stuff comes from.

I'm in the Napa Valley looking for correspondences to my vineyard over the mountains in Sonoma County, and for clues to the attitude the best growers and home winemakers in this wine-drenched culture carry to their task. The attitude, I'm finding, is one of love for the grapevines: one must really care for them as well as take care of them.

"Handle the vine like a man, the wine like a woman," Ed Lino told me. Ed retired from the sea to grow grapes in Calistoga in the northernmost part of the valley over 35 years ago. He talks to his vines. "Now little feller," he says to a spindly chardonnay, "you'll have to do better than this." He pours another glass of Portagee Pete, as he calls the pink wine he makes from lightly crushed cabernet sauvignon, and declares, "The best wine to drink in the whole world is homemade wine." He should know. And I agree with him.

I'm writing this book to express my enthusiasm for the backyard vineyard and basement bodega. It's ritual: doing the same things year after year at their prescribed times. It's myth: some spirit of the wine definitely joins the party if the door's not closed. It's sacrament: the miraculous transformation of rainwater into grape juice into wine gets my blessing. The way is open for anyone with the proper conditions to discover this great plant-human collaboration.

INTRODUCTION: MAKING WINE

Before we strike off into grape-growing and winemaking territory, an orientation will be helpful. First, I've included a glossary of all terms you will encounter. Second, table 1 (page 6) shows the major steps in the process, describes their purpose, and lists special equipment you may need to carry them out. All these steps are explained in detail in the chapters that follow.

Glossary

Acetobacter. A bacterium that changes alcohol to acetic acid (vinegar) in the presence of air; hence the need to keep air away from wine.

Aging. Storing wine to allow it to mature.

Airlock. A device that allows gas to escape from a vessel containing wine, but allows no air to enter.

Aisle. The vineyard floor between the rows of grapes.

Anther. The male structure of the grape flower. It produces pollen.

Arm. Permanent wood on a grapevine from which fruiting wood is grown. The French term is *cordon*.

Aroma. The smell of the grape variety used in a given wine. If there's no varietal smell but there is a grapey smell, the aroma is termed *vinous*.

Basal. Toward the base, or older wood on a grapevine.

Bed. The prepared soil in which the grapevines are planted.

Berry. An individual grape.

Bleeding. The running of sap from a cut-off cane, arm, or trunk.

Blending. Mixing two or more wines together for adjustment of flavor, acid, or aromas in the finished wine.

Body. A certain fullness of feel in the mouth imparted by a well-made wine; a full structure in the taste of a wine.

Botrytis. A mold that attacks grapes. Under special climatic conditions, it can concentrate the flavors and sugars and produce superior wine.

Bouquet. The smells in wine that develop in the bottle and are especially detectable when a wine is well aged.

Brix. A measure of the percentage of sugar in the grape juice or must.

Calcareous. A soil with a lot of calcium compounds in it, such as limestone or chalk soils. Preferred in Europe for fine wine grapes.

Calyptra. The covering of the emerging grape flower.

Cane. One-year-old grape wood.

Cap. Residue of skins and grape particles that float on the must during primary fermentation.

Capsule. A foil covering for the top of a wine bottle.

Carboy. A 5-gallon (19 L) bottle, such as that used for bottled-water coolers. Used extensively in the home wine-making process.

Chaptalizing. Adding sugar to crushed grapes of deficient natural sugar.

Cluster. Flowering and, subsequently, fruiting organ of the grapevine.

Cluster thinning. Technique whereby some clusters are removed early in the year from emerging shoots. Used to control the size of the eventual crop and to hasten ripening.

Cold stabilization. Chilling wine to about 30°F (−1°C) so that potassium bitartrate crystals precipitate out.

Compost. Partially rotted vegetable matter used as a fertilizer and soil conditioner under the vines.

Cordon. See *arm*.

Corolla. Individual grape flower before it blossoms.

Cover crop. Plants grown in a vineyard's aisles to cover the soil.

Crushing. Crushing and smashing fresh grapes to a pulp to release the juice prior to fermentation.

Cultivar. Horticultural shorthand for "cultivated variety." Same meaning as *variety;* i.e., a kind or type of grapevine, such as cabernet sauvignon.

Cultivation. Weeding, fertilizing, and otherwise caring for a plant.

Disgorgement. The process of removing sediment from sparkling wine that has been fermented in the bottle.

Dry wine. A wine in which almost all the sugar, or all the sugar, has been fermented to alcohol. Any wine with less than 0.5 percent sugar.

Enology. The science of winemaking.

Extended maceration. The practice of delaying the pressing of red wine to increase the extraction of flavor and color components.

Fertilization. Adding plant nutrients to the soil.

Filtering. Running wine through a filter to remove sediment or yeast.

Fining. The process of adding a substance to wine to clear it of cloudiness.

Fruitful bud. A bud that will grow into a shoot with flowers and fruit on it.

Fruiting cane. A cane of one-year-old wood that has fruitful buds.

Graft. To splice together two different grape woods.

Herbaceousness. In wine tasting, a vegetable taste. In grape growing, herbaceous growth is green and succulent.

Humus. Fully decayed organic matter that adds structure and nutrients to a soil.

Hydrometer. An instrument for measuring the specific gravity of liquid.

Internode. The portion of a shoot or cane between the nodes.

Lateral shoot. A shoot that develops from another shoot during the growing season. Usually trimmed off.

Lees. Sediment in the fermenting or finished wine.

Legs. Rills of wine that form on the sides of a wineglass.

Malolactic fermentation. A beneficial fermentation in wine caused by *Oenococcus oeni* bacteria. It changes malic acid to lactic acid, softening the taste. It may happen naturally but is usually induced by the winemaker.

Mulch. Any covering for bare soil, from black plastic to grass clippings or spoiled hay.

Must. A mixture of crushed grapes, juice, stems, and skins. The term refers to this mixture from the time the grapes are crushed until the mixture is pressed.

Node. The lumpy, regularly spaced places on a cane or shoot from which leaves and fruit clusters form. Where the buds are.

Oaking. Adding oak flavors to a wine by aging the wine in an oak barrel or soaking chips of oak in the wine.

Overcropping. Allowing too many fruit clusters to form, which will weaken the vine.

Oxidation. The combination of air with components of fresh juice or wine. Some oxidation is desirable in the early part of the fermentation, but oxidation is not desirable at all later in the process, as it causes browning and reduces wine quality.

Pedicel. The stem that attaches the grape berries to a cluster.

Peduncle. The stem that attaches the grape cluster to the shoot.

pH. A measure of the intensity of acidity in a liquid, such as wine. It measures the concentration of hydrogen ions.

Pomace. The solid waste left after the juice is pressed out of the must.

Pressing. Using a grape press to squeeze the juice or wine from a must.

Primary fermentation. The initial, rapid fermentation during which about two-thirds of the sugar in the must is converted by yeast to alcohol.

Pruning. Cutting off any portion of a grapevine. Usually refers to the cutting back of aerial parts in the late winter to control vine size, vigor, or crop.

Punching down. Mixing the cap on a must down into the juice or ferment- ing wine. Done at least twice a day during the primary fermentation.

Racking. Siphoning wine from one container to another to separate the wine from the lees.

Residual sugar. Sugar left in a wine after fermentation is finished.

Retronasal aromas. The smells of a wine that are detected when they enter the nasal cavity from the back; that is, they waft into the nose from behind the palate.

Riddling. Periodically shaking and tilting bottles of sparkling wine before disgorgement to settle the sediment against the crown cap.

Rim. The thin edge of a wine in a tilted glass. The rim color is a measure of age and quality.

Rootstock. Roots of a grape variety to which fruiting wood is grafted. Rootstocks are usually chosen for their resistance to soil-borne diseases or pests, or because they grow well in certain soil types.

Row. A length of lined-up grapevines.

Scion. Wood that's grafted to a rootstock or to aerial parts of a growing vine.

Secondary fermentation. The slower fermentation, accomplished away from air, that reduces sugar left after primary fermentation to alcohol.

Shoot. The growing structure that emerges from buds on a grapevine and becomes summer's fruiting cane. Shoots are herbaceous and carry leaves, fruit clusters, and tendrils.

Shoot thinning. Pruning out extrane- ous shoots during the growing season so more light can reach the clusters.

Spur. Dormant fruiting cane pruned to five buds or less.

Stemmer-crusher. A machine that removes stems from clusters of grapes and crushes grapes to make a must.

Stemming. Removing stems from clus- ters of grapes before or after crushing.

Sticking. A stoppage of fermentation before the sugar is entirely converted to alcohol, usually due to yeast dying off from lack of nutrients or to chill- ing. Stuck fermentations can often be restarted.

Stigma. The female portion of a grape flower that accepts a pollen grain.

Stock. Vegetative material for planting, such as grape stock for planting in a vineyard. Also short for *rootstock*.

Sulfiting. Adding potassium metabisulfite to a must to kill or stun unwanted yeasts. Wine yeasts are tolerant of the amounts of sulfite added to a must.

Tannin. A bitter phenolic substance contained primarily on grape seeds and in grape stems. Tannin preserves long-lived wines, eventually linking with other compounds in the wine to produce color, aroma, and flavor compounds when the wine reaches maturity.

Teinturier. A grape variety used to add color to a wine.

Tendril. A grapevine's anchoring growths. They arise from shoots and wind around trellis wires.

Titratable acidity. A measure of the amount of total acid in a must or wine, expressed as its tartaric acid content.

Topping up. Adding a second and similar wine to a vessel to fill it up, when the wine you have doesn't reach the top.

Trace elements. Plant nutrients that are needed in very small amounts but are crucial to plant health nevertheless. Zinc, manganese, iron, and magnesium are examples.

Training. Tying and pruning vines to achieve a desired shape on a trellis.

Trellis. A support for grapevines that maximizes the amount of sunlight the vines receive.

Trunk. The aerial part of the grapevine that emerges from the soil and gives rise to arms and their fruiting canes.

Variety. Same as *cultivar.*

Véraison. The point in a grape berry's development when it first begins to turn color during ripening.

Vigor. Intensity of a vine's growth.

Vinify. To ferment; i.e., to charge a solution containing sugar with yeast. The yeast then converts the sugar to alcohol and carbon dioxide gas.

Vintage. There are several meanings. *Vintage* may refer to the crop of any given year. It is sometimes used to refer to the crops of years of exceptionally fine quality, such as with vintage Port or vintage Champagne. It also may refer in general to the harvest of grapes from a vineyard.

Viticulture. The science of growing grapes.

Yeast. One-celled plants that grow naturally on grape skins and convert sugar to alcohol. Yeast is the catalyst that changes grape juice to wine. Special strains of yeast are used in fine winemaking and are available commercially.

Table 1: An Overview of the Major Steps

	STEP	PRIMARY OBJECTIVE	SPECIAL EQUIPMENT
VINEYARD PREPARATION	Selecting the grape variety	To find a grape that will produce wine to your taste, and that will ripen properly in your climate and on your soils.	
	Choosing a vineyard site	To find the place on your property that will get optimum sun to the vine while minimizing frost dangers.	
	Preparing the soil	To prepare the soil for the grapevines in advance. It should be dug deeply, and fertilized if necessary, for young vines to make their best growth.	The digging can be done by hand, but a backhoe will save your back.
	Constructing a trellis	To give grapes proper trellising to achieve maximum berry quality. The trellis type will depend on the grape variety.	Stakes, end posts, wire, and wire anchors

The steps above should be done prior to planting and are best completed the fall before new vines are planted.

	STEP	PRIMARY OBJECTIVE	SPECIAL EQUIPMENT
TRAINING THE VINES	Planting the vines	To give bare-rooted planting stock the best possible start.	Pruning shears
	Training the vines to the trellis	To help the vines develop a strong trunk and arms that can support fruiting canes, and train them for optimum sun exposure on the trellis.	

Training can take from two to four years, although three years is most common. There is little grape production during this time.

	STEP	PRIMARY OBJECTIVE	SPECIAL EQUIPMENT
VINEYARD MANAGEMENT	*Cluster thinning	To prevent overcropping and subsequent weakening of the vines, and to hasten ripening.	
	Controlling pests	To prevent diseases and pest damage.	A sprayer
HARVEST DAY	Harvesting ripe grapes	To pick the wine grapes when they have optimum levels of sugar, acid, and pH.	A hydrometer, an acid test kit, and access to a pH meter
	Crushing the grapes	To release juice, color, and flavor components from the grapes in preparation for fermentation.	A grape crusher is useful for large batches (over 50 gallons), but the crushing can be done by hand (or foot).
	Adding sulfite	To stun or kill wild and unwanted yeasts in the crushed grape must.	Potassium metabisulfite powder or tablets

*Cluster thinning takes place in the spring, and harvest in late summer or fall.

	STEP	PRIMARY OBJECTIVE	SPECIAL EQUIPMENT
PRIMARY FERMENTATION	Adding the yeast	To add yeast suited to your grapes and winemaking goals.	Special wine yeasts
	Primary fermentation	To produce a rapid fermentation of about two-thirds of the grape sugars; this takes a week or so.	A primary fermentation vat, open topped, such as a stainless steel 55-gallon (208 L) drum
	Pressing the grapes	To separate the wine from the skins, seeds, stems, and sediment. (Note that the pressing of white grapes is usually done before the primary fermentation.)	A grape press, fine-mesh plastic pressing bag, funnel, and plastic hose

	STEP	PRIMARY OBJECTIVE	SPECIAL EQUIPMENT
SECONDARY FERMENTATION	Secondary fermentation	To ferment the remaining grape sugar to alcohol over two or three months.	Five-gallon (19 L) glass carboys or an oak barrel, with airlocks
	Racking	To remove the wine from the deposits of sediment in the bottom of the secondary fermentation vessels.	An extra carboy and a plastic siphon hose

The primary and secondary fermentations and the first racking or two will take place from harvest through late fall or early winter.

	STEP	PRIMARY OBJECTIVE	SPECIAL EQUIPMENT
AGING	Aging	To allow the young wine to settle down and begin to mature.	A cool, dark storage area, not subject to wide temperature fluctuations

White wines need at least six months and red wines a year of aging between the end of the secondary fermentation and bottling. Several rackings will be done during this period.

	STEP	PRIMARY OBJECTIVE	SPECIAL EQUIPMENT
BOTTLING	Blending	To correct color, acidity, or overly tannic wines, or to adjust oak flavors. Unless the blend will be better than any component wine, don't blend.	
	Bottling	To get the wine into handy bottles for further storage and drinking.	A siphon hose, corks, hand-corking machine, labels, and foil capsules

After bottling, the wine can age toward peak maturity in your cellar. Storage conditions must be cool, dark, and not subject to wide temperature changes. Most white wines will reach peak maturity in two or three years. Fine tannic reds may take five or more years. Good but ordinary reds will reach their peak anywhere from a year to three years after bottling.

Important Note

The information about winemaking contained in this book is, naturally enough, subject to differences of opinion and interpretation. Storey Publishing and I are not engaged in rendering legal, accounting, or other professional services through the sale of this book. When expert assistance is required, the reader should seek the services of a competent professional.

PART 1

SELECTING THE VINES

The right wine-grape variety for you is the one that ripens well in your area.

——————————

Being a home winemaker is a lot like being an amateur opera singer. Both activities entertain friends. When done badly, reaction can range from disgust to token tolerance. When done competently, reaction ranges from enjoyment to admiration for the performer. When done with excellence, the audience will stare in disbelief, rise to applaud, and demand more.

The purpose of this book is to bring the reader swiftly and surely to the goal of excellence. As I am a longtime grower and winemaker myself, be prepared to hear me say how I did it, but don't be tempted to follow. Rather, digest the information you find here and proceed as you see fit. Handling a living being such as a grapevine calls for skill and attention to detail. So does making wine. Both, to achieve excellence, must be done artfully. As all artists know, what works for one doesn't necessarily work for another. Same materials, same physical laws, but — *voilà!* — here a Picasso, there a Van Gogh. There's no way to teach the art; that comes from within. But if your enthusiasm waxes strong enough, art will break through. I've met many artists of the grape in my travels. All shared one common trait: they were determined, no matter what, to do their very best. It's my hope that the material in this book will help you do your very best with this delicate task of home winemaking.

THE SECRETS OF GOOD WINE

There's a maxim among traveled wine drinkers that any wine tastes best in the region it comes from (and with that region's food). If that's true, then homemade wines must taste best when drunk at home, so if you are making exceptional wine to begin with, it doesn't get any better than that. There are not many peak experiences available to us for the dollar or so our homemade wine costs. My personal peak experience came during a lunch a few years ago on a sweet, dry, sunny summer day. I knifed a ripe cheese made from our goat's milk and slathered it on chunks of bread fresh from the oven, bread made from grain I'd ground by hand that morning. I washed it all down with a thick, oaky homemade Chancellor. All three foods are the product of predigestion by yeasts or bacteria. All three involve triple partners: goat, bacteria, and human; wheat, yeast, and human; grape, yeast, and human. Lunching in the center of such a maelstrom of interspecies cooperation and pregnant numerology, I never felt more at home nor more in the right place.

Auspicious years for humankind are often years of great excellence for wine, as the destinies of human and grape do seem forever intertwined. The immensely great year of 1945 springs to mind. Human and grape collectively sighed in relief at the end of the Second World War and went back to celebrating life with the finest vintage of the century.

"The secret of the wine is the grapes it's made from," says Bill Wagner, a longtime New York State winemaker whose Finger Lakes chardonnays can give any white wine a run for its money. The winemaker's role is to protect and preserve the quality of good grapes right into the bottle. Jim Mitchell of Sakonnet Vineyards in Rhode Island, who does as good a job with French-American hybrid grapes as anyone, quotes these maxims:

- The most important elements of great wine are, first, the grape; second, the climate; third, the soil; and fourth, the skill of the winemaker — in that order.

- The best wines are made as far north as a particular grape variety will grow.

- To produce great wines, the vines must suffer, rather like athletes.

Pondering this last, Robert Weaver, professor of viticulture and enology at the University of California at Davis, says, "One viticultural theory is that a struggling vine produces better wine than one that has better growing conditions. If this is true, the reason may be that the struggling vine has smaller berries than the vine growing under more favorable conditions. Thus there is more skin (which contains more pigments, flavor, and tannins) per gallon of wine than when the grapes are larger."

The elements for great wine are just the same for the home winemaker as for commercial wineries: The right grape variety in the right climate and soil achieves the right balance of sugar, acid, pH, and flavor components. When all these things come together, the results can be spectacular indeed. The world's foremost example is the Sauternes produced at Château d'Yquem south of the city of Bordeaux. Speaking of this wine — an incredibly luscious, sweet, long-lasting, golden drink fit for toasting the Second Coming — Émile Peynaud, the renowned French enologist, said, "If you could measure a taste, an odor, you would find a number value for Yquem that is ten times greater than for a white wine. There is an intensity, a concentration, a richness, a complexity of odor and flavor completely unique." Most wines can be imitated: "One can always copy them elsewhere," Peynaud said. "But Yquem is absolutely inimitable. We haven't even been able to imitate it in Sauternes."

Wherever the property, there is a variety of grape that will produce the most excellent wine possible. Your task, long before the first bottles come to life in your cellar, is to identify that vine, for, as Doug Knapp, former president of the American Wine Society, says, "The grape makes the wine." Attempts to produce a rich Napa-style cabernet in Minnesota may be doomed to failure, but perhaps that property could be the home of the finest Sabrevois in the world. So what if it's not Yquem? It's probably a much better Sabrevois than they can produce in Sauternes.

THE ORIGIN OF CLASSIC WINE GRAPES

In order to find the perfect variety for you, it's valuable to look for a moment at the original home of *Vitis vinifera*, the classic wine grape, to see what its habits and needs are and evaluate its potential for your place. *V. vinifera* varieties have the potential to make the greatest wines. In areas where they don't ripen well or are otherwise hard to grow, hybrids of vinifera and American grapes (French-American hybrids) are often grown. American wine grape varieties by themselves can also be used.

Interestingly, vinifera is native to the same area of southwestern Russia as the original Indo-European peoples, whose prehistoric migrations carried the Indo-European language and the vinifera grape to all parts of the ancient world. Some scientists say the original home was around the Caspian Sea, while legend and tradition favor ancient Armenia. The philologists have the last word, however. The ancient Indo-Europeans most likely came from an area southeast of Poland and north of the Caspian Sea. The word sleuths know this because as the tribes migrated east to India, west to Greece, and north into Europe, they carried with them their language. They've discovered, for example, that there is a word for beech in Sanskrit, although no beech grows in India. It was obviously carried there by a people who came from a land where beech does grow. By closely examining words for flora and fauna in the modern Indo-European languages (current in all of Europe save for Finland, Hungary, and Turkey, and through much of the Middle East to India), they've located the original home in the place where that flora and fauna grow without cultivation. And it is precisely in this area that *V. vinifera* still grows wild. The vines grow wild in the trees. (Incidentally, I know a farmer near Bordeaux who grows vines on his fruit trees to this day.) According to the late Maynard Amerine, a foremost wine scientist in the United States, "The fruit of wild

The Evolution of Modern Wine Grapes

Winemaking as we know it began with native European vines of the species *Vitis vinifera*. Early explorers in the Americas found native North American grapes of the species *V. labrusca*, which seldom produced good wine.

Crosses between *V. vinifera* and *V. labrusca* were made in both North America and Europe to produce hybrids. Because most of this breeding work was done in France, many of these crosses are called French-American hybrids. They were developed to combine the wine quality of *vinifera* with the superior disease and cold resistance of *labrusca*.

Today the finest wines are still made from *V. vinifera* varieties, but there are also excellent French-American hybrids that grow well in the eastern United States.

vinifera is palatable and the wine is of a quality comparable to that made from present cultivars."

There's evidence of vine cultivation six thousand years ago in the Near East, although there's no evidence of any cultivation west of Greece until 1000 B.C. The westward movement of the vine then followed the ancient Phoenician sea routes. By the time of Christ, the first vineyards were being established along the Mosel River in Germany. The westward movement continued; it was only in 1958 that *Vitis vinifera* traveled across the Pacific from California and was first introduced to the Philippines.

As vinifera moves, local growers tend to cross it with native vines. This happened in the eastern United States in the eighteenth and nineteenth centuries, producing some excellent hybrids. In the Caribbean and Venezuela, vinifera and native *V. caribaea* vines have produced vigorous races of Criollas that suit that climate, opening the potential for a true grape culture.

Physical evidence of the migration of Indo-Europeans carrying their beloved grapes is supported by the philologists. In India, the Sanskrit word for wine is *vena*. In Italy, *vino*. It acquired an intercalary *h* as it became *vinho* in Portugal. Up north it became *vin* in France, *wein* in Germany, and *wine* in English. Although the words are different, they're obviously variations of the original Indo-European word for wine. What that word was, nobody knows.

There are many biblical references to vines. One of the most well known is found in Numbers 13:23–24: "They came to the valley of Eshcol; there they cut off a vine branch with a cluster of grapes, which two men carried away on a pole, as well as pomegranates and figs. This place was called the valley of Eshcol after the clusters which the sons of Israel had cut there." *Eshcol* is the Hebrew word for cluster. According to L. H. Bailey, the horticultural taxonomist, "*Syrian* is said to be the variety that the spies found in the land of promise. Clusters of 20 to 30 pounds (99–14 kg) are common to this coarse-growing kind, but its quality is so poor that it is now rarely grown." After 40 years in the desert, I suppose the Israelites thought Syrian was just fine.

After thousands of years of history and migration, about six thousand varieties of grapes are now grown on 22 million acres (9 million hectares) worldwide. Despite this welter of grapestock, you *can* find the variety suited to your taste and land.

The Spirit of Grape Growers

But before looking for the perfect grape to marry, be aware that you're entering into a human endeavor with a long history and a fine tradition of good humor. "The world of wine is united by a marvelous spirit of sharing and friendliness," says Bern Ramey in his book on the great wine grapes. And I remember what one grape grower said to me as I browsed the equipment shelves in the Compleat Winemaker in St. Helena, California. Without prompting, he offered this cheerful observation: "It's wonderful here. Everybody's involved in winemaking in one way or another. Nobody's jealous. Competitors share their knowledge, and they know how to have fun." Having fun is what this is all about.

A SELF-EDUCATION IN WINE

Winemaking is an immediate, year-to-year business. Finding the right vine, on the other hand, can take years — although if you select the vines carefully, it's possible to find the ideal vine on the first try. Then you must establish the vineyard and wait several years before it bears the kind of crops needed to make wine. When your vineyard does produce good crops, be prepared for them. Find a local source of fresh wine grapes now and start making wine as soon as it's feasible. By the time the vineyard is producing, you'll know how to treat the grapes after they ripen as well as before. The testing and waiting time will be a lot more fun if wine is flowing in this interim.

Recognizing Wine Quality

Understand from the outset that there's no possibility of making a fine red Bordeaux unless you live there. Good California cabernet will forever come only from California. The pursuit of quality will not necessarily be furthered by imitating any existing wine. What we're doing here is looking for unique wine of the highest quality.

To do that, it's necessary to recognize the quality in your glass. And so, I'm setting you a pleasant task, which can be dispensed with only if your palate is already well educated — that is, if it's familiar with the aromas and taste of a great Rheingau, a great Mosel, a great Champagne, a superb Burgundy (from Burgundy, of course), a great Médoc, a great Graves, and the best that Australia, Chile, Argentina, South Africa, California, and New York have to offer. There are many other fine wines from other areas, but knowing the quality that's found in the best of these places leaves you in a position to recognize quality wherever it's met and to go for it in the vineyard. The discriminating palate is the critical palate, and it's sad to see someone wrinkle up his or her nose at a fine wine, not because it's bad, but because of the lack of education of that palate. Cheap, drinkable jug wines are to be had, and serve their purpose. But quality bears an inverse relationship to the size of the advertising budget. The task, then, is to invest in the refinement as well as the education of your palate, especially by looking for properly aged wines from the best years. It will do no good to buy a bottle of the finest Bordeaux at high cost if it comes from a dismal year. Rather, if you're going to spend on the best, consult a vintage chart to help make sure it is the best — that is, a first-growth from a good year with enough age to be at its peak. Areas like Bordeaux, Burgundy, the eastern United States, and the Pacific Northwest have chancy summer weather. Some years are great, some good, some not so good, and some are just awful. California's wine country, on the other hand, has fairly reliable and steady summer weather. That means that almost every year is a great year there, and the vintage dates, while meaningful, are not as important as they are in the areas of variable weather.

For some years I didn't think California reds aged as well as French reds. That was, perhaps, because not enough time had elapsed that it was possible to taste older California reds. Now I've tasted many, and they indeed age beautifully, although perhaps faster than classic French reds. Great French reds are very much like flowers in their aging process. For years they are like buds: tightly closed, filled with promise. Slowly the tannins fall away, and the flower opens, spilling its perfume and fruit. And then its moment passes; it slowly fades into unpalatability. For my parents' 50th wedding anniversary, I bought two bottles of 1926 Pichon Lalande, a very high-class Pauillac. I decided to keep one and give them the other. My bottle had faded and wasn't worth drinking. Miraculously, theirs was glorious, like their marriage, which truly was golden. Once the bottle was opened, though, it faded within a half hour. Similarly, a rather wealthy friend who lives in New York City invited me to share a bottle of 1918 Haut-Brion with him. The treasure was intact, a veritable dowager empress of a wine, with full, if short-lived, powers. Like the woman in *Lost Horizon* who leaves Shangri-La and ages several hundred years in a few minutes, the wine died within a half hour. With great French reds, 10 to 15 years of bottle age usually brings the wine to perfection, although exceptional vintages (like the 1918, another year that, like the 1945, saw the end of a terrible war) keep going for decades. The taste and smell of a properly aged Bordeaux (cedar, wood smoke, antebellum New York City apartments) or Côte d'Or Burgundy (fields of wildflowers, bee propolis) are core curriculum for any educated palate. While California reds don't age exactly like the French, a good five or seven years of bottle age does improve them greatly.

I like California cabernet sauvignons when they have 10 to 12 years of age. Charbono, also, needs time. Pinot noirs are best from five to seven years old, while zinfandels are varietally unique when young and fruity and become more like generic old reds as they age. I like them from three to five years old. But that's just me. As you explore the world's wines, you'll develop your own taste and critical judgment. The key is how much pleasure the wine is giving you.

Courses on Wine Appreciation

The cost of a self-education will run to several hundred dollars at least, but that's what it takes. There are also excellent wine education courses given in major cities, where knowledgeable people preselect wines for their quality. This route may cost less and take less time, and you'll be assured that the wines you're tasting are first-rate. The danger is that you may be unduly influenced in your taste by the teacher or others in the class — that is, you'll be more inclined to like what the "expert" likes. Self-education has this virtue: your favorite wines will really be *your* favorites. For in this final analysis, *liking* the wine makes all the difference. People who like sweet Italian pop wine are every bit as entitled to their opinion as is the connoisseur to his or her affection for Montrachet. One would hope, though, that education means refinement, and that taste will change with experience. For someone contemplating making fine wine at home, acquiring a love and knowledge of good wine is a prerequisite for success. Otherwise, one gets stuck in the trap of the dilettante and takes the scrawl of a monkey for high art.

The vine you eventually plant for wine will be determined both by your taste (cultivated through sampling) and by your local climatic considerations. Viniferas, unfortunately, require rather special conditions to do their best, although they can be grown most anywhere. The French-American hybrids and American types do well through great chunks of North America, but their wines don't have the potential to transform themselves into the elixirs that are top-notch viniferas. I tiptoe through the last statement because

A Grape Variety Sampler

You can become familiar with the taste of some of the classic *Vitis vinifera* grape varieties by trying these several categories.

The Red Bordeaux Varieties

(Cabernet sauvignon, merlot, cabernet franc, malbec, petit verdot)

Bordeaux

California (Napa, Sonoma, Mendocino, Central Coast)

Chile

Argentina

Australia

South Africa

Washington State

Pinot Noir

Burgundy (but not Beaujolais)

Northern California (especially Russian River Valley and Sonoma Coast)

California Central Coast and Santa Barbara

Oregon

Sparkling Blanc de Noirs from any region (white or rosé)

Sangiovese

Northern Italy (Tuscany)

California

The Red Rhône Varieties

(Grenache, syrah, mourvèdre)

Northern Rhône regions (e.g., Côte-Rôtie, Cornas, Hermitage)

Southern Rhône regions (e.g., Châteauneuf-du-Pape, Gigondas)

California

Zinfandel

Northern California

California Central Coast (e.g., Paso Robles)

Chardonnay

Burgundy (White Burgundy)

France (Chablis)

California coast

Sparkling Blanc de Blancs from any region

Washington State

Gewürztraminer

Alsace

Northern California

Sauvignon Blanc

Long Island

Northern California

New Zealand

South Africa

Graves

Riesling

Rheingau

Mosel

Finger Lakes region of New York State

Washington State

a well-made French-American hybrid wine or even American grape wine will beat an ordinary vinifera, no problem. Just because vinifera has great potential in special, favored areas doesn't mean it will make the best possible wine on a given acre of soil. When it came time to choose a variety for my Pennsylvania vineyard, for instance, I chose a red French-American hybrid. On my California property, zinfandel is the choice.

VINIFERA IN THE UNITED STATES

After tasting your way through the recommendations made earlier, you'll probably be tempted to test some vinifera grapes on your site. To me (and many, many others), they simply make the best-tasting wine. And you can probably succeed, especially if you're willing to take great pains, even in the far north, to take the vines down from their trellises and bury them over the winter. But all this will avail you little if the berries don't ripen properly, or the plants succumb to disease. If you're interested in vinifera, definitely include them in your group of test vines, just to see how they do. As a home viticulturalist and winemaker, the bottom line is the quality of the wine, unencumbered by the necessity for profit, and the extra handwork vinifera varieties require may pay off.

Vinifera on the Eastern Seaboard

Because of the booming interest in vinifera plantings in the East, there are some spectacular success stories, such as the developments with chardonnay on the North Fork of Long Island's eastern end, and the plantings made by growers in southeastern Pennsylvania.

The area from the Virginia coast northward, along Delaware, through southern New Jersey and eastern Long Island, on to the coast of Rhode Island, along Narragansett Bay, and out to Martha's Vineyard, holds the greatest chance of success for commercial or home plantings of vinifera because of the winter warming effect of the Gulf Stream. Many acres of cabernet sauvignon and other viniferas have been planted here. Similarly, the eastern side of Lake Michigan, the north shore of Lake Erie, and the Finger Lakes have good winter snow cover and temperatures moderated by the water. Proximity to a large body of water is a definite plus for the grape grower. One old farmer's saying that "grapes like to see water" is perhaps a recognition that the mass of water levels out temperature highs and lows for the delicate grapes. But as one old-timer explained to me, it is more that "when the grapes are planted so they see water to the south, the sunlight bounces off the water and up under the leaves, and that helps ripen them, dries them, and keeps the mold away."

Problems in the South

The South, from Norfolk to Miami and west to Texas, Oklahoma, and Kansas, is home to more species of wild grapevines than any other similar-sized region in the world. These grapes are seldom known for the quality of their fruit, but they are exquisitely suited to the climate, which can give vinifera a rough time. Much of the region is subject to warm winters with occasional cold blasts from the north. Vinifera tends to go weakly into those mild winters, not really prepared for the odd night when temperatures get down to 10 to 15°F (−12 to −9°C). Buds swell during warm winter days, then freeze at night. Vinifera pumps sap early, and late freezes can then split canes and trunks. Pests, mildews, molds, rots, crown gall, and especially Pierce's disease (caused by a rickettsia-like organism; it destroyed large plantings of vinifera along Alabama's Tombigbee River in the 1820s) all attack vinifera in the South. Most wild grapes in the Gulf States are resistant, and some are immune, suggesting that the area is the original home of Pierce's disease. Grafting vinifera to the rootstocks of these native species can prevent soil-borne problems, but not the disease itself, which attacks the aerial parts of the vine. It is the biggest problem with vinifera in the South. Yet vintners from Tennessee to Georgia are plunging ahead with plantings of the classic wine grapes.

Vinifera at Home on the West Coast

Californians, with their perfect climates, tend to snicker at these eastern attempts to grow vinifera, secure in the knowledge that no matter what easterners do, they'll never be able to rival the soils and the weather of the Golden State and the Pacific Northwest. And they're right.

Vinifera in the Rest of America

In the most northern states, vinifera can be grown only with difficulty because of the intense cold. The Southwest, on the other hand, is blooming with new plantings of vinifera in the higher elevations. The Midwest shares many of the problems of the South, and the Rocky Mountain States support plantings at the lower elevations. Luckily, breeding programs in Minnesota, Iowa, and New York State are developing exciting new varieties with vinifera in their parentage.

IDENTIFYING WINE-GROWING AREAS

The French wine laws are the strictest in the world. In France, the term "controlled appellation" means that the wine was grown in a specially delimited area that alone has the right to use the regional name. Examples of controlled appellations are "Bordeaux," meaning that the grapes are from anywhere within that large region; "Haut-Médoc," which means that the grapes are from the specific upper Médoc area of Bordeaux, and "St. Julien," meaning that the grapes are from that commune in the Haut-Médoc district of Bordeaux. The appellations, then, cut the pie finer and finer. America, too, is delimiting viticultural areas by law, but in a different way. The process is under the control of the Treasury Department's Alcohol and Tobacco Tax and Trade Bureau (TTB). The TTB establishes new viticultural appellations all the time. New ones just named as I write this include the Moon Mountain District appellation in Sonoma County and Ballard Canyon in Santa Barbara County.

The Value of Regional Designations

The TTB designates special regions as "viticultural areas." No wine label can now carry the designation "estate bottled" (meaning that the grapes were grown and the wine was made on a single estate) unless the winery is in an official viticultural area. And no label can carry a geographical designation unless that designation is a government-approved viticultural area. For instance, if you live in Nuns Canyon, California, you can't use that name on your commercial label until you get the TTB to designate Nuns Canyon an official viticultural area. That doesn't stop us home winemakers, but a look at the official viticultural areas is interesting because it gives you, at a glance, those areas where winemaking is in full flower, where there are commercial growers nearby who can share their experiences and save you a lot of trial-and-error learning. It's a good idea to visit local vintners — commercial or home-style — whether or not you're in a viticultural area.

TTB Viticultural Areas

The list on pages 23–25 shows the approved and proposed viticultural areas to date. You'll notice there's a Shenandoah Valley, California, and a Shenandoah Valley, Virginia. Growers in these places were in a dispute over which area would get the right to the name. The agency gave a nod to the East by ruling that California's Shenandoah Valley must include the name of the state.

You'll also notice there are several multistate areas. One of the most interesting of these is the Ohio River Valley, comprising parts of West Virginia, Kentucky, Ohio, and Indiana. The designation was proposed and promoted by the Indiana Winegrowers Guild (now the Indiana Winery and Vineyard Association) and the Ohio Wine Producers Association. The Ohio River Valley was once known as the "Rhine of America," before Prohibition wrought havoc upon viticulture in this country. The area runs from Cairo, Illinois, to just south of Wheeling, West Virginia, near the Pennsylvania border. It includes 30,000 square miles (77,700 square km) on both sides of the Ohio River, bounded by high ridgelines. There's a 175-day frost-free growing season here, and the prevailing winter winds are from the southwest. A distinctive "Ohio-type" rain pattern means that the weather is changeable and moist. Gray-brown podzol soils dominate the slopes and hilltops where grapes will be most at home. The character of the valley was created by glacial erosion, which means that ground rock flours are prevalent in the soil, supplying good mineral nutrition to the vines. The slopes create the good air drainage that is so necessary in such a moist region, and there are warm microclimates that face south on these slopes, just as they do on the Rhine.

Your Single Most Important Decision

Identifying the grape that gives wine you like and grows well and ripens consistently in your climate is perhaps the single most important decision you'll make in your quest for fine homemade wine. My decision to forgo vinifera in favor of planting French-American hybrids — Chancellor and several Colobel *teinturier* vines (the latter for color, in which Chancellor can be deficient in poor years) — at my Pennsylvania property was based on the fact that the best wine I made there was a Chancellor, and the best commercial French-American hybrid wine I ever encountered was a Chateau Esperanza (Finger Lakes) Chancellor. I also knew that while Chancellor could have some mildew problems, it grows well in Berks County, isn't prone to winter kill, has no undue problems with pests, and gave me a good gut feeling.

Official American Viticultural Areas (AVAs)

The following AVAs are currently approved by the U.S. Alcohol and Tobacco Tax and Trade Bureau.

ARIZONA

Sonoita

ARKANSAS

Altus

Arkansas Mountain

CALIFORNIA

Alexander Valley

Alta Mesa

Anderson Valley

Antelope Valley of
the California High
Desert

Arroyo Grande Valley

Arroyo Seco

Atlas Peak

Ballard Canyon

Ben Lomond Mountain

Benmore Valley

Bennett Valley

Big Valley District–
Lake County

Borden Ranch

California Shenandoah
Valley

Calistoga

Capay Valley

Carmel Valley

Central Coast

Chalk Hill

Chalone

Chiles Valley

Cienega Valley

Clarksburg

Clear Lake

Clements Hills

Cole Ranch

Coombsville

Cosumnes River

Covelo

Cucamonga Valley

Diablo Grande

Diamond Mountain
District

Dos Rios

Dry Creek Valley

Dunnigan Hills

Edna Valley

El Dorado

Fair Play

Fiddletown

Fort Ross-Seaview

Green Valley of
Russian River Valley

Guenoc Valley

Hames Valley

Happy Canyon of
Santa Barbara

High Valley

Howell Mountain

Inwood Valley

Jahant

Kelsey Bench–Lake
County

Knights Valley

Leona Valley

Lime Kiln Valley

Livermore Valley

Lodi

Los Carneros

Madera

Malibu-Newton
Canyon

McDowell Valley

Mendocino

Mendocino Ridge

Merritt Island

Monterey

Moon Mountain
District Sonoma
County

Mt. Harlan

Mt. Veeder

Napa Valley

North Coast

North Yuba

Northern Sonoma

Oak Knoll District of
Napa Valley

Oakville

Pacheco Pass

Paicines

Paso Robles

Pine Mountain–
Cloverdale Peak

Potter Valley

Ramona Valley

Red Hills Lake County

Redwood Valley

River Junction

Rockpile

Russian River Valley

Rutherford
Saddle Rock–Malibu
Salado Creek
San Antonio Valley
San Benito
San Bernabe
San Francisco Bay
San Lucas
San Pasqual Valley
San Ysidro District
Santa Clara Valley
Santa Cruz Mountains
Santa Lucia Highlands
Santa Maria Valley
Santa Ynez Valley
Seiad Valley
Sierra Foothills
Sierra Pelona Valley
Sloughhouse
Solano County Green
   Valley
Sonoma Coast
Sonoma Mountain
Sonoma Valley
South Coast
Spring Mountain
   District
St. Helena
Sta. Rita Hills
Stags Leap District
Suisun Valley
Temecula Valley
Tracy Hills
Wild Horse Valley
Willow Creek
York Mountain
Yorkville Highlands
Yountville

COLORADO
Grand Valley
West Elks

CONNECTICUT
Western Connecticut
   Highlands

ILLINOIS
Shawnee Hills

INDIANA
Indiana Uplands

MARYLAND
Catoctin
Linganore

MASSACHUSETTS
Martha's Vineyard

MICHIGAN
Fennville
Lake Michigan Shore
Leelanau Peninsula
Old Mission Peninsula

MINNESOTA
Alexandria Lakes

MISSOURI
Augusta
Hermann
Ozark Highlands

NEW JERSEY
Outer Coastal Plain
Warren Hills

NEW MEXICO
Middle Rio Grande
   Valley
Mimbres Valley

NEW YORK STATE
Cayuga Lake
Finger Lakes
The Hamptons, Long
   Island
Hudson River Region
Long Island
Niagara Escarpment
North Folk of Long
   Island
Seneca Lake

NORTH CAROLINA
Haw River Valley
Swan Creek
Yadkin Valley

OHIO
Grand River Valley
Isle St. George
Loramie Creek

OREGON
Applegate Valley
Chehalem Mountains
Dundee Hills
Elkton Oregon
Eola–Amity Hills
McMinnville
Red Hill Douglas
   County
Ribbon Ridge
Rogue Valley
Southern Oregon
Umpqua Valley
Willamette Valley
Yamhill–Carlton
   District

PENNSYLVANIA

Lancaster Valley

Lehigh Valley

TEXAS

Bell Mountain

Escondido Valley

Fredericksburg in the
Texas Hill Country

Texas Davis
Mountains

Texas High Plains

Texas Hill Country

Texoma

VIRGINIA

Middleburg Virginia

Monticello

North Fork of
Roanoke

Northern Neck
George Washington
Birthplace

Rocky Knob

Virginia's Eastern
Shore

WASHINGTON

Ancient Lakes of
Columbia Valley

Horse Heaven Hills

Lake Chelan

Naches Heights

Puget Sound

Rattlesnake Hills

Red Mountain

Snipes Mountain

Wahluke Slope

Yakima Valley

WEST VIRGINIA

Kanawha River Valley

WISCONSIN

Lake Wisconsin

Wisconsin Ledge

MULTI-STATE REGIONS

Central Delaware
Valley (New Jersey,
Pennsylvania)

Columbia Gorge
(Oregon,
Washington)

Columbia Valley
(Oregon,
Washington)

Cumberland Valley
(Maryland,
Pennsylvania)

Lake Erie (New York,
Ohio, Pennsylvania)

Mesilla Valley (New
Mexico, Texas)

Mississippi Delta
(Louisiana,

Mississippi,
Tennessee)

Ohio River Valley
(Indiana, Kentucky,
Ohio, West Virginia)

Ozark Mountain
(Arkansas,
Missouri,
Oklahoma)

Shenandoah Valley
(Virginia, West
Virginia)

Snake River Valley
(Idaho, Oregon)

Southeastern
New England
(Connecticut,
Massachusetts,
Rhode Island)

Upper Mississippi
River Valley (Illinois,
Iowa, Minnesota,
Wisconsin)

Walla Walla
Valley (Oregon,
Washington)

New AVAs are being added all the time. For an up-to-date list of all the AVAs in the United States, as well as the rest of the world, visit the TTB website (see page 214).

Table 2: Recommended Wine Grapes for U.S. Regions

This table summarizes variety recommendations from growers and grape scientists for regions from coast to coast, excluding California, which is covered in tables 3, 4, and 5.

WHITE VINIFERA	RED VINIFERA	WHITE HYBRID	RED HYBRID	AMERICAN GRAPES
New York State: Finger Lakes and the Hudson River Region				
Chardonnay	Blaufränkisch	Aromella	Arandell	Catawba
Gewürztraminer	Dornfelder	Cayuga White	Chancellor	Delaware
Riesling	Zweigelt	Chardonel	Corot Noir	Himrod
		Marquis	Geneva Red 7	Isabella
		Melody	Maréchal Foch	New York Muscat
		Ravat 51	Noiret	Niagara
		Seyval Blanc		
		Traminette		
		Valvin Muscat		
		Vidal 256		
Southern New Jersey, Eastern Long Island, and Coastal Rhode Island				
Chardonnay	Cabernet Sauvignon	Aromella	Arandell	Catawba
Gewürztraminer		Cayuga	Chancellor	Delaware
Riesling	Merlot	Seyval Blanc		
Sauvignon Blanc	Pinot Noir	Vidal 256		
Northwestern Pennsylvania				
Riesling		Ravat 51	Chancellor	
		Seyval Blanc	Chelois	
		Vidal 256	De Chaunac	
			Maréchal Foch	

WHITE VINIFERA	RED VINIFERA	WHITE HYBRID	RED HYBRID	AMERICAN GRAPES
Southeastern Pennsylvania				
Chardonnay Gewürztraminer Riesling	Cabernet Franc Pinot Noir	Cayuga Seyval Blanc Vidal 256	Chancellor De Chaunac Maréchal Foch	Delaware
Ohio				
Chardonnay Gewürztraminer		Seyval Blanc Vidal 256	Chambourcin De Chaunac Maréchal Foch	Delaware
Virginia				
Chardonnay Gewürztraminer Riesling Sauvignon Blanc	Cabernet Franc Cabernet Sauvignon Merlot	Aurora Cayuga Seyval Blanc Vidal 256	Chambourcin Chancellor Maréchal Foch Villard Noir	
Arkansas				
		Aurora Ravat 51 Seyval Blanc Verdelet Blanc Vidal 256 Villard Blanc	Baco Noir Chancellor Villard Noir	Delaware Niagara
Oklahoma				
		Aurora Seyval Blanc Villard Blanc	Rougeon	Delaware

WHITE VINIFERA	RED VINIFERA	WHITE HYBRID	RED HYBRID	AMERICAN GRAPES
Texas Hill Country				
Chenin Blanc	Barbera	Ravat 51	Baco Noir	
Colombard	Carnelian			
Central Midwest				
		Aurora	Baco Noir	Delaware
		Ravat 51	Chancellor	
		Seyval Blanc	Chelois	
		Vidal 256	De Chaunac	
			Maréchal Foch	
Arizona–New Mexico				
Chardonnay	Cabernet Sauvignon			
Riesling	Pinot Noir			
Sylvaner	Ruby Cabernet			
Zinfandel				
Oregon–Southern Washington				
Chardonnay	Cabernet Sauvignon			
Chenin Blanc	Malbec			
Riesling	Merlot			
Pinot Blanc	Pinot Meunier			
Sauvignon Blanc	Pinot Noir			
Sémillon				

WHITE VINIFERA	RED VINIFERA	WHITE HYBRID	RED HYBRID	AMERICAN GRAPES
Southwestern Idaho				
Chardonnay	Pinot Noir	Seyval Blanc	Chelois	
Gewürztraminer				
Gray Riesling				
Riesling				
Sylvaner				
Northern Cold Tier*				
		Aromella	Arandell	
		Aurora	Corot Noir	
		Brianna	Frontenac	
		Edelweiss	Geneva Red 7	
		Frontenac Blanc	King of the North	
		Frontenac Gris	Léon Millot	
		Louise Swenson	Maréchal Foch	
		La Crescent	Marquette	
		LaCrosse	Noiret	
		Prairie Star	Sabrevois	
		Ravat 51	St. Croix	
		Seyval Blanc	Swenson Red	
		St. Pepin	Valvin Muscat	
		Swenson White		
		Zilga		

Includes Eastern Washington, northern Idaho, Montana, North Dakota, South Dakota, Nebraska, Iowa, Minnesota, Wisconsin, northern Michigan, Illinois, Indiana, central Ohio, northern New York, Vermont, New Hampshire, Maine, and the southern parts of Canada's provinces. Michigan home winemakers should check with wineries in their area about the possibility of growing varieties of Vitis vinifera, as riesling, pinot noir, chardonnay, pinot gris, and cabernet franc have been shown to grow well in the warmer and lake-moderated parts of the state.

Southeast and Gulf States

Due to special conditions, varieties of muscadine (*Muscadinia rotundifolia*) are recommended for this region. They are classified as bronze, black, or white. Bunch grape varieties that will grow in the Southeast include Moored, Alwood, Delaware, Rougeon, and Rosette.

Bronze	Black	White
Carlos	Bountiful	Dearing
Magnolia	Chief	Dixie
Scuppernong	Cowart	Higgins
	Noble	

Table 3: Heat Summations at Various Towns and Cities in California by Climatic Regions

Grapes just love California, and you can grow just about anything in this state. But there are wide climatic differences within the state, and the various grapes do best in different regions. The following table lists cities and towns by region and heat summation (total degrees above 50°F/10°C over the growing season).

Region 1 (less than 2,500)	
TOWN OR CITY	HEAT SUMMATION
Branscomb	1,810
Lompoc	1,970
Watsonville	2,090
Bonny Doon	2,140
Campbell	2,160
Blocksburg	2,230
Riverside	2,240
Santa Cruz	2,320
Woodside	2,320
Gonzales	2,350
Betteravia	2,370
Hayward	2,370
Peachland	2,380
Ben Lomond	2,390
Suyamaca	2,410
Santa Maria	2,490

Region 2 (2,501–3,000)	
TOWN OR CITY	HEAT SUMMATION
Willits	2,520
Santa Clara	2,550
Weaverville	2,550
Palo Alto	2,590
San Luis Obispo	2,620
Gilroy	2,630
Sebastopol	2,630
Covelo	2,710
Petaluma	2,740
Dyerville	2,750
San Jose	2,760
Crocket	2,840
Atascadero	2,870
Redwood City	2,870
Los Gatos	2,880
Napa	2,880
San Mateo	2,880
Santa Barbara	2,880
Soledad	2,880
Hollister	2,890
Kelseyville	2,930
Santa Rosa	2,950
Placerville	2,980

Region 3 (3,001–3,500)	
TOWN OR CITY	HEAT SUMMATION
Oakville	3,100
Paso Robles	3,100
Ukiah	3,100
Calistoga	3,150
Hopland	3,150
King City	3,150
St. Helena	3,170
Santa Margarita	3,180
Healdsburg	3,190
Poway	3,220
Clear Lake Park	3,260
Pinnacles	3,330
Cuyama	3,340
Santa Ana	3,360
Camino	3,400
Livermore	3,400
Mokelumne Hill	3,400
Potter Valley	3,420
Cloverdale	3,430
Ramona	3,470
Mandeville Island	3,480
Martinez	3,500

Region 4 (3,501–4,000)	
TOWN OR CITY	**HEAT SUMMATION**
Escondido	3,510
Upland	3,520
Colfax	3,530
Suisun	3,530
Turlock	3,600
Linden	3,620
Vista	3,660
Pomona	3,680
Lodi	3,720
Nacimiento	3,740
David	3,780
Vacaville	3,780
Sacramento	3,830
Delta	3,850
Clarksburg	3,860
Sonora	3,880
San Miguel	3,890
Fontana	3,900
Auburn	3,990

Region 5 (4,001 or more)	
TOWN OR CITY	**HEAT SUMMATION**
Modesto	4,010
Ojai	4,010
Oakdale	4,030
Brentwood	4,100
Stockton	4,160
Antioch	4,200
Woodland	4,210
Merced	4,410
Reedley	4,410
Chico	4,450
Fresno	4,680
Red Bluff	4,930
Bakersfield	5,080

Source: Winkler et al., *General Viticulture*

Table 4: Vinifera in California — Habits & Regional Suitability

VARIETY	WINE COLOR	MOST SUITABLE VITICULTURAL REGION(S)	TIME OF MATURITY*
Barbera	Red	III, IV	Midseason
Burger	White	IV, V	Late
Cabernet franc	Red	I–III	Midseason
Cabernet Sauvignon	Red	I–III	Late midseason
Carignane	Red	III, IV	Late midseason
Charbono	Red	II–IV	Midseason
Chardonnay	White	I–III	Early
Chenin Blanc	White	II–V	Midseason
Colombard	White	III–V	Midseason
Emerald Riesling	White	II, III	Late
Flora	White	I–III	Early
Gamay	Red	II, III	Late midseason
Gamay Beaujolais	Red	I, II, cooler parts of III	Early
Gewürztraminer	White	I	Early
Grenache	Rose	II–V	Late midseason
Grignolino	Red	II–IV	Early
Malbec	Red	II, III	Midseason
Malvasia Bianca	White	III, IV	Midseason
Marsanne	White	II	Early midseason
Merlot	Red	II, III	Midseason
Mission	Red	III–V	Late midseason
Mourvèdre	Red	II, III	Late midseason
Muscat of Alexandria	White	IV, V	Late midseason
Nebbiolo	Red	III, IV	Late
Palomino	White	IV, V	Late midseason
Petit Verdot	Red	II, III	Late midseason
Petite Sirah	Red	II, cooler parts of III	Early midseason
Pinot Blanc	White	II, III	Early midseason
Pinot Noir	Red	I	Early

VARIETY	WINE COLOR	MOST SUITABLE VITICULTURAL REGION(S)	TIME OF MATURITY*
Riesling	White	I, cooler parts of II	Early midseason
Roussanne	White	II	Early midseason
Royalty	Red	IV, V	Midseason
Rubired	Red	IV, V	Midseason
Ruby Cabernet	Red	IV, V	Late midseason
Saint-Émilion	White	II, III	Late
Salvador	Red	IV, V	Late midseason
Sangiovese	Red	II, III	Midseason
Sauvignon Blanc	White	II	Midseason
Sémillon	White	III	Early midseason
Sylvaner	White	II, III	Early
Syrah	Red	II–IV	Midseason
Tinta Madeira	Red	III–V	Early
Zinfandel	Red	I–IV**	Early midseason

Sources: Winkler et al., *General Viticulture*; Weaver, *Grape Growing*;
Jackson and Schuster, *Grape Growing and Winemaking*.
*Early grapes require heat summations of at least 1600 to ripen. Late grapes require at least 3500.
**Gives a different style in each region.

Table 5: Superior Wine Grapes for California's Hot Regions

These grape varieties are suitable for zones IV and V, where heat summations
rise above 3,500 degrees Fahrenheit.

WHITE TABLE WINES	WHITE DESSERT WINES	RED TABLE WINES	RED DESSERT WINES
Chenin Blanc	Mission	Barbera	Carignane (for port)
Colombard	Muscat Blanc	Carignane	Rubired
	Muscat of Alexandria	Grenache	Tinta Madeira
	Palomino (for sherry)	Rubired	
		Ruby Cabernet	

Source: University of California at Davis

---------------------------- **PART 2** ----------------------------

GROWING THE GRAPES

The sun, with all those planets revolving around it and dependent on it, can still ripen a bunch of grapes as if it had nothing else in the universe to do.
— Galileo

After the selection of a grape variety, the next most important factor in achieving fine wine at home is the selection of a site. It's entirely possible to plant the right variety in the wrong place and end up with poor wine at best, while a site 100 feet away that would ripen the grapes to perfection lies fallow. It happens all the time. Thousands of years of trial and error with French sites have brought us to an era when we can identify by name the few precious acres that produce the world's finest wines. To show how proper site conditions can affect the value of property, ask the price of an acre of Château Lafite Rothschild, or talk to a real estate agent in Napa County about per-acre prices in 1970 compared with the current rates for vine-growing land. You couldn't buy an acre of Lafite, and there are similarly priceless acres developing up and down the coastal spine of California.

In California, the process of fine-tuning site selection is in full swing. The recurrence of phylloxera in the late 1980s and 1990s forced the replanting of huge amounts of vineyard land — expensive, but a blessing. Vineyardists who otherwise wouldn't have touched a vineyard replanted to more suitable varieties on better rootstocks at closer spacings. We will be reaping the benefits in our wineglasses for years to come.

Imagine a property for sale on a hill above a river. Four acres and a nice house. On the south slope of the hill is a 2-acre (0.8 ha) vineyard, and the seller pulls the cork on a red wine he made from that vineyard's grapes. It's delicious. How much do you add to the value of the place? Give the buyer another glass and think big.

PARTS OF THE GRAPEVINE

A grapevine has a surprising amount of nomenclature. Here you'll find illustrated the specific parts that will come up in our discussions of vineyard and winemaking operations. Of course, other vine anatomy, mostly microscopic or internal, though not shown here, abounds.

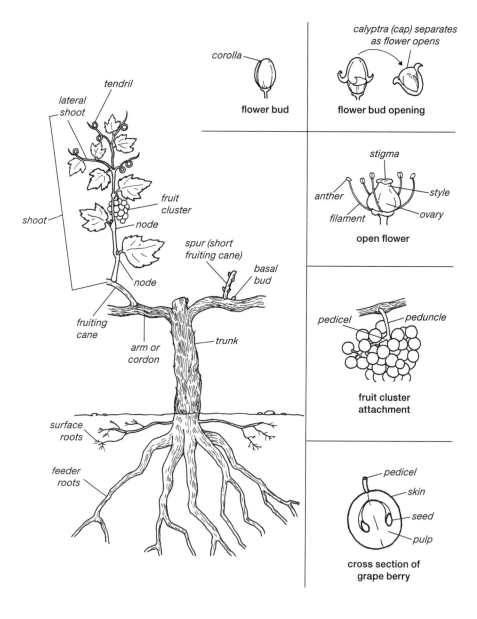

calyptra (cap) separates as flower opens

corolla

flower bud

flower bud opening

tendril

lateral shoot

stigma

anther

style

filament

ovary

open flower

fruit cluster

shoot

node

spur (short fruiting cane)

basal bud

node

fruiting cane

arm or cordon

trunk

pedicel

peduncle

fruit cluster attachment

surface roots

feeder roots

pedicel

skin

seed

pulp

cross section of grape berry

HOW MUCH WINE TO MAKE

Selecting a site begins with deciding how many gallons of wine you want to make each year. That decision affects all the others.

One gallon (3.8 L) fills 5 bottles of wine. You'll have to wash 500 bottles to antiseptic purity if you make 100 gallons (380 L) of wine. Ponder for a moment the triple washing and rinsing of 500 bottles. Now think again about how much wine you want to make. (You can, of course, avoid this task by buying new wine bottles.) Personally, I make about 40 gallons (151 L) most years.

Computing the Size of a Vineyard

In computing the size of the vineyard needed to produce the amount of wine you've decided on, let's begin with a few assumptions:

- A mature grapevine yields from 8 to 12 pounds (3.6–5.4 kg) of grapes.

- 11 to 12 pounds (5.0–5.4 kg) of grapes yields 1 gallon (3.8 L) of finished wine.

- Vines are planted 6 feet (1.8 m) apart in rows 10 feet (3.1 m) apart, totaling 650 vines per acre (267 vines per hectare).

And you'll need to know the following variables:

x = gallons of wine desired

z = number of vines in each row

a = number of rows

y = pounds of grapes per vine

In general, you can assume yields-per-vine of 8 pounds (3.6 kg) for classic vinifera and low-yielding varieties; 10 pounds (4.5 kg) for most French-American hybrids; 12 pounds (5.4 kg) for Cayuga and high-yielding American vines; and 16 pounds (7.3 kg) for Mission, Thompson Seedless, and muscadines.

Calculating the Number of Vines

To determine the number of vines you need to make x gallons of wine:

$$\frac{x \times 11}{y}$$

For example, to make 25 gallons (95 L) of Cayuga, which yields 12 pounds (5.4 kg) per vine, you'd need:

$$\frac{25 \times 11}{12} = 22.9, \text{ or 23 vines}$$

Calculating the Size of the Vineyard

Only you know whether your property allows for a square, a rectangular, or an odd-shaped vineyard. Assuming that space is not constricted, you can achieve a good-looking rectangular arrangement by having about as many rows as vines in a row.

With 100 vines, for example, you could have a vineyard of 10 rows ($a = 10$), with 10 vines in the row ($z = 10$). With 60 vines you could have a vineyard of 7 rows, with 8 vines in a row (with a few gaps; or you could plant 64 vines by making an eighth row).

When computing the dimensions of the vineyard, add 6 feet on all sides to accommodate end posts for the trellises and to allow space for mowers and other equipment. This formula does that for you:

$$[(z - 1) \times 6] + 12 = \text{length of each row}$$
$$[(a - 1) \times 10] + 12 = \text{width of all the rows}$$

Multiply the length of each row by the width of all the rows to get the number of square feet the vineyard will take up.

Here's an example of the whole process, based on the needs of someone who wants to make 40 gallons (151 L) of chardonnay per year:

$$\frac{40 \times 11}{8} = 55 \text{ vines}$$

For a rectangular vineyard, the closest we can get to 55 vines is 56 (7×8). So we will plant 56 vines in 7 rows, with 8 vines per row.

$$[(8 - 1) \times 6] + 12 = 54 \text{ feet (16.5 m) for the length of each row}$$
$$[(7 - 1) \times 10] + 12 = 72 \text{ feet (22.0 m) for the width of all the rows}$$

The vineyard will be $54 \times 72 = 3,888$ square feet (361 m²), or less than one-tenth acre.

Determining Vine Spacing

In the computations above, I've assumed "6 × 10" spacing — vines 6 feet (1.8 m) apart in rows 10 feet (3.1 m) apart, but you may want to modify that arrangement. Six by ten spacing is common in the East, where water usually isn't a problem. In California, however, viticulturalists at UC Davis recommend 100 square feet (9.3 m²) per vine for vigorous vines in the hot regions, and about 60 square feet (5.6 m²) for vines of sparse to moderate vigor in the cooler coastal and Sierra regions.

Many growers in the Napa Valley plant their vines 8 feet (2.4 m) apart in rows 8 feet (2.4 m) apart. One longtime Napa grower remarked, "I'm planting 8 by 12 nowadays. I noticed that the vines on the ends of the rows were always the healthiest, and I figured that's because they have the most room to grow." Where water must be competed for, the extra space is needed for the roots to forage and drink.

Spacing doesn't seem to have any effect on quality according to American scientists, but spacing vines too far apart can reduce the quantity per acre. As a home grower, achieving top yields per acre isn't very important, so you can leave more or less room as your situation requires. Since a fully mature, vigorous vine will fully use 60 square feet (5.6 m²) and more, spacings closer than 6 × 10 feet (1.8 × 3.1 m) for wine grapes aren't usually recommended in America, except for the far north. There are always exceptions, though: Muscat of Alexandria produced 32 percent more total crop over eight years when spaced at 4.5 feet (1.4 m) than at 7 feet (2.1 m).

The typical acre (0.4 ha) of California vinifera carries from 440 to 600 vines, a very low number by European standards, where 3,000 (and sometimes many more) vines are crammed onto an acre of — for instance — Champagne's soil. In France, close spacings and low training squeeze every last drop of wine from the acreage. In America, scientists recommend no more than 650 vines per acre trained to a high trellis. They maintain that yields are as high or higher than in Europe, even with the fewer vines. The Europeans, on the other hand, maintain that close spacings reduce yield per vine but improve the quality and maximize yield per acre. Americans counter that reducing spacings have no effect on quality, and so back and forth the argument goes. As with almost every other facet of grape growing and wine making, there are many and varied ideas about spacing.

The trend in California in recent years has been toward the European style of spacing, with vines every 4 feet (1.2 m) in a row. In the home vineyard, however, wider spacing makes cultivating and training easier.

Table 6: A Guide to Vine Spacing

LOCALE	FEET BETWEEN VINES	FEET BETWEEN ROWS
West of the Rockies		
Vigorous vines in hot, dry regions	8	12
Medium-vigor vines	6 or 8	10
	6 or 8	8
Low-vigor vines in cooler regions	6	8 or 10
East of the Rockies		
Vigorous vines in dry regions	8	10
Low to medium-vigor vines	6	10
Muscadines	20	12

Note: For spacing equivalents in meters, multiply each number by 0.3.

FINDING A FAVORABLE SITE

Now that you know the size and shape of the vineyard, where should you put it? To evaluate your property — or a piece of land you may consider buying for planting — it's important to know the site characteristics favorable to grape growth and wine quality, considering factors such as slope, solar radiation, frost and heat pockets, water, wind, and soil type, drainage, and depth.

You may have no choice about where to locate your vines, because of space limitations on your property. In that case, the descriptions that follow should help you get the most out of what you have. If your property, on the other hand, has many acres of varying flats and slopes, or you want to identify a parcel of land to buy for a vineyard, this information is a guide to site selection.

Evaluating Slope and Sunlight

What you're looking for is a slope, oriented anywhere from the southeast to the southwest in cooler areas, or from the northeast to the northwest in areas where sunlight and heat are intense. The best place for the vines is three-quarters of the way up the hill.

On clear, cool nights, when the earth's heat is radiated away from the ground quickly, the layer of air near the soil is cooler than the air mass above. Because this air is cooler, it's denser, and on slopes with a grade steeper than 2 percent, it starts to slide downhill. The coolest air thus collects in pools in the lowest places or behind barriers, and when temperatures on the slopes are hovering just above freezing, vegetation in the pockets can be blackened by frost. Temperatures on the valley floor run from two to four degrees colder than on slopes at night, but about two degrees warmer during the day, since air movement is less, and heat buildup occurs in the low spots.

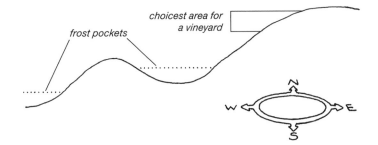

On any slope, rows must follow the contour to prevent gullies and erosion. This automatically produces east-west rows on slopes facing either south or north, and north-south rows on slopes facing east or west. On level land, you see some growers with north-south row orientation and others with east-west.

Why do some level-land growers choose one orientation over the other? The orientation and spacing of the rows have a significant effect on vineyard temperatures and the acid levels in the grapes. In general, vineyard temperatures are higher at closer spacings than at wider spacings.

Orientation governs the amount of sunlight that falls on the exposed soil between the rows. More sunlight on the soil causes higher vineyard temperatures and less acid in the grapes, while more sunlight on the leaves produces higher sugar in the grape berries. So in areas where sugar is adequate but acid too high, you'd want to achieve higher vineyard temperatures with a wider spacing oriented so that as much sunlight as possible falls on soil; in areas where sugar is too low (such as in the north), closer spacings are indicated to get as much vineyard sunlight on the leaves as possible.

Recent computer-aided studies show that closely spaced north-south rows intercept the most sunlight. In the most northerly areas, then (say, above 42° north latitude), 7-foot (2.1 m) north-south rows on southeastern slopes are probably optimal.

Tables 7 and 8 give a good idea of the magnitude of the effects we're discussing.

Table 7: Index of Sunlight Received by Various Slopes
(45° North Latitude)

SLOPE	JUNE 21	SEPTEMBER 21
0° (no slope)	100	100
South 15°	107	122
South 10°	105	115
South 5°	103	108
North 5°	96	91
North 10°	91	81
North 15°	86	70

Table 8: Index of Sunlight Received at Various Latitudes
(15° Slope)

LATITUDE	NORTH SLOPE	SOUTH SLOPE
June 21		
50°	83	109
45°	86	107
40°	89	104
35°	91	101
30°	93	99
September 21		
50°	65	127
45°	70	122
40°	75	118
35°	78	114
30°	81	111

Vineyard Soil and Grape Quality

All grapes have an affection for gravel, flint, slate, or stony soils, and the best acres are so infertile and stony that a corn farmer wouldn't take them as a gift. In Bordeaux, Château Ducru-Beaucaillou is so named because of its "beautiful pebbles." Graves, the great region to the south of Bordeaux, takes its name from the French word for gravel. Good California grape soils are flecked with flint, obsidian, and volcanic debris. In the East, the hills of the Hudson River valley and shores of the Finger Lakes are stony and poor, without much of the rich humus that most other crops love. One reason why steep hillsides are so good for grapes is that erosion has scoured the land to its poorest, stoniest constituents. Bottomland soils are nearly always richer — often too rich. In addition, those low areas have cold air pockets, poorer water drainage, higher humidity, less air movement, and, consequently, more disease.

Types of Soil

Soil is classified as clay, sand, or silt, usually in combinations of these. Vines grow well in all three types, as long as water drainage is good. Look at the soil types in well-known wine regions of France (see table 9).

It's universally believed in Europe that calcareous (limestone or chalk) soils produce the best wines. This may be true, but not, American scientists say, because they contain large amounts of calcium. Calcareous soils are almost always well drained. Well-drained soils are warmer, and hence promote better vine growth and ripening. In any event, in the Cognac region of France, the growers in the most calcareous zones get a higher price for their grapes and wines because of it.

Arguments about calcareous soils aside, the soil makeup has been proved to have significant direct effects on the quality of wines. High-iron soils can produce wines with a ferric *casse*: a slight cloudiness that's impossible to get rid of without sophisticated equipment. Red soils are usually high-iron soils, and they are not necessarily good soils for red wines, as legend has it. Too much boron in the soil may hasten maturity and increase sugar content, but it's also known to raise the grapes' pH. An abundance of potassium also raises pH levels — a problem in areas that produce less acidic grapes. Soils high in phosphorus produce wines with a higher iron content.

German studies showed that grapes grown on alkaline chalk were higher in potassium and magnesium than grapes from neutral or slightly acid soils. They also underwent a more complete malolactic fermentation.

Table 9: Soil Types in Wine Regions of France

WINE REGION	SOIL TYPE
Bordeaux	Predominantly sandy, gravelly loam; some clay soils; calcareous subsoil
Burgundy	Calcareous in Côte d'Or; granitic in southern Burgundy
Chablis	Clay
Champagne	Modified chalk
Mosel	Slate loams

Testing Soil pH

Generally, vinifera likes a slightly alkaline soil, American types like a slightly acid soil, and French-American hybrids like a slightly acid to neutral soil. You can test the pH of your soil with a simple soil test kit, or you can have a more extensive soil test undertaken, with readings of pH, available nutrients, and organic matter, by your local county extension office, land-grant university, or state agricultural college. A pH under 6.0 shows an overly acid soil, correctable with ground limestone. A pH approaching 8.0 shows an overly alkaline soil, correctable with gypsum.

Determining Your Soil Type

Your soil type will probably be a loam: a mixture of clay, silt, and sand, plus stones and organic matter. Grapes would most prefer something like a gravelly, sandy, clay, or silt loam, if they could have their druthers; that is, the best soils are a mixture of all the elements. Soil with too much sand, silt, or clay generates problems. An easy way to find out what kind of soil mixture you have is to fill a jar one-third full of soil from the area where you intend to plant. Take the soil sample as a slice from the surface to 6 to 8 inches (15–20 cm) deep. Fill the jar to the top with water, then give it a good shake. Put the jar on a windowsill, or anywhere you'll be able to observe it without disturbing it. The heavy sand will settle out first, followed by silt and then clay. Organic matter will float. Within two or three days, most of the clay particles will have settled out, and you'll have a good picture of your soil's composition. Good loam contains 45 percent sand, 35 percent silt, and 20 percent clay. If more than 70 percent of your soil sample settles as the bottom layer, you have a sandy soil. If more than a third settles as the clay layer, or as silt, then you have clay or silt soil. Neither is desirable. Very sandy soils lose moisture quickly and are also frost prone, due to their low heat capacity and thermal conductivity. They warm up too quickly on sunny days in late winter, encouraging buds to push, but then cool off fast at night, promoting freezing of tender new tissue. Heavy clay or silt soil gives poor drainage and ventilation because of its relatively small pore spaces. Soils rich in humus are also undesirable; they are often too high in nitrogen for grapes, creating rank, weak growth that's susceptible to pests and diseases. A soil that is more than 75 percent sand, clay, or silt, or that is rich in humus, is a problem soil for grape cultivation. We'll talk about correcting these problems later.

Determining Soil Depth

Most grape varieties are deeply rooted plants, sending their roots 6 feet (1.8 m) or more into the soil. Good drainage sends moisture down to the deepest roots, washes the soil free of injurious salt accumulations, drains away rainfall so that it doesn't pond and deprive the surface roots of oxygen, and carries oxygen deep to the roots.

Because of the deep-rooting habit of grapes, vineyard soils have to be deeper than about 30 inches (76 cm). That is, there should be no bedrock, hardpan, or impenetrable layer within 30 inches (76 cm) of the surface. Up to a depth of 70 inches (178 cm), the deeper the soil, the better it is for vines. Soils deeper than 70 inches (178 cm) don't seem to improve grapes any further, meaning that's about the limit of their root length.

To check a site for soil depth, you may want to dig a hole 3 feet (91 cm) deep and inspect the soil profile for a hardpan or rock layer. Hardpans are compacted, impervious layers that act like cement — roots can't grow through them, water can't penetrate. Less-compacted layers can still cut water penetration by 80 percent. Both hardpans and compacted layers have to be broken up by a backhoe if they exist where you intend to plant grapes. A standard soil percolation test will also reveal a hardpan or compacted layer. You can also dig a smaller hole to inspect the first foot or so, then drive a rod into the ground to see if it penetrates easily to 30 inches (76 cm) or more. And you can consult soil maps at a local county extension office; many are even available online. These amazingly detailed maps show your property, the various soil types on it, and whether it's over shallow bedrock or is deeply drained. Also, check the plants that are growing on the site; they can tell you a lot about its composition and drainage. If moss and wild strawberries cover the ground, for example, you've got a poorly drained, acid soil.

Vineyard Drainage

This matter of drainage is supremely important to your eventual success. Grapes do not like wet feet. Every grower and scientist I have spoken with says the same thing: Warn people not to plant in badly drained, wet areas. New York State grape scientists go so far as to say that "the site characteristics of rainfall, soil nutrients, organic matter, high lime, soil texture, and pH are minor compared with *soil depth, temperature*, and *replant status.*" Soil depth means soil's ability to drain water. Temperature means winter minimums and the length of the growing season. Obviously, planting a tender variety in an area with a −25°F (−32°C) winter minimum, or planting a 180-day grape in a 150-day region, spells disaster. Replant status becomes important if you want to plant where grapes have grown within the past three years. For the first three years after a vineyard is pulled out, it just won't support new vines. This is probably an allelopathic effect; that is, a chemical exuded by grape roots to reduce competition keeps working for three years after the roots are pulled.

——————— Rootstocks for Problem Soils ———————

Some soil problems can be overcome by using the right rootstocks. In the highly alkaline soils of the Southwest, for instance, Dog Ridge rootstock will grow well and support good grafts of vinifera and hybrids. In rich, humusy eastern soils, a *Vitis riparia* rootstock will hold down vigor. In all but the sandiest areas, vinifera will need rootstock that resists phylloxera, the soilborne root louse. No rootstock, however, will grow in wet, badly drained soil.

Preparing the Soil for Grapes

Whenever the soil is in distinct strata, water percolation and root growth problems show up. For example, if a fine topsoil is underlaid by a poor subsoil, vine roots will tend not to grow across the interface. However, there is a solution, as I learned from one of the experts.

On my first visit to Dr. Konstantin Frank, the renegade Russian émigré who showed the world that vinifera could grow well in the Finger Lakes region of upstate New York, I saw him preparing Pinot Noir vines for planting. I asked if I could purchase some for planting at home.

"Do you have your soil prepared?" he snapped.

I stammered something to indicate that I hadn't.

"Go home and get a backhoe. Dig a trench three feet wide and three feet deep and refill it with the soil. Let it sit over winter. Then ask me for vines," he said. "Then, maybe."

He wasn't about to let me take his precious vines home and dig up a few holes in the backyard for them. He was telling me, in his irascible way, that preparing the soil for grapes means loosening, breaking up, and mixing soil layers well below ordinary cultivation depth. The procedure breaks apart man-made compaction layers in the first couple of feet caused by foot traffic as well as wheeled vehicles, plus claypans, hardpans, and dense layers below that. In addition, deep mixing disrupts strata of varying soil textures that interrupt root growth.

This can be done by hand, if you like heavy work. More feasible for most of us will be a backhoe that can do the job quickly and well. Just make sure that the backhoe never drives across a turned-up bed. And make sure you never walk on these beds. Feet can and do cause dense layers that turn aside roots and water. A tractor with deep chisel plows can also do the job, but the soil mixing won't be as complete as with a backhoe.

On a slope too steep for equipment, preparing the soil will mean hand-work. The process is no less necessary, but you are assured of better water drainage on a slope, so subsoiling doesn't have to be quite as deep. A couple of feet will do.

The planting trench, or holes, as it may be, should be a good 3 feet (0.9 m) wide, if possible. This large zone of loosened soil allows the vine roots to grow well the first year. In scientific studies of fruit growth in orchards, both grapes and fruit trees responded well to large planting holes. Soil improvement, such as adding manure and compost or other fertilizers, had no beneficial effect, much to the surprise of the researchers. In fact, when the holes were filled with improved soil that differed greatly from the poorer base soil, one of those interfaces that deters root growth was formed at the boundary. Not only that, but fine wine grapes, in particular, don't favor rich soil. Like the herbs that grow most fragrant in poor soil, quality wine grapes are suited to earning their living the hard way. So soil improvement isn't usually necessary unless you want to loosen a thick, heavy clay soil by adding sand to open up larger pore spaces. Any amendments can be added when the backhoe is replacing the soil in the trenches. One ton (0.9 metric ton) of sand will help loosen about 100 feet (31 m) of 3-foot-wide (0.9 m) trench in heavy clay soil. If your soil pH needs correction, add ground limestone or gypsum at rates recommended by your county agent.

The trenching or handwork should be done in the autumn before the spring in which you'll plant. Rains, snows, frosts, and a little time alone are all good for the soil. Trenching in the autumn after weed growth gives you a weed-free planting bed in the spring. On steep slopes, bare soil is extremely prone to erosion, so you may want to terrace now, or at least cover the soil with a mulch that you can remove before planting.

If the planting site must be in a poorly drained area, or the water table is within 2 to 3 feet (0.6–0.9 m) of the surface, you may want to add ditches to drain away excess water. A tile drain field under the vineyard may also work. Tile for drainage is pretty much like that for a septic system and just as expensive. Your local county extension office will have literature on installing one.

Proximity to Forested Land

Timber too near your site can negatively influence the quality of the grapes. A forest clearing is not a good area for a vineyard. Such sites are subjected to cool, moist air flowing into the vineyard from under the trees during the day and to cool airflows from the tree crowns at night. This effect is more pronounced if the forest is at a height above the planting. Cool, humid air promotes fungus and disease attacks, and the forest is a reservoir of such spores. Edges of forests and woods also harbor multifarious insects. Near large forests, deer can be a nearly impossible problem.

Consider the Prevailing Winds

When picking a site, consider the wind. Very windy sites can mean broken canes during the growing season and dehydrating cold winds in the winter. In northerly areas especially, choose sites that are sheltered from the prevailing winds. In much of the East, the winds are from the northwest in the winter. Thus a southeastern slope is the most protected. You can also plant windbreaks here and there as needed. A line of arborvitae might do it on the northwest side of a home vineyard. Just don't plant Russian olive or other shrubs that might attract birds. Stone walls and terraces are ideal for wind protection and heat retention.

GRAPE TRELLISES

Now's the time to erect permanent trellises for the grapes. It'll be two years before the vines really need the kind of trellis you'll put in, but if you wait to do it, you'll be digging and working around the young grapes, compacting soil, cutting roots, and generally disturbing the plants. Young plants of almost any type don't like to be disturbed as they take off smoothly into adulthood. Little setbacks frustrate them, and they give up easily. So, after the planting trenches are dug, with no grapes to worry about and the soil loose and easy to work, at least set posts. Stringing wire on the posts can wait for the grapes, although stringing now gives you a year to tighten any slack that may develop as posts settle in.

If you don't erect trellises now, you'll at least need to insert tomato stakes or something similar when planting your stock. First-year grapes need to be tied up off the soil. Never allow young vines to run on the ground.

Types of Trellis Systems

There are dozens of trellising systems used around the world, each suited to different climates and varieties. Behind them all is a desire to get the vine up off the ground. In areas with cold winters, high trellises keep the fruiting parts away from colder air that tends to lie along the ground. In warm areas, vines are often trained lower. Some trellising systems require four or five wires, cross arms, posts, and end posts. Others require no supports at all after the vine is established.

Probably the best way to help you select the proper trellis for your grapes is to describe the most common types of supports in the United States, and which varieties and climates they're best suited for. We won't be considering arbors and espaliering, as these are for appearance, or shade, or purposes other than the production of fine wine grapes.

Single Stakes

Both head-trained vines and vertical-cordon vines need no wires at all. Head-trained vines are found mostly in northern California, where they are sometimes called goblets. They require a stake for the first few years, and after that, they are supported by the trunk itself. The system is being abandoned in most California vineyards, although it's a sentimental favorite with me.

The vertical cordon also requires only a stake. Head training is used mostly for petite sirah, zinfandel, Carignane, and older California varieties. Vertical cordon is used for chardonnay and less for cabernet sauvignon. UC Davis viticulturalists currently frown on both systems. That's because they're out to maximize production for commercial growers, and in vertical-cordon systems, grapes and foliage can bunch together and promote molds, rots, and fungus. There are some real advantages to no-wire systems, however. Arnold Tudal of Tudal Winery in St. Helena used vertical cordon for both chardonnay and cabernet sauvignon and liked it because he could rototill his acres both ways — that is, up and down the rows of vines and up and down the files of vines running perpendicular to the ranks — without interference from wires. "Keeping the ground turned up all around the grapes keeps the soil warmer. My grapes ripen sooner, and I usually harvest two or even three weeks before other growers around here," he said. These systems can be used only in an area where trunks won't freeze — that is, in areas with close to a 300-day growing season. (See table 10 for the growing seasons of some selected cities.)

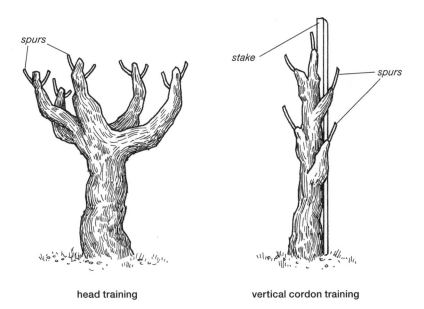

head training   vertical cordon training

Table 10: Growing Seasons

The growing season is the number of days of average daily temperature over 50°F (10°C).

CITY OR REGION	DAYS IN THE GROWING SEASON
Napa, California	300
St. Helena, California	290
Fresno, California	285
Livermore, California	285
Sherman, Texas	270
Montpellier, France	235
Hutchinson, Kansas	225
Bordeaux, France	220
Mountain Grove, Missouri	220
Lyons, France	195
Sandusky, Ohio	194
Omaha, Nebraska	189
Reading, Pennsylvania	180
Westfield, New York	173
Madison, Wisconsin	170
Minneapolis, Minnesota	170
Geneva, New York	162
Ithaca, New York	160
Morris, Minnesota	160
Penn Yan, New York	149
Bismarck, North Dakota	145
Duluth, Minnesota	130

One-Wire Trellis

While you occasionally see one-wire trellises, they're best for raisin or table grape production, not fine wine grapes. With only one wire for support, the new canes droop. Also, without a second wire for tying up canes, the grapes' arms can twist under a load of fruit and break. I wouldn't recommend this system.

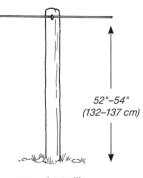

52"–54"
(132–137 cm)

one-wire trellis

Two-Wire Trellis

This is the most common type of trellising in the United States today, both in California and in the East. It's the simplest, most effective system for most grape varieties in most areas. The height of the two wires above the ground differs from warm areas to cold, with the wires higher in the colder areas. An average height is shown here.

Three-Wire Trellis

This system takes a little more work and a little more wire, but it gives the grower extra places to tie loose canes and is especially suited to American grape varieties that tend to sprawl and grow downward. It's also a good system for vigorous French-American hybrids anywhere east of the Rockies, and it is the most common trellis for new vinifera plantings in California.

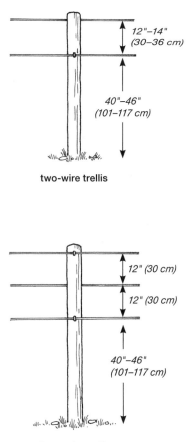

12"–14"
(30–36 cm)

40"–46"
(101–117 cm)

two-wire trellis

12" (30 cm)

12" (30 cm)

40"–46"
(101–117 cm)

three-wire trellis

Lyre or Movable Wire Trellis

This system has many variations, but all of them serve to raise the new year's growth vertically upward so that the grape clusters hang in filtered sunlight in the open air underneath. This trellising system cuts down on rot and mildews and prevents the development of vegetative flavors that occur in grapes grown in too much shade. It's specifically designed for wine grapes and is gaining in popularity in California's fine wine regions.

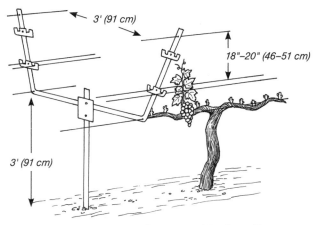

lyre or movable wire trellis

Geneva Double-Curtain Trellis

This system is excellent for northern areas when very vigorous vines are grown. The Geneva double-curtain system has the advantage of allowing more sunlight in the renewal area, the uppermost shoots that will make next year's fruiting canes. Scientists have found that when the renewal area is shaded too much, subsequent canes are weaker and less fruitful. The Geneva double curtain also provides maximum sunlight for the greatest number of leaves and gets the vine high off the ground into the warmest air zone in the vineyard microclimate. This same system can be used as a T-trellis in warm areas where vigorous grapes like Chenin blanc are grown.

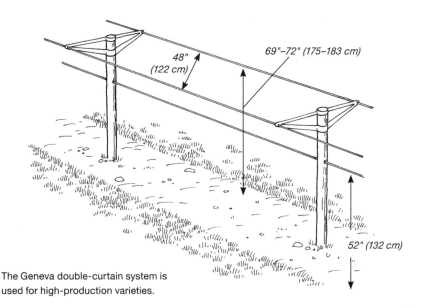

The Geneva double-curtain system is used for high-production varieties.

Choosing the Trellis System

We'll see how grapes are set up on these trellises when we look more closely at pruning and training systems for the vines. You may want to read over that material (pages 69–101) before you finally decide on a trellis system for your grapes. Table 11 gives an overview of the trellising styles available and the vines and training systems they're good for.

Table 11: Trellising Systems

TRELLIS TYPE	TRAINING SYSTEMS	APPROPRIATE VARIETIES
Single stakes	Head training; vertical cordon	Low-vigor vines in California and other regions with growing seasons of 300 days or more
One-wire trellis	Double-arm cordon	Low-yield, low-vigor vinifera. Not recommended
Two-wire trellis	Double-arm cordon; four-arm cordon; umbrella Kniffen; Hudson River umbrella	All types of grapes in all regions. The standard trellis, and the least support possible for vigorous American and French-American hybrids
Three-wire trellis	Same as two-wire, plus Keuka high renewal and six-arm Kniffen	Same as two-wire, except gives more support points for a better display of the leaf canopy to sunlight
Lyre or movable wire	Same as three-wire	The best system for varieties of *Vitis vinifera*
Geneva double-curtain trellis (T-trellis)	Geneva double curtain; cordon-cane pruning	American and French-American hybrids of high vigor. Excellent for cold-winter areas. Also good trellis for very vigorous warm area varieties

CONSTRUCTING A TRELLIS

To construct a full-scale vineyard trellis, you'll need the following materials. See Appendix 3 for sources of supplies.

End posts. Use 8-foot (2.4 m) wooden end posts, treated with a wood preservative. Wood allows a solid anchor for cordon wires when it is drilled and fitted with Wirevise tensioners (see the top diagram on page 59). Pressure-treated commercial posts are also good, as are naturally rot-resistant woods such as redwood, which will last for 10 years in the coastal parts of California, and black locust and cedar, which are excellent choices for end posts or stakes in the East. For rows that are over 100 feet (31 m) long, the end posts should be 6 to 8 inches (15–20 cm) in diameter. For shorter rows, sturdy steel pipes at least 3 inches (8 cm) in diameter or 5- to 6-inch-diameter (13–15 cm) wooden posts will suffice.

Stakes. Sturdy steel fence stakes are excellent and never rot out. As for wood stakes, I've seen vineyards with 2 × 2s, 2 × 4s, and even 4 × 4s. Round posts that are 4 to 5 inches (10–13 cm) in diameter look nice. Check what's available at your lumberyard or building supply store. The part that touches the soil must be preserved or pressure treated. If you preserve the stakes yourself, do the job in the fall, so that fresh preservative does not contaminate the soil near spring-planted vines. Each stake should be 8 feet (2.4 m), allowing 2 feet (0.6 m) in the ground and 6 feet (1.8 m) of aerial part — high enough to support any wires you intend to string.

Wire. High-carbon or other high-tensile-strength wire of at least 13 gauge is necessary. Wires that are 11 or 12 gauge are thicker and hold more weight, but they aren't likely to be needed unless you plan to grow long rows of very high-yielding vines like Concord, muscadine, or viniferas such as Mission.

Earth anchors. End posts are wired to earth anchors at the ends of each row. Earth anchors are large screws with rings on top. You twist them into the ground with a bar. If you have long rows of heavy crops, an even sturdier anchor is a steel reinforcing rod with a ring on top set into 4 square feet (0.4 m²) of concrete poured into a hole at the end of the row. If all this seems like overkill, consider that the trellis under the full weight of summer canes, fruit, trunks, and leaves, standing up to a stiff breeze, will exert tons of pressure along the row. Nothing looks worse or damages trunks and canes more than a jerry-built trellis sagging and swaying with each breeze.

Staples. Large galvanized staples or brads are used to attach the wire loosely to the stakes. If the staples are driven down tight on the wire, they can nick and break it; also, the wire can't be tightened from the end posts. The staples should be driven down to just hold the wire lightly. Plastic wire anchors that are nailed to stakes are also available. They are designed to hold the wire with the proper tension.

Wirevise tensioners. These little devices go in the end posts and firmly hold the wire, keeping it from slipping under the full weight of the vines and their fruit. The wire can be drawn through them for tightening, but it can't slip back. They're well worth their cost. The Wirevise people also make Wirelinks, which are handy for splicing broken wires.

Tools. You'll need the following tools: a drill to make holes in the end posts to thread the wires through; a good, large pair of pliers; a breaker or crowbar for twisting the earth anchors into the ground; a hammer for stapling the wires to the stakes; a sledgehammer or hand sledge for driving in stakes; and a shovel or post-hole digger to dig holes for posts and wooden stakes, or a farmer with a tractor equipped with an earth augur.

With your materials and tools at hand, now you're ready to get to work. Set one of the end posts and the earth anchor assembly first. Set the post at a 60-degree angle, leaning away from the row, at least 24 inches (61 cm) into the ground. Set the post in its hole, then block it in place with soil and rocks until the hole is about one-third full. Tamp. Fill another third, blocking the post with more rocks and soil. Tamp. Fill to the top and tamp again. Mound up some soil around the post so there's no water-holding depression left.

Set the first stake 8 to 10 feet (2.4–3.1 m) from the end post, at least 24 inches (61 cm) into the soil. Metal stakes can be driven into unbroken ground (just drive them in straight), but wooden posts need to be dug, set, and tamped in, just like the end posts. Attach the wire to the stake, leaving enough to be put through the end post and the Wirevise tensioner. You'll use staples or plastic wire anchors to attach wires to a wooden stake; steel fence stakes have hooks that can be crimped lightly onto the wires. Set the rest of the stakes in the same manner, spacing them 18 feet (5.5 m) apart in the row, and stringing wire as you go. The 18-foot (5.5 m) spacing accommodates a 6-foot (1.8 m) vine spacing, allowing three vines between stakes, as shown in the lower diagram. For vines 8 feet (2.4 m) apart, stakes can be set at 16-foot (4.9 m) intervals, with two vines between stakes, or at 24-foot (7.3 m) intervals, with three vines between stakes. Twenty-four feet (7.3 m) is a long run of wire, though, and could need support in the middle.

Stringing the wire for each stake right after you set it helps to keep the rows straight, but you may also want to stretch a cord down the length of the rows to make sure you're setting the stakes in a straight line. Crooked rows will put extra strain on the wires at the staples and cause breakage.

When you reach the end of the row, string the last stake, then set and string the end post. Now go back to the first end post and string that. Pull the wires tight with a breaker or crowbar. Now attach the end posts to the earth anchors, as shown in the diagram on page 59. This work is best done in the fall preceding the spring in which you'll plant.

A STURDY TWO-WIRE TRELLIS

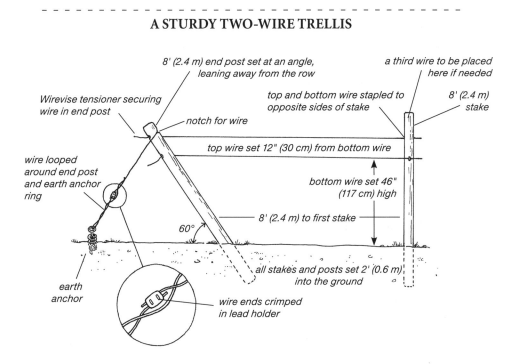

Wirevise tensioner securing wire in end post

8' (2.4 m) end post set at an angle, leaning away from the row

a third wire to be placed here if needed

top and bottom wire stapled to opposite sides of stake

8' (2.4 m) stake

notch for wire

wire looped around end post and earth anchor ring

top wire set 12" (30 cm) from bottom wire

bottom wire set 46" (117 cm) high

8' (2.4 m) to first stake

60°

all stakes and posts set 2' (0.6 m) into the ground

earth anchor

wire ends crimped in lead holder

TYPICAL SETUP OF VINES ON TWO-WIRE TRELLIS

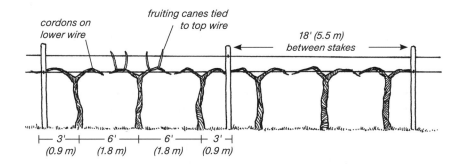

cordons on lower wire

fruiting canes tied to top wire

18' (5.5 m) between stakes

├─ 3' ─┼── 6' ──┼── 6' ──┼─ 3' ─┤
(0.9 m) (1.8 m) (1.8 m) (0.9 m)

With only a few dozen vines or a very small vineyard with short rows, you won't need your trellis to be as sturdy as the one shown in the diagram. However, overbuilding won't hurt, and it will save you the trouble of having sagging wires with no easy way to tighten them.

ORDERING AND PLANTING GRAPESTOCK

Let's suppose that the trellis is up and wired by the end of October. By the end of December your vines should be ordered from a reliable supplier. By reliable, I mean a nursery whose stock is guaranteed virus free, has a reputation for supplying strong grafts and vigorous vines, and guarantees to replace any vines that die within a month — free. Studies show that one-year-old vines have a higher success rate in surviving transplanting than two- or three-year-olds, so look for a supplier of young vines. You'll find a list of mail-order suppliers in appendix 4. Nurseries send the stock at the proper time for planting — from May in the most northern regions to February in California and the Deep South.

When your stock arrives, you'll be ready for it. Now the real adventure begins. Suddenly these babies are in your care. As you watch them flower, fruit, senesce, and shiver their way through the seasons, you'll come to know them very well. The vines will tell you what they need. You just have to learn how to listen to them.

Handling Bare-Rooted Stock

Chances are you'll be getting bare-rooted stock, wrapped in damp excelsior of some type, then wrapped in the mailing package. *Never let the roots dry out.* If you can get right to the planting job, all the better.

The plants will be okay in the mailing package for a day or two, but if it's going to be longer than that before you plant them, dig a shallow trench and lay them down in it out of direct sun. Cover the roots with soil or wet sand, and keep them moist until planting time. This is called heeling in, and your plants can last for weeks in fine condition this way.

Whether you've heeled in or not, before you plant, soak the roots in a bucket of water for at least 6 hours but not more than 12 hours. Then carry the water bucket with the plants to the vineyard. Take the plants from the water and with a pair of sharp cross-cut pruners (anvil-type pruners tend to crush plant tissue when even a little dull), cut back the top, if any, above the graft to two or three buds. Cut straight across, at least ½ inch (1 cm) above the bud you want to be topmost. (Cuts too close to buds will dry and kill them.) With a sharp thumbnail or penknife, nick out all but the bud or buds you want to keep. Make sure to get the whole bud out.

Some growers cut their bare-root vines back to only one bud before planting, but I think that's dangerous. If that bud turns out to be damaged or dead, the plant can die or be severely set back. I leave two or three buds, which gives me a choice when selecting a shoot to train into a trunk after the vines are planted and start growing.

Trimming the Roots

Many years of scientific testing have shown that although trimming roots encourages new root growth, the more of the roots you remove, the more stored carbohydrate food you're taking from the plant, and the poorer growth it makes in the first year. So trim all roots back to 6 to 8 inches (15–20 cm), but no more, and remove all roots within 8 inches (20 cm) of the top of the

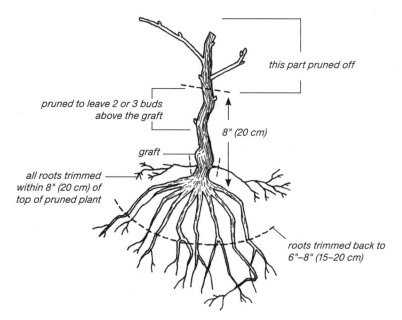

TRIMMING BARE-ROOTED STOCK BEFORE PLANTING

this part pruned off

pruned to leave 2 or 3 buds
above the graft

8" (20 cm)

graft

all roots trimmed
within 8" (20 cm) of
top of pruned plant

roots trimmed back to
6"–8" (15–20 cm)

pruned plant. These cuts will leave plenty of root for the plant and stimulate root production at the cut ends when they contact the soil.

Planting the Grapevines

The hole for each plant should be just deep enough that the buds will be about 2 inches (5 cm) above the soil surface. If you're planting grafted vines, then the graft should be about 2 to 3 inches (5–8 cm) above the soil surface. (Roots should never grow from above the graft, or some of the chief purposes of grafting will be circumvented.) Place each plant in its hole with the roots spread out evenly all around. You can place a mound of soil in the bottom to set the depth and to array roots evenly around it. Try not to let any roots overlap. Press the roots firmly onto this mound, cover with soil, and press

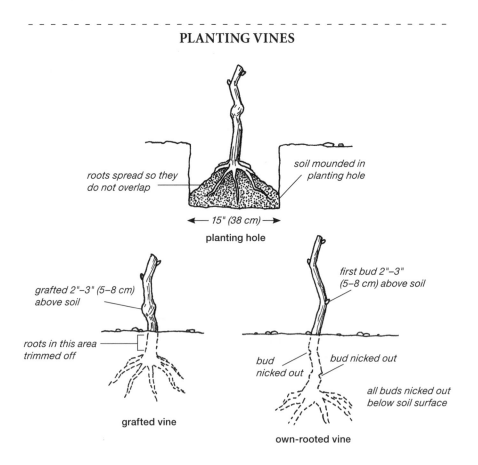

PLANTING VINES

roots spread so they do not overlap

soil mounded in planting hole

← 15" (38 cm) →

planting hole

grafted 2"–3" (5–8 cm) above soil

roots in this area trimmed off

grafted vine

first bud 2"–3" (5–8 cm) above soil

bud nicked out

bud nicked out

all buds nicked out below soil surface

own-rooted vine

again. It's essential that the roots are fully in contact with the soil, including the space under the center of the roots.

Fill in the rest of the hole and gently but firmly step it down. You may want to leave a slight depression at the surface to catch extra rain or hose water.

Watering and Protecting Young Vines

After planting, soak each vine until the soil in and around the hole is thoroughly wet well past the bottom roots. Keep the soil moist for the first month, if possible. Droughty soil is the primary reason that newly set-out grapes die. In a month, new roots will be striking out for available soil moisture, and constant watering after that will only delay new root growth.

For grafted vines, growers in drought-prone areas often cover the entire new plant for several weeks with soil or dip the aerial parts in paraffin heated just to the melting point to prevent the graft from drying out. This gives the plant a chance to get settled in before it has to transpire water. These techniques are recommended in cool, dry regions and are *necessary* in hot, dry regions. The buds have no trouble pushing through the soil or the paraffin. Once growth starts in earnest, the mounded soil should be pulled away from the plant until the graft and buds (now turning into shoots) are again properly above ground level. Another way to protect grafted vines in their first few weeks is to cover them with pots or boxes of whatever types are available. Own-rooted vines will do well if the soil is kept moist, and will need no hilling or waxing.

While tying a vine to a support isn't absolutely necessary the first year, you should do it — especially in the East, where warm, wet weather promotes fungus on vines on the ground. If you haven't constructed a trellis, a slender bamboo cane about 5 feet (1.5 m) long, sunk into the soil next to the plant, will do. Tie the strongest shoot to it with a plastic twist tie, twine, or a strip of cloth. Don't tie it so tightly that you damage the tender young shoot — just snug it enough to hold the shoot to the stake.

Managing First-Year Growth

If you want to try to train a future trunk up to the trellis in the first year, you can remove all but one shoot from the plant after frost danger is over, leaving the single shoot to carry the first year's growth. Doing this will stimulate that shoot's growth. With vigorous varieties, this shoot should reach at least the bottom wire, if not the top, in the first year.

On the other hand, you may want to let all three buds grow the first year to produce as much leaf area as possible. This will promote photosynthesis and the growth of strong roots during the first year. In the second spring, you can prune the plant back to one bud again. This one bud, supported by a large root system, will explode into an extremely vigorous shoot that will speed toward the top wire and make it with ease. This method can delay fruit production, but that isn't crucial in the home vineyard. I choose the two-year method in my vineyard, but you can use either in establishing yours. I think the two-year method is safer and surer.

Some very fruitful varieties — Chancellor is one — will send out a few tentative flower clusters the first year. Nick them off with your thumbnail before they flower. You want all the strength of the vine for the first two years to go into root and leaf production. A strong start repays you in the long run.

For more in-depth discussion of training and pruning in the first two years, see pages 69–75.

MANAGING VINEYARD ROWS AND AISLES

The vineyard resembles a new construction site at this point, with the young vines and trellises in place. Vine rows will be planted in the middle of the 3-foot-wide (0.9 m) beds dug by the backhoe, leaving 7-foot (2.1 m) aisles. The beds should be kept in bare soil through the spring and most of the summer.

Cover Crops for the Beds

Toward the end of July, weeds or a cover crop like grass should be allowed to grow in the beds. This helps the grapes slow down and helps the fruit and wood to mature. Annual grasses, which will be killed by frosts, are a good cover crop. Make sure they're *annual*, not perennial, grasses, or you'll never get rid of the grass. Allowing weeds to grow is simpler. Just make sure to cut them before they can set seed, or you're creating future weed problems for yourself.

To Mulch or Not to Mulch

Mulching the area under the vines is not recommended for any except the very hot and dry areas. The mulch keeps the soil moist, which can stimulate

late vine growth — growth that will be weak, tender, and immature heading into cold weather, with a much greater chance of winterkill. Such late growth takes carbohydrates that would better be pumped into the ripening grapes. Also, mulches decay over the summer, washing soluble nutrients down to vine roots, stimulating even more undesirable late growth. Mulch also prevents you from letting weeds grow in the beds after July.

After killing frosts have arrived in late fall and the vine loses its leaves and goes dormant, any weeds in the beds should be turned under. Under no circumstances should weeds be allowed to set seeds. The vine bed goes through the winter with bare soil. This allows frost to penetrate deeply into the ground, preventing early bud burst, and the consequent danger of frost damage, in the spring. Dr. John McGrew of the USDA told me that he had two rows of vines along his driveway in Maryland. One was mulched over the winter and through the spring, and the other had bare soil. The mulch kept the soil warmer, and vine growth began there before it did in the unmulched bed. This early growth was killed by late frosts, while the bare-soil vines had no injury at all.

Handling Weeds in the Beds

Bare soil in the beds allows beneficial air movement around the vines in spring and early summer when warm, wet weather can stimulate fungus growth and diseases. Weeds or cover crops allowed to grow under the vines before July can act as a reservoir of insects that attack the vines directly or carry viruses and diseases to the leaves. Many growers use herbicides to keep the soil free of growth, but these chemicals prevent late-season weed growth in the beds and can have an adverse effect on the grapes, to say nothing of the health of the winemaker. Cultivation is best done with a hoe or with a good rear-tined rotary tiller set to a shallow depth. Only the top 2 inches (5 cm) of soil should be cultivated, or too many vine roots will be destroyed.

Techniques for Managing Aisles

The 7-foot (2.1 m) aisles are a different story. There, growth is often desirable. In the Napa Valley area, spring brings a pale yellow bloom to the wildflowers that grow in the aisles, creating a special beauty with the black trunks and fresh green of new grape leaves. Wildflower mixes specific for various areas of the country are marketed by several firms. One for California, sold by the

Clyde Robin Seed Company of Castro Valley, California, includes strawberry and white Dutch clover, California poppies, cosmos, bachelor's buttons, Shasta daisies, lupines, coreopsis, gaillardia, rudbeckia, and fescue grass. Ordinary sod grass will do, and can be mowed easily to look good. A pure stand of white Dutch clover is excellent because it mows well and adds nitrogen to the soil. On a visit to Bordeaux, I stopped by Château le Puy near Saint-Émilion and found turnips growing in the aisles. I asked Monsieur Amoreau, the owner, about it, and he explained that turnips strike deep roots and bring subsoil nutrients to the surface. When the turnips are fully grown in the fall, he tills them, chopping them to bits, and tosses some around the vines to decay over-winter and add subsoil micronutrients to the root zone of his grapes.

BEDS AND AISLES

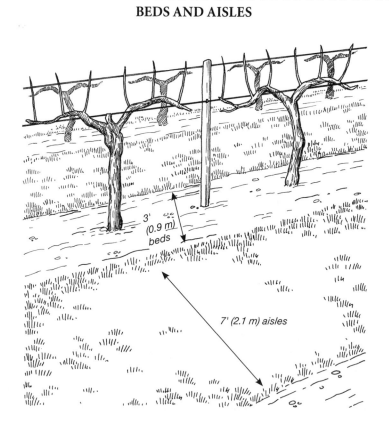

3'
(0.9 m)
beds

7' (2.1 m) aisles

The 3-foot (0.9 m) vine beds should be kept in bare soil through the spring and midsummer.
The 7-foot (2.1 m) aisles should be planted with a cover crop, such as sod grass.

Grasses tend to creep into bare-soil beds, so some sort of barrier to their underground rhizomes, such as yearly edging, is ideal though time-consuming. The permanent cover for the aisles is important for stopping erosion as well as for looks. I use grass, keeping it mowed and edged carefully.

Cover crops that support beneficial insects are especially valuable in the aisles. These include all types of clover, radishes allowed to seed, dill, and vetch. The beneficials they attract will help curb pest problems.

A stone mulch in the bed prevents weed growth early in the growing season and helps keep the soil evenly warm as the grapes ripen.

Stone Mulches

One final note about bare-soil beds: a stone mulch is perfect. That is, stones are laid in the 3-foot (0.9 m) beds to completely cover the soil. This keeps the weeds down, and the stones retain the heat of late summer and early fall days. There's no way to allow the weeds to grow after July, but the advantages of the stones far outweigh this disadvantage. The trouble is that laying that much stone is a task beyond the ambition of most of us, including me.

IRRIGATION

Irrigation is used mostly by commercial growers, who want to control every aspect of their crop's growth to ensure getting a marketable harvest to help repay the bank the money lent to put in the irrigation system. Small vineyard owners going for fine wines are out of this vicious cycle. Besides, the home vineyardist isn't interested in turning out a standardized product year after year. If a season is wet and dreary and the leafhoppers eat up the vines, then you'll probably have underripe grapes. That's what vintage wine is all about: the good years are the hills and the poor years are the valleys. There's no way to capitalize on the rare climatic conditions that make truly great vintage years if you're going to standardize everything by irrigating routinely. The best wines are made from vines that have held on during a dry growing season to ripen a crop of undersize, intense berries to perfection.

That said, irrigation may be necessary in desert areas (those that receive less than 12 inches/30 cm of rain in a year), where heat and dryness could kill vines. Using drip irrigation — simply a system of water lines laid along the rows, with emitters near the base of the vines — will take half as much water as an overhead sprinkler system. The main advantage to an overhead sprinkler is that you can use it on cold spring nights to prevent a frost.

Only enough water to keep the vines from dying or being permanently damaged should be applied. Since vine roots strike so deep, it has to be plenty dry to call for irrigation. You'll see shoot growth slowing in a spring drought, when it should be raging along, with the spaces between the nodes shortening toward the ends of the shoots. Tendrils will become flaccid and wilty, and grape flower clusters will dry out. If you see any of these symptoms, it's time to irrigate. Give the roots a good soaking, rather than watering them just a little. The good soaking will penetrate to the bulk of the plant's root system. Shallow watering promotes the growth of surface roots. Then the next time the soil dries out down through the first few inches, the whole vine suddenly has no water. It could quickly be damaged.

A warning: If the year starts out with low to adequate water but turns very dry during grape maturation, don't be tempted to irrigate on the theory that a good soaking will plump up the berries. They will be smaller than usual in a dry year, and soaking them after veraison (when the fruit starts to color) will pump the berries full of water, lessening quality and very possibly splitting them. Water only to save vines, not fruit. Install permanent irrigation when you're building trellises and preparing the vineyard for grapes.

PRUNING IN THE FIRST TWO YEARS

Now we come to training and pruning the young vines to establish a good fruiting framework on the trellis. This is the heart of grape growing, and the process on which everything else depends.

It took me a while to understand how to prune grapes, because I picked up my information piecemeal. Now I've achieved a reputation as someone who is privy to the mysteries of grape pruning, and I'm asked several times each spring to rescue vines that have grown into thickets from neglect.

- -

HOW AN UNPRUNED VINE GROWS

A vine grows primarily from buds on last year's wood. Without pruning, it soon becomes a chaotic tangle of geometrically multiplying canes and buds. I've used three-bud increments (shown on dormant vines, without foliage or fruit) to illustrate the growth pattern, but unpruned canes actually carry up to 15 or more buds, and each bud will throw out another cane, making the tangle even more dramatic than is shown here.

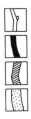

New wood with buds

1-year-old wood

2-year-old wood

3-year-old wood

End of first year's
growth (3 buds)

End of second year's
growth (9 buds)

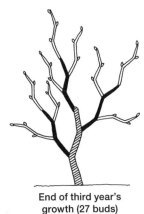

End of third year's
growth (27 buds)

End of fourth year's
growth (81 buds)

How a Vine Grows

To prune properly, whether to train a young vine or maintain a mature one, it's necessary to understand how a grapevine grows. Otherwise, a vine is an unintelligible jumble of trunks, arms, canes, shoots, leaves, tendrils, and fruit clusters. The illustration on page 69 shows how a vine grows: from last year's growth, for the most part. Sometimes buds will arise from older wood, but these are suckers and should always be removed unless you want to use one to start a new arm or trunk.

Sometimes new shoots will give rise to branch or lateral shoots. These laterals will seldom, if ever, be fruitful in the following year and are routinely removed. Removing them helps keep the canopy open and directs growth into the main cane, which will then grow a little longer. If you have the time and inclination, especially in the first year, look for these lateral branches as they arise and pinch them off to keep growth in the main cane.

- -

GROWTH OF A SHOOT

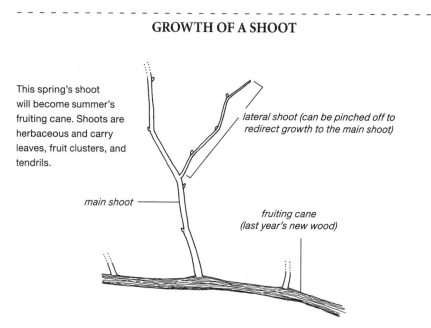

This spring's shoot will become summer's fruiting cane. Shoots are herbaceous and carry leaves, fruit clusters, and tendrils.

lateral shoot (can be pinched off to redirect growth to the main shoot)

main shoot

fruiting cane (last year's new wood)

Training the Vines to the Trellis

How you prune will depend, of course, on the training system you're using on the trellis. We'll discuss all these systems later (see page 96), but in the first two years after setting out new vines, all varieties for all training systems are handled the same way.

If the vine has made vigorous growth in the first season and reached the bottom wire, prune back to one cane. If growth has not been vigorous, or you want to produce a strong cane that will surely reach the top wire in the second season, prune back to one bud at the start of the second year.

- -

PRUNING BACK TO ONE CANE

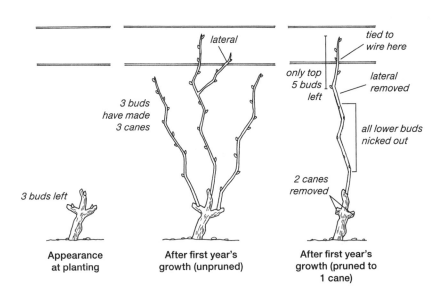

3 buds have made 3 canes

lateral

3 buds left

only top 5 buds left

tied to wire here

lateral removed

all lower buds nicked out

2 canes removed

Appearance at planting

After first year's growth (unpruned)

After first year's growth (pruned to 1 cane)

PRUNING BACK TO ONE BUD

laterals

3 buds left

3 buds
have made
3 canes

this bud
retained

**Appearance
at planting**

**After first year's
growth (unpruned)**

**After first year's growth
(pruned to 1 bud)**

prune off shoot when
it gets 10" (25 cm)
past the top wire

top 5 buds left

laterals

all laterals
removed

all lower buds
nicked out

Whenever a vine's first
cane reaches the top wire,
cut it off about 5 to 10
inches (13–25 cm) above
the top wire and tie it to the
wire. This cut allows more
of the plant's energy to be
channeled into the portion
that will eventually be the
main trunk.

vine is ready for a
vigorous third year

**After second year's
growth (unpruned)**

**After second year's growth
(pruned to 1 cane)**

TYING CANES TO TRELLIS WIRES

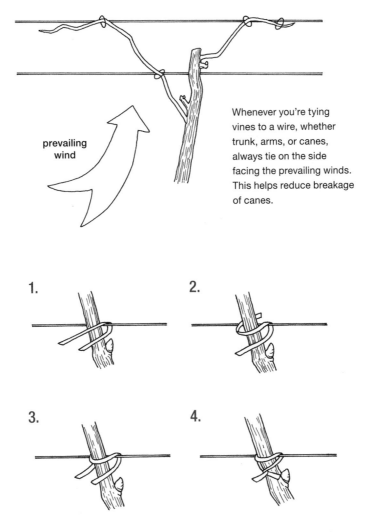

prevailing wind

Whenever you're tying vines to a wire, whether trunk, arms, or canes, always tie on the side facing the prevailing winds. This helps reduce breakage of canes.

1.

2.

3.

4.

Here's a method of tying canes to wires using plastic-coated twist ties. (Paper-covered ties disintegrate.) Tie loosely rather than tightly.

PRUNING AN ESTABLISHED MAIN CANE

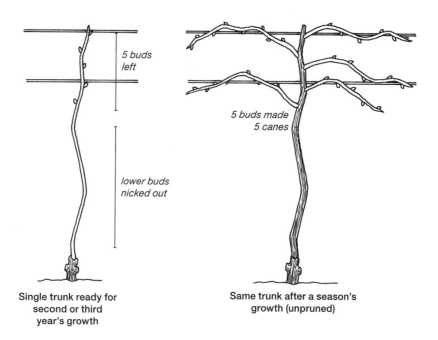

5 buds
left

5 buds made
5 canes

lower buds
nicked out

Single trunk ready for
second or third
year's growth

Same trunk after a season's
growth (unpruned)

Single vs. Multiple Trunks

The single-trunk training described here will be the easiest to handle and adequate for all but the coldest regions. But in the East, especially when working with cold-hardy varieties, some Geneva scientists recommend having no trunk more than five years old, with up-and-coming trunks at four, three, two, and one years old. In other words, each year a cane is brought up from a spur at the base of the vine, which becomes a trunk that bears fruiting wood after five years. New trunks are constantly coming, reducing the problems that old vinifera has with virus, crown gall, and other grape diseases in the East. An additional advantage is that if a hard freeze kills one or more trunks, there will most likely be one that survives. Double trunking is not seen in the West, as far as I know.

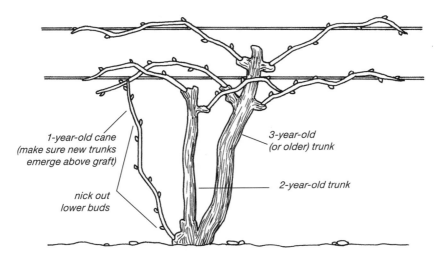

PRUNING TO MAINTAIN MULTIPLE TRUNKS

1-year-old cane
(make sure new trunks
emerge above graft)

nick out
lower buds

3-year-old
(or older) trunk

2-year-old trunk

Allow No Fruit in the First Years

Any flower clusters that show during these first two years should be taken off with clippers or a thumbnail. These are the years when proper training is much more important than whatever small fruit yield the vine will bear. Since fruit yield and vegetative growth compete for the vine's resources, allowing fruit to develop will slow down the training and you'll get less fruit in the long run.

ESTABLISHING A TRAINING SYSTEM

After the first two years of vine growth, pruning methods will diverge based on the training system you intend to use. What's cut off and what's retained is different with different training systems, such as cordon-spur, cordon-cane, umbrella Kniffen, Geneva double curtain, and so on.

If you know the variety you'll be planting, consult table 11 (page 56) so you have an idea of which training system you're going for. Or use the rules on page 77.

Recognizing Winterkill

If you live in the northern part of the East and Midwest, you'll have to come to know the appearance of living wood from dead wood. Winterkill usually nips the end of canes, because that portion of the shoot often doesn't enter winter with fully matured wood. The cut end of live wood is green and white inside, and the cane is resilient. Dead wood is dark and brittle. Winterkilled buds are brown in the center when nicked off; live buds are green.

To minimize the risk of winter injury to vine trunks, follow these simple rules:

- Avoid wet growing sites, which reduce root development and consequently vine vigor, making the grapes more susceptible to winter injury. Excess ground water can also raise the moisture level of the trunks prematurely, reducing hardiness.

- Avoid cold sites, such as in hollows and flatlands at the base of hills, which prevent canes and wood, as well as grapes, from maturing properly, and properly matured wood is a requisite for warding off winterkill. These place are prone to early and late frosts — both detrimental to vine vigor, hence to hardiness. Lucky is the grower whose site is near an unfrozen body of water that moderates temperatures.

- Avoid windy sites. Wind exacerbates the drying effect of subzero temperatures.

- Avoid overcropping vines, which robs them of the essential carbohydrate phloem sap antifreeze they need to survive the winter.

- Choose varieties that have the earliest-maturing wood when all other factors are equal.

- Employ good cultural practices, especially keeping vines free of disease, to help their wood to mature properly.

- Hill up vines enough in cold areas to help insulate surface feeder roots, grafts, and the lower parts of trunks; make sure they're unhilled when buds swell in the spring. Hilling also helps them avoid "wet feet."

- **Vinifera:** In California, use head, lyre or movable wire, vertical cordon, cordon-spur, or cordon-cane. In the East, use cordon-cane, Kniffen systems, Keuka high renewal, or Geneva double curtain — often with multiple trunks.

- **French-American hybrids:** Use cordon-cane or lyre in warmer areas, such as California and the Northwest, and Kniffen, Keuka high renewal, and Geneva double curtain in the East.

- **American varieties:** Use Geneva double curtain, four- to six-arm Kniffen, or umbrella systems.

Training and pruning proceed together, but we'll look at the essentials of pruning first, since you must know them to train a vine properly. For an illustrated guide to the training systems, see page 96.

PRUNING MATURE VINES

John McGrew, former wine-grape specialist for the USDA, gives us six rules that help explain the facts of grape growth and the central ideas behind pruning.

1. There are two kinds of buds on a grapevine: those that give rise to shoots that bear fruit, and those that do not.

2. Buds formed on wood of the previous season's growth are fruitful buds.

3. Training puts the crop in an economical and convenient position.

4. A renewal spur gives rise to a vigorous shoot this year that will be retained to become a fruiting cane the next year.

5. Pruning controls the size of the crop.

6. Fruit production competes with vegetative growth.

When to Prune

The best time to prune is when the buds start looking plump, but before they swell rapidly toward bud break. In any case, make sure your pruning is done before bud break. Not pruning until the last minute delays bud break and is a good practice to help vines avoid damaging late frosts in the spring. I used to prune in late March in Pennsylvania; now in California, I prune in January.

FRUITFULNESS OF BUDS ALONG A CANE

The fruifulness of buds varies with variety. The cane here shows the fruitfulness typical for a French-American hybrid. Examine your own vines when they are mature to see which buds are producing flower clusters.

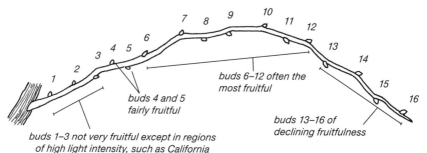

buds 1–3 not very fruitful except in regions of high light intensity, such as California

buds 4 and 5 fairly fruitful

buds 6–12 often the most fruitful

buds 13–16 of declining fruitfulness

In the Napa Valley, pruning starts in mid-December and continues through February, although late pruning is often done in March. Vines will start to grow when the average daily temperature gets above 50°F (10°C), so watch your vines carefully in the spring.

Recognizing Fruitful Buds

You'll be able to easily tell last year's wood from older wood. Last year's canes are smooth with obvious buds, below which are the scars of last year's leaves. The bark on older wood is shaggy and stringy. The best canes for fruit production are those that received good sun exposure in the previous season and are between the size of a pencil and a little finger in diameter, depending on the inherent vigor of the vine. This brings us to the fact that, in general, buds on canes that grew in the previous season are fruitful while other buds are usually not (with some notable exceptions, such as De Chaunac, whose buds on older wood can indeed be fruitful).

Scientists have found that the fruitfulness of particular buds is dependent on their distance from the trunk, and temperature and light conditions. In the East and North, for example, fruitfulness increases as you go out the cane, away from the trunk, especially in French-American hybrids and American grapes. As can be seen from the illustration above, buds 6 through 12 are usually the most fruitful. Fruitfulness in buds closer to the trunk is enhanced by higher temperatures and intense sunlight — the kind of conditions found in California. That's why cordons with spurs of 4 or 5 buds are often found there, while in the East, cordons or Kniffen systems with long canes of up to 12 buds are found. In any event, an open canopy and careful positioning of the shoots that will form next year's fruiting canes are important. A common mistake made by new grape growers is pruning and tying their vines in the spring and then letting them grow as they will during the year. It's important to visit the vines every few weeks during rapid growth to place next year's fruiting canes, the ones that come from renewal spurs, in the open sun. The trigger mechanism for flower bud formation is sunlight, with heat also a factor. Thus next year's fruit is being formed in the primordial stage during this year's growth, starting right from the time when shoots are elongating past their tenth bud.

Pruning Prevents Overcropping

Overcropping in a given year reduces the fruitfulness of buds in the subsequent year. So the best way to guarantee that your vines produce adequately year after year is to prune them properly year after year. You may have noticed that old unkempt apple trees have the habit of bearing large crops of small fruit one year, and few if any apples the next. I at first figured that this was the tree's way of interrupting the yearly cycle of the bugs. And it may well be. But the primary reason is that the tree has run riot, and been left unpruned and neglected. The off year is the tree's attempt to regroup and build up its resources. The same holds true for a vine. An unpruned vine will have from 10 to 100 times the buds necessary for a good crop of quality grapes. The vine struggles for quantity, thus maximizing its chances to reproduce. The vintner struggles for quality, maximizing his or her chances for *vin parfait*. Pruning is the way to avoid overcropping.

How Much to Prune

Depending on the fruiting capacity of the vine variety, your training system, and your growing conditions, you will prune this season's fruiting wood (generally the 1-year-old wood) to spurs (with 2 to 5 buds) or canes (with 6 to 12 or more buds). Cordons and head-trained vines can be pruned to either spurs or canes. Kniffen systems and other eastern training schemes use canes, because spur buds near the trunk under the lower light and heat conditions of the East may not be fruitful (and also because cordon arms may winterkill and are avoided). In addition to the fruiting spurs or canes, many growers leave renewal spurs of two buds — one renewal spur for each fruiting cane on the vine. This year's fruiting cane will be cut off at next spring's pruning, and the shoots that form from the renewal spurs will be next year's fruiting canes.

It can be even simpler. Rather than use renewal spurs, it's possible to prune fruiting canes back to several buds each spring. I've seen this method done with cordon-spur pruning in California, where the vintners can get away with it. I might try it experimentally in the East, leaving 10-bud canes rather than 4-bud spurs. It's certainly an elegant, simple way to prune. (See illustrations on page 88.)

I like the way Mike Grgich of Grgich Hills Cellar in the Napa Valley sums up pruning: "Pruning every vine in the same style is a mistake," he said. "You can't put the same suit on you and me. I prune all of my vines according to the vine itself." I looked at some of his nearby chardonnay, recently pruned. He used renewal spurs with canes of about eight buds. "That's because the most fruit comes from the fourth, fifth, and sixth buds," he said. Zinfandel, on the other hand, requires a different suit and gets spur pruned.

Balanced Pruning

The most important relationship in pruning is between crop and vegetative growth. One is grown at the expense of the other. If you overcrop by leaving too many fruitful buds, the next year's vegetative growth, including fruiting canes, will be weak and depressed and the fruit inferior. If you overprune, the crop will be reduced, but the vegetative growth will respond with increased vigor. The idea is to find the right balance that allows the vine plenty of wood, where its food resources are stored, and a moderate crop. Grapes of moderate crops are of a much higher quality than those from overcropped vines.

"Balanced pruning" is a way for growers to make sure that they're getting a good balance between vigor and crop. At least until they develop a feel for a vine's reaction to pruning, growers can calculate the number of buds to leave on a vine by weighing the cane prunings from that vine. To do it, you'll need a small hanging scale that you can hold in your hand and that measures up to 5 pounds (2.3 kg) of weight. Tie the canes pruned from a vine with a piece of twine and hang them from the scale.

Table 13 (page 83) gives the formula for balanced pruning for growers in the Mid-Atlantic and northern-tier states (above the Mason-Dixon Line and west to the Dakotas). Generally, fewer buds are left than is shown in the "Maximum Buds" column, particularly for growers in California and other areas with mild winters. Forty buds is about average for most vinifera varieties. Cordon spurs are usually 4 buds on 5 spurs on each arm, making 20 buds an arm and 40 for both arms. Cordon canes are ordinarily 10 buds long, and 4 canes is a typical number retained at pruning. A study at UC Davis recommended that 10 buds be retained for each pound (0.5 kg) of cane prunings on small-clustered, cane-pruned varieties like pinot noir and chardonnay.

You can expect to get about 2 pounds (0.9 kg) of cane prunings from vines of low to moderate vigor; 2 to 3 pounds (0.9–1.4 kg) from moderate to somewhat vigorous vines; and 3 to 4 pounds (1.4–1.8 kg) from vigorous vines. Vines producing more than 4 pounds (1.8 kg) of cane cuttings a year are very vigorous and should have their canopy divided into a Geneva double curtain to allow more light to get to the shoots that will be next year's fruiting canes.

After you've cut and weighed the canes, burn them. Insects and insect eggs, parasites, and diseases such as Eutypa dieback can overwinter in the canes.

Table 12: Cane-Length Pruning Recommendations for Eastern Regions

LC = long cane (12+ buds)	MC = medium cane (7–11 buds)	SC = short cane (up to 6 buds)

Southern Region

Cabernet Sauvignon SC

Catawba MC

Chambourcin SC

Chardonnay SC

Chancellor SC

Chelois SC

Delaware SC

Golden Muscat MC

Joannes-Seyve 23–416 MC

Landort 244 MC

Niagara LC

Pinot Noir SC

Riesling SC

Seibel 10868 MC

Steuben MC

Verdelet SC

Vidal 256 SC

Villard Blanc SC

Villard Noir SC

Central Region

Aurora LC

Buffalo LC

Cascade MC

Concord LC

De Chaunac MC

Fredonia LC

Maréchal Foch MC

Ontario LC

Ravat 51 MC

Schuyler SC

Seneca MC

Seyval Blanc SC

Van Buren LC

Worden LC

Northern Region

Beta LC

Edelweiss MC

Swenson Red MC

Table 13: Balanced Pruning for Mature Vines in Mid-Atlantic and Northern-Tier Regions

GRAPE VARIETY	NUMBER OF BUDS TO RETAIN FOR FIRST POUND OF CANE PRUNINGS		NUMBER OF BUDS TO RETAIN FOR EACH ADDITIONAL POUND OF CANE PRUNING	MAXIMUM BUDS PER VINE AT 6 × 10 OR 8 × 8 SPACING*
American Grapes				
Concord	30	plus	10	60
Fredonia	40	plus	10	70
Niagara	25	plus	10	60
Delaware, Catawba, Ives, Elvira, and Dutchess	20	plus	10	50
French-American Hybrids				
Small-clustered types such as Maréchal Foch and Léon Millot	20	plus	10	50
Medium-clustered types such as Aurora, Cascade, and Chelois	10	plus	10	40
Large-clustered types** such as Seyval Blanc, Chancellor, Verdelet, and Villard Blanc	20	plus	10	45
Vinifera				
All types***	20	plus	20	60

Source: Misc. Bull. III, New York State College of Agriculture and Life Sciences, Cornell University.
Metric equivalents: *6 × 10 = 1.8 × 3.1 m   and   8 × 8 = 2.4 × 2.4 m
**Large-clustered types need pre-bloom cluster thinning to one cluster per shoot.
***In years of excellent fruit set, or on weak vines, cluster thinning is indicated for all vinifera types.

HOW TO PRUNE A GRAPEVINE

1.

Let's start with this situation and call it year one. It's early spring, just before the season's growth begins.

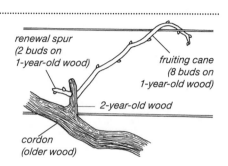

renewal spur
(2 buds on
1-year-old wood)

fruiting cane
(8 buds on
1-year-old wood)

2-year-old wood

cordon
(older wood)

2.

After the season of growth, the leaves drop, and winter reveals this situation. We want to prune so that we're left with a fruiting cane and a renewal spur, just as in year one. Dotted lines show where I'll cut to do this. Cane X will becomes the 8-bud (or up to 12-bud) fruiting cane, and cane Y will become the 2-bud renewal spur.

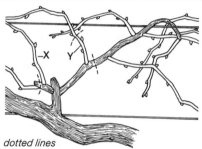

dotted lines
show where to make
pruning cuts

3.

Here's how it looks after the actual pruning. The vine is ready for growth in year two.

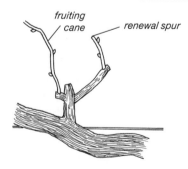

fruiting
cane

renewal spur

4.

Let's see what happens in year two. Each bud has grown a shoot that matures into a cane when the foliage drops. The dotted lines show where I'll prune to get back to a renewal spur and fruiting cane in year three.

5.

And here's the same area after the cuts are made, ready for growth in year three. Notice that the arrangement is getting longer and more cluttered with old wood. Eventually we will want to get back to the situation in year one, where we're working with relatively new wood.

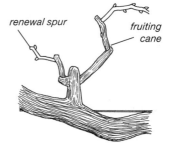

renewal spur

fruiting cane

6.

This is the same situation as in step 5, except that sucker buds have formed on the cordon at A and on three-year-old wood at B, and a basal bud has formed on two-year-old wood at C. To get back to a less elongated and cluttered situation, we could use either bud A or B for renewing the area. Using C wouldn't allow us to clean up the situation very much. You'll notice such sucker and basal buds forming almost every year in various places on old wood. None, as a rule, will be fruitful. They should be removed when growth starts, unless you use them for renewal. Now let's see how things would look if we used bud A to clean things up.

7.

Here's the same area from step 6 after a season's growth. Bud A becomes a cane that will be fruitful if it gets enough sun; such renewal canes should be positioned for full sun as they grow. Buds B and C were removed before the season's growth started.

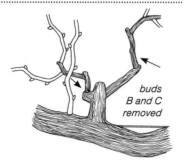

buds B and C removed

8.

To prune for year four growth, the old renewal area is removed and the renewal cane is cut to 8 to 12 buds. Let's see what happens when we grow this out during year four.

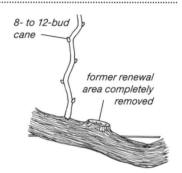

8- to 12-bud cane

former renewal area completely removed

9.

After year four growth, it looks like this. By pruning at the dotted lines, we're back at the situation in step 1 for year five.

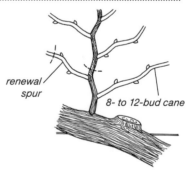

renewal spur

8- to 12-bud cane

10.

Look back at step 6. What would the situation be if we had selected bud B for renewal and nicked off buds A and C? Here we see what we'd have at the end of the growing season (year four) if we'd kept bud B.

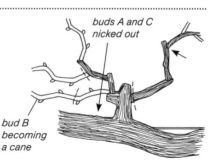

buds A and C nicked out

bud B becoming a cane

11.

Here's step 10 after pruning. The vine is ready for growth in year five.

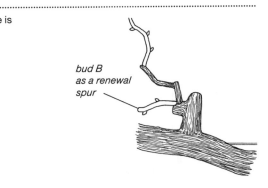

bud B as a renewal spur

12.

Growth in year five produces this situation. Now we can simplify the growing area by pruning as shown by the dotted lines.

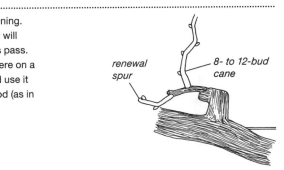

13.

Here's what it looks like after pruning. The growth area is simplified but will become awkward again as years pass. Watch for a sucker bud somewhere on a cordon near the growth area and use it to replace the entire knob of wood (as in steps 7, 8, and 9).

renewal spur

8- to 12-bud cane

CORDON-CANE SYSTEM

Now we can better see how to train a vine into a cordon-cane system.

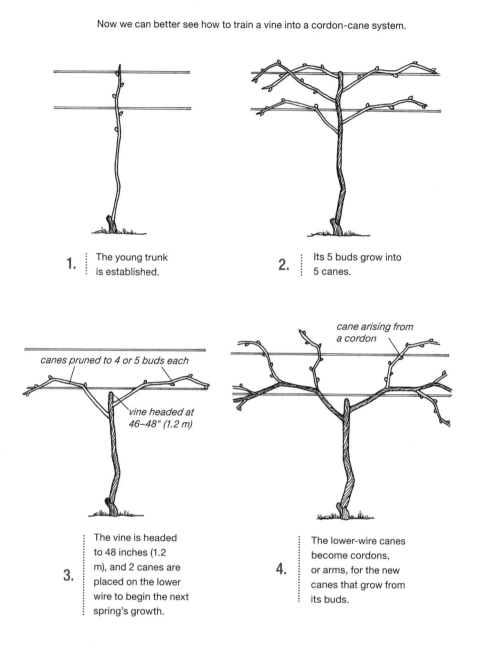

1. The young trunk is established.

2. Its 5 buds grow into 5 canes.

canes pruned to 4 or 5 buds each

vine headed at 46–48" (1.2 m)

cane arising from a cordon

3. The vine is headed to 48 inches (1.2 m), and 2 canes are placed on the lower wire to begin the next spring's growth.

4. The lower-wire canes become cordons, or arms, for the new canes that grow from its buds.

5. After a season's growth, each new cane is ready for pruning. The dotted lines show where to prune to achieve a cane-and-spur renewal system. Often California growers will prune at the solid line, leaving a cane and no renewal spurs.

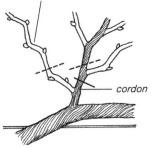

previous year's cane (step 4) now with its own shoots

cordon

KNIFFEN SYSTEM ILLUSTRATED

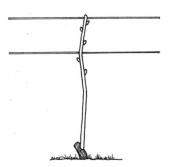

1. Cordons are dispensed with when starting a Kniffen system, preferred in the East. Here's a typical 5-bud young trunk.

this cane removed

2. The four best-positioned canes are retained after a season's growth. Canes are pruned to 10 buds.

3. When these buds grow out the next year, they will leave canes as shown above. Dotted lines show where pruning cuts will be made to establish 4 fruiting-cane and renewal-spur growing areas.

SPUR PRUNING SYSTEM

1. Five 4-bud spurs are on each of two cordons.

2. This is a close-up of 1 spur.

trim to 4 buds

3. This is the same spur afer a growing season. Dotted lines show how the pruner renews the area to a 4-bud spur.

4. Here's how it looks after the pruning cuts are made.

Pruning Muscadines

In the southern states, where *Muscadinia rotundifolia* is being grown, a unique pruning method is used. Muscadines produce scattered berries rather than bunches, and they carry an enormous profusion of wood. Thus they tend not to overcrop themselves if left to run unpruned. Pruning a muscadine is more akin to hedge trimming than to ordinary grape pruning. Because of the profusion of fruiting spurs along the vines' arms, moderate pruning means clipping all wood back to about 12 to 15 inches (30–38 cm) from the trellis wires in all directions. Light pruning would be clipping back only the tips. Heavy pruning would be forcing the muscadine to a four-arm Kniffen or similar system. Such Procrustean training methods aren't for the muscadine. Since the vine doesn't harm itself if left to fruit at will, the job of pruning is more that of keeping it generally in place on the wires so you can get through the vineyard. A Geneva double curtain trellis is excellent for muscadines.

Delayed and Double Pruning

In areas where late freezes occur, pruning is normally delayed until the buds just start to swell. Such late pruning delays vine growth, often until freeze danger is passed. Some variations of this tactic make sense in the very coldest areas. It appears that delayed bud burst is an in-cane, rather than an in-vine, phenomenon. Therefore, double pruning is often practiced in cold areas on tender varieties and those susceptible to late freezes. At the normal pruning time, twice the number of 10-bud canes are left as are wanted. If no winter damage is evident after the buds start to swell, the extra canes are then removed. If winter damage has occurred, as shown by dead buds, the extra canes are cut back, but not completely, to make up for killed areas. An even simpler method, and one that works just as well, is to prune to the desired number of canes at pruning time, but don't cut the canes back to 10 buds, or however many buds you want to develop. Let these canes hang full length until the buds swell, then assess the damage and prune to the required number of buds. Since delayed growth results from this late pruning of the canes, the effect works to get your vines past freeze danger before major green growth starts.

A New Zealand viticulturalist, Ross Turkington, delayed pruning a group of vines until well after bud burst. As is typical of grapevines, the buds farther out the shoots burst first, while the lower buds, toward the trunk, were still tight. The canes were then pruned back to the unburst buds, usually the first five. Two weeks later, these buds burst. Turkington found that although the crop started to ripen later, final berry maturity was reached at about the same time as conventionally pruned vines. The grapes, although reduced in quantity by about 50 percent from the conventional vines, were of higher quality. Wine made from the late-pruned grapes scored consistently higher in blind tastings, he reported.

In cold-winter areas, I'd recommend at least delaying pruning until the buds start to swell, or double pruning or late cane pruning. It prevents freeze damage, improves quality, and helps keep vines from overcropping.

Managing Vine Vigor

Sometimes growers who've seen the severe European pruning systems will cut back the tips of shoots, or even remove whole shoots, during the summer growing season to manage overvigorous vines with extra-light crops. This forces sugars to the grapes where otherwise the very vigorous vine would use the sugars to keep growing shoots. But summer pruning cuts away leaf area and food reserves the plant needs to create fruitful buds for next year's crop. There are other, better ways to manage vigor. First, start the vines with any training system you think is appropriate. If they overrun that trellising system, next year move to a top-wire cordon system with fruiting canes hanging down. If they're still running wild, go to a four-arm Kniffen or cordon system on both wires. If they're still too vigorous, go to the Geneva double curtain.

Management of nitrogen and water in the vineyard also manages vigor. Too much nitrogen creates weak, lush growth in excessive amounts. Too much water can have the same effect. Both problems can be corrected by using cover crops rather than by summer pruning. The more vigorous the vines, the earlier you should start the cover crops of clover and annual grasses, or the earlier you should allow the weeds to grow. These cover crops and weeds will compete with the vines for nitrogen and water and help reduce vigor.

The very best way to manage vigor is to allow more buds to push shoots — but how is this done without allowing the vine to overcrop? Cluster thinning is the answer.

CLUSTER THINNING

Cluster thinning is the removal of flower clusters before they bloom. Combined with lighter pruning, it is a perfect way to manage vigor, keep crops to the proper, moderate levels, and get the highest-quality wine grapes. I highly recommend it. I've seen some Alden grapes that had never matured properly for me ripen perfectly, with plenty of time to spare, after being cluster-thinned. For very fruitful wine grape varieties like Chancellor, cluster thinning is a must.

A vine doesn't like to be shorn of its food reserves. "Traditional pruning is too severe. If vineyardists will prune 10 to 15 percent lighter, and thin the clusters early in the spring, they'll have healthier, larger vines and a larger, finer crop," says grape scientist C. J. Alley, who works at UC Davis. It was at Davis about 50 years ago that scientists proved that a combination of lighter pruning and cluster thinning produces crops up to 50 percent larger than with traditional pruning, with an *increase* in grape quality and no loss of vine health.

If you would ordinarily leave 40 buds on 4 canes, next year leave 48 and cluster-thin. If you'd leave 60 buds, leave 75. You may even leave an extra cane. Leave more buds on vigorous vines than on weak ones. (By removing *all* the clusters and allowing a very weak vine to grow foliage freely, you can rejuvenate it, although you may pass up a crop.)

Timing of Cluster Thinning

The right time to cluster-thin is in early spring, before the clusters' flowers open. As buds break and shoots start to elongate, you'll see little rosy whorls of leaves unfold and tiny clusters appearing. Most shoots will have two or three clusters. Pinch off one or two clusters on shoots that bear three, or one on shoots that bear two. Large-clustered varieties should always be thinned to one cluster per shoot.

Waiting until after flowering to remove clusters — even just *three days* after flowering — will lessen the improved growth you'd otherwise expect and will not improve the final quality of the grapes.

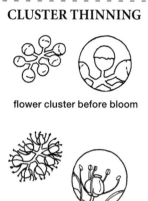

flower cluster before bloom

The lightly pruned and cluster-thinned vine leafs out several weeks earlier than the traditionally pruned vine, due to the lighter pruning. In areas where late frosts can be a problem, delaying the light pruning until buds swell will delay this tendency toward faster leafing. Vines handled this way start the year with more buds and a greater reserve of wood, and thus food, and throughout the season make more growth. The greater growth and longer season in the sun make more nourishment for the grapes, which in turn grow larger and sweeter, and ripen earlier. I realize that larger grapes means less color and skin extractives in the musts, due to less skin per pound of grapes, but a little longer time in the vat will help overcome that drawback. The sweeter fruit and better acid-sugar balance are blessings that more than make up for larger berry size.

flower cluster after bloom

Positioning Cluster-Thinned Shoots

Lightly pruned, cluster-thinned vines will be stronger growers and may overrun a two-wire trellis and shade themselves. Careful positioning of shoots so that next year's fruiting canes get the maximum sunlight is a very important corollary technique that goes with this method.

Other Benefits of Cluster Thinning

Cluster thinning and lighter pruning also reduce bunch rot in tight-clustered varieties like Chenin blanc, California scientists have found. In fact, many tightly bunched vinifera would have looser clusters and less rot if pruned to 60 rather than the standard 40 buds, and then cluster-thinned to control the size of the crop.

Another beneficial effect of cluster thinning is improved berry set: the remaining clusters will contain more berries and larger berries, in a looser cluster.

Some French-American hybrids are prone to produce clusters from basal buds that arise on older wood — De Chaunac is typical of these. Cluster thinning here is essential to remove any fruit on these suckers, if not the suckers themselves, so that the crop is kept to the buds you've counted. Otherwise, the extra fruit set could mean overcropping, with delayed maturity, higher acid levels, and lower sugar levels.

Cluster thinning can advance the maturity of the grapes by as much as a month, although two weeks is more common. This means late-maturing varieties can possibly be grown where growing seasons are shorter. It can also mean that midseason or early-maturing varieties may ripen in the hot summer days, which will reduce fruit and wine quality. Thus cluster thinning isn't recommended on early-maturing eastern varieties, such as Aurora, unless the vine has put out so many clusters that it's obviously going to overcrop, or unless you want to help restore vigor to a weak vine.

Which Clusters to Remove

Let's say that a shoot has two or three clusters emerging. Which of the clusters should be pinched off? The ones closest to the cane or those farther out on the shoot? I could find no research on this, so I did some of my own.

One spring I pinched shoots on the east side of my row to leave the cluster nearest the cane. On the west side of the row I left the cluster farthest out on the shoot. I tasted both sides at harvest, and though I must admit that the call is very subjective, I think the clusters closest to the cane were better, everything else being equal. For one thing, they were shaded a little more from the direct sun.

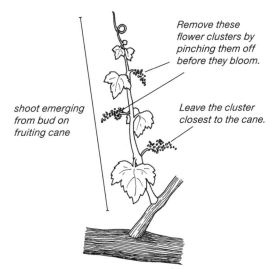

Remove these flower clusters by pinching them off before they bloom.

shoot emerging from bud on fruiting cane

Leave the cluster closest to the cane.

Second, those closest received sugar from one more set of leaves than the clusters farther out. Third, the weight of the grapes was a little closer to the stronger parts of the vine. If the cluster closest to the cane looks small, weak, or damaged, however, leave a better-looking one.

TRAINING SYSTEMS ILLUSTRATED

As we've discussed, the training system affects how the canes, leaves, and fruit are displayed regarding sun exposure, and this has great bearing on sugar production, ripening, and production of fruitful buds for the following year. Choose a training system for practical purposes first, and then for aesthetics.

- -

HEAD TRAINING

Though old-fashioned, this method is still found in California's northern counties, where it's used for varieties like Carignane and zinfandel.

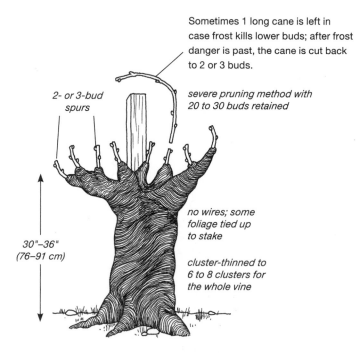

Sometimes 1 long cane is left in case frost kills lower buds; after frost danger is past, the cane is cut back to 2 or 3 buds.

2- or 3-bud spurs

severe pruning method with 20 to 30 buds retained

no wires; some foliage tied up to stake

cluster-thinned to 6 to 8 clusters for the whole vine

30"–36" (76–91 cm)

VERTICAL CORDON

The vertical cordon is used in California to save space and avoid wires. It's passing out of favor.

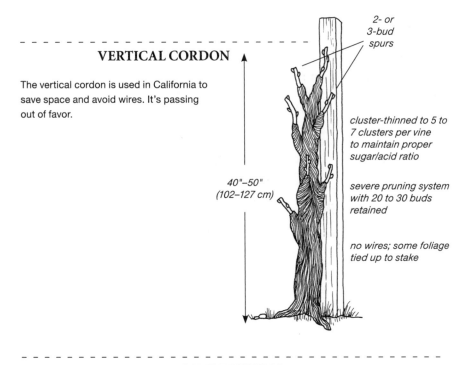

2- or 3-bud spurs

40"–50" (102–127 cm)

cluster-thinned to 5 to 7 clusters per vine to maintain proper sugar/acid ratio

severe pruning system with 20 to 30 buds retained

no wires; some foliage tied up to stake

CANE PRUNING

Often seen in California, cane pruning produces a high head-trained vine with canes instead of spurs. If using 2-bud renewal spurs, choose positions where their shoots can be tied for maximum exposure to sunlight.

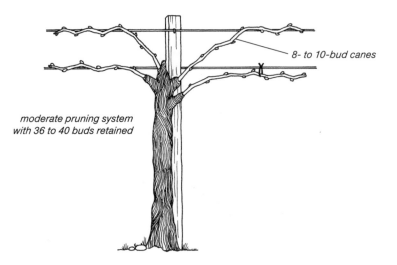

8- to 10-bud canes

moderate pruning system with 36 to 40 buds retained

CORDON-SPUR/CORDON-CANE PRUNING

Cordon-spur systems (below, left) use five 4-bud spurs on each cordon, for a total of 40 buds on the vine. Cordon-cane systems (below, right) typically use two 10-bud canes on each cordon, for a total of 40 buds on the vine.

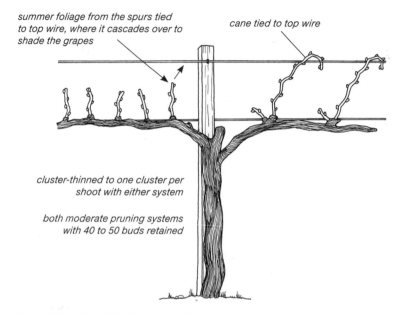

summer foliage from the spurs tied to top wire, where it cascades over to shade the grapes

cane tied to top wire

cluster-thinned to one cluster per shoot with either system

both moderate pruning systems with 40 to 50 buds retained

FOUR-ARM KNIFFEN TRAINING

Widely used in the East for all types of grapes, this system provides good shade to the fruit growing on the lower wire.

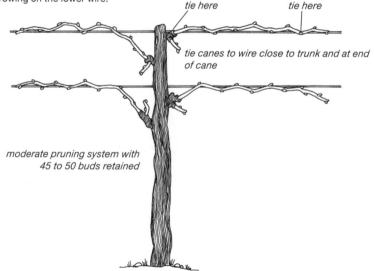

tie here

tie here

tie canes to wire close to trunk and at end of cane

moderate pruning system with 45 to 50 buds retained

HUDSON RIVER UMBRELLA

Also called curtain training, The Hudson River umbrella takes advantage of the tendency of French-American hybrid grapes to grow downward, and it gets renewal spurs into the sunlight.

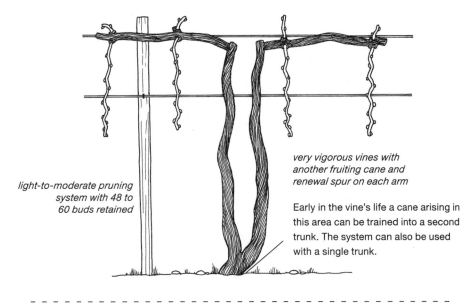

light-to-moderate pruning system with 48 to 60 buds retained

very vigorous vines with another fruiting cane and renewal spur on each arm

Early in the vine's life a cane arising in this area can be trained into a second trunk. The system can also be used with a single trunk.

LYRE OR MOVABLE TRELLIS SYSTEM

Here's the hottest new trellis system in California, which should work well in most climates across the country. Cordons run along a central wire. Shoots are trained between close-set wires, which are moved upward as the shoots elongate during growth. This keeps the leaves up in the sun and the fruit hanging in bright shade below.

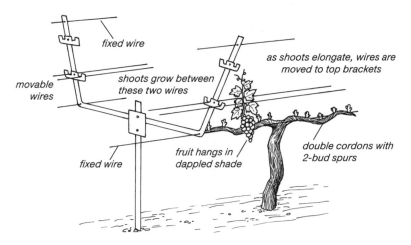

fixed wire

as shoots elongate, wires are moved to top brackets

movable wires

shoots grow between these two wires

fixed wire

fruit hangs in dappled shade

double cordons with 2-bud spurs

GENEVA DOUBLE CURTAIN

This system is used on vigorous and very vigorous varieties to keep foliage separate. The trellis stakes and vines are planted down the middle of the row, and alternate vines are brought to opposite sides of the trellis.

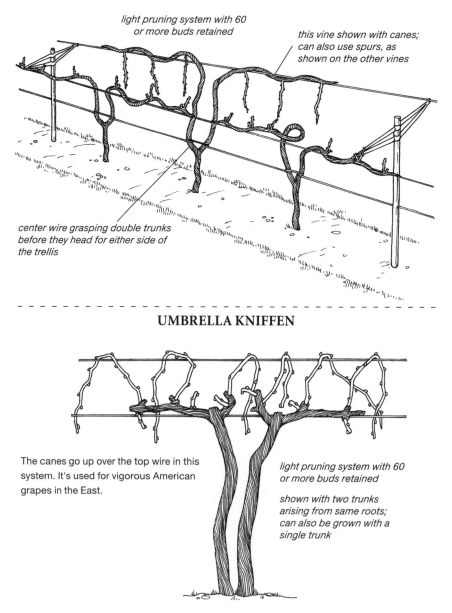

light pruning system with 60 or more buds retained

this vine shown with canes; can also use spurs, as shown on the other vines

center wire grasping double trunks before they head for either side of the trellis

UMBRELLA KNIFFEN

The canes go up over the top wire in this system. It's used for vigorous American grapes in the East.

light pruning system with 60 or more buds retained

shown with two trunks arising from same roots; can also be grown with a single trunk

BILATERAL THREE-WIRE TRAINING

This system uses the Geneva double curtain trellis but places the fruiting canes along the lower center wire. As shoots arise they are alternately brought to opposite wires. It's used in California for low-vigor vines like pinot noir.

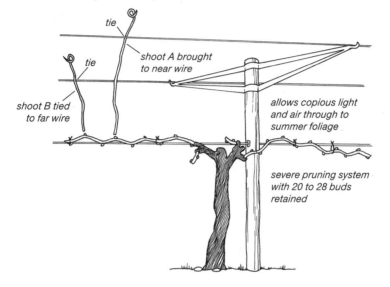

tie

tie

shoot A brought to near wire

shoot B tied to far wire

allows copious light and air through to summer foliage

severe pruning system with 20 to 28 buds retained

MODIFIED KEUKA HIGH RENEWAL TRAINING

This system is adapted to varieties such as Aurora that have an upright growth habit and bear heavily from the first buds on the cane.

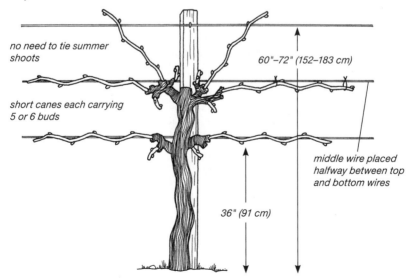

no need to tie summer shoots

short canes each carrying 5 or 6 buds

60"–72" (152–183 cm)

middle wire placed halfway between top and bottom wires

36" (91 cm)

PEST CONTROL STRATEGIES

All your pests are food for their parasites and predators. You want to knock an infestation's numbers back down to acceptable levels, where naturally occurring controls can keep them in check, rather than eliminate them completely. If you eliminate them, you'll also eliminate the beneficials that exist by eating or parasitizing them.

Institute no controls unless your vines or crop are in danger. Learn to tolerate a certain amount of insect presence and damage. Use the most benign control first. Only an intractable infestation of insects that threatens to destroy vines and crops would be reason for broad-spectrum insecticides. And maybe not even then: nature may be telling you to find another site for the vineyard.

For specific pest, disease, virus, and other vineyard problems, see appendix 5.

There are many weapons in the vintner's armamentarium, ranging from benign to very deadly. They're listed here, starting with the most benign. They should be applied in the same order.

Naturally Occurring Controls

Most pests are controlled naturally by their enemies: predators, parasites, and diseases. These beneficials should be protected, because they'll provide 80 percent or more of the control that goes on in the vineyard. That means avoiding broad-spectrum insecticides and giving beneficials good habitat, which essentially means a bit of old field or meadow nearby.

Applied Biological Controls

Parasites and predators of major grape pests can be purchased from insectaries for release in the vineyard. Your county extension agent may know of firms that supply beneficial insects or parasites for your region; you can also find suppliers online.

If your vineyard suffers from infestation by larval worms and caterpillars, look for preparations of the bacterium *Bacillus thuringiensis* (Bt), which are sold at garden supply stores under trade names such as Dipel and Thuricide. Bt affects only caterpillar-like larvae. To be effective, the worms must eat the bacteria, which you disperse by spraying on the leaves. It kills within three days.

It's possible to make your own anti-pest culture with sick or dead caterpillars. Sick caterpillars will lose color and move slowly, if at all. At death, they often hang limp and darkened from a leaf by a spot of "glue." Several of these are all you need to treat an acre (0.4 ha) of vines. Whiz them in a blender with a quart (1 L) of water, strain, and dilute to spray your vines. Use right away, as this mixture will start to putrefy after 12 hours. It's a bit grisly, but very cheap and very effective. Just don't forget to clean the blender.

Feeding Repellents

These are safe and sometimes effective — which means that sometimes they're not. You have to discover ones that work for you. The idea is to spray something on the vines that your target pest can't stand. It drives the pest away; your problem is solved. Very few commercial products of this type are available. Some of the new products made from neem tree seeds are extremely effective repellents. But look around: What plant in your area is seldom, if ever, eaten by insects? Put some of the leaves in a blender with water, puree, strain the slurry well, and spray it undiluted on your vine leaves. Catnip, tansy, pine, garlic, and sassafras are good choices to try. Make sure you know the plant you're spraying isn't something poisonous to you, like elderberry canes or poison ivy. It may take you a while to find something that repels troublesome pests, but when you do, the remedy is safe, cheap, and effective.

Traps

Sex-lure attractants are effective and are widely marketed in the East for Japanese beetles and gypsy moths. In some, the sex lure is bolstered by food odors. Japanese beetles can quickly turn vine leaves to lace, reducing photosynthesis, and therefore sugar production, berry quality, and plant growth. These traps can be a real help. The pervasive scent of a female interferes with the males' ability to locate females for mating, and the traps actually capture hundreds of males.

Another kind of trap — effective against flea beetles, white fly, and some other insects — is a variation of flypaper. Gallon plastic jugs are painted bright yellow or yellow-orange. When dry, they're coated with a thin coat of Tanglefoot, the sticky stuff put on your tree trunks to catch crawling insects and ants. They can be set among the vines just before buds swell to catch emerging flea beetles, especially. For some reason, the bright yellow attracts them. One every 15 feet (4.6 m) of row will do a good job. Set them on the ground (some water inside will keep them from blowing over), or hang them from trellis wires.

Dormant Sprays

Dormant oil spray is a good preventive and remedy for mites and scale insects. It's applied in northern states when the sun coaxes the late winter or early spring daytime temperature up to the 50s (Fahrenheit; equal to the teens in Celsius) but nighttime temperatures plunge below freezing. Both mites and scale insects begin to stir under the brightening sun, and their respiration quickens. At this stage, they're vulnerable to a thin coat of oil, which covers and suffocates them. The coating is very thin. One cup (237 mL) of fresh 10-weight motor oil and 1 cup (237 mL) of a liquid dishwashing soap or detergent are stirred together in 2 gallons (7.6 L) of water. Commercial dormant sprays are available, too, and these usually mix more easily with water. Make sure that the oil is thoroughly dispersed and emulsified. Once I halfheartedly stirred the oil and detergent in my sprayer, then sprayed my apple trees. Everything was okay until I did the last three trees. They looked too shiny. I soon figured out that the oil, not well dispersed, had settled to the bottom of the tank, and I was giving the trees a heavy coat of oil, which could penetrate to the cambium and kill them. I emptied the tank and cleaned it, then refilled it with hot water and detergent, and sprayed the trees again, trying to wash the oil off. I was lucky — there were no apparent ill effects from the overdose.

So be sure to mix up the dormant oil spray (which means an oil spray for dormant wood, not a spray made from something called "dormant oil") in a clean can or large bucket, and then pour the emulsified oil mixture into the tank. My mistake was trying to mix right in the sprayer tank. Then spray the entire vine until it's wet. Drenching isn't necessary. Spray *before* bud burst, as the oil will kill new leaf tissue.

Botanical Insecticides

These include rotenone, ryania, and pyrethrum — sometimes found in combination, usually as a dust that's dissolvable in water. These are broad-spectrum insecticides and should be used as a last resort. Their advantage over chemicals such as carbaryl and malathion is that they are safer for people to be around.

Chemical Insecticides

The pyrethroids — chemical analogs of pyrethrum — are relatively safe but still toxic to humans. Lime-sulfur and flowable sulfur are sometimes used as misting agents and are safe to use. There are thousands of chemical insecticides. Personally, I avoid them. If you want to go this route, your county extension agent can advise you about which are effective for your particular pest problem. Be aware that they often cause as many problems as they solve in the tight-knit ecosystem of the healthy vineyard. They can be very dangerous to the person applying them. And some will eventually work their way into the finished wine. If you use chemical pesticides, it's wise to wear protective clothing and a mask.

FERTILIZATION

Observe how your vines grow when young. If the leaves are deep green and they're making good growth, you don't need to fertilize the first year or so. Most ground that's lain fallow for more than three years has enough nutrients to support at least the first year's growth, especially if it's been under sod or meadow grass. If you're planting where nothing was growing, where the soil was rocky or poor, or in what was recently a heavily cropped field, fertilize with compost by digging about 4 to 6 inches (10–15 cm) of it into the top 2 to 3 inches (5–8 cm) of soil in a 4-foot-diameter (1.2 m) circle around each young vine. If all looks well with the young vines, plan to fertilize in the third year and every year or two thereafter. Spread 2 to 3 inches (5–8 cm) of compost around each vine in a 6-foot-diameter (1.8 m) circle and mix it into the top 2 inches (5 cm) of soil with a rake or hoe. This is best done about two to three weeks before bud burst.

When most wine grape varieties are mature and properly fertilized, they'll produce between 3 and 4 pounds (1.4 and 1.8 kg) of cane prunings each year, or between 2.5 and 3.5 pounds (1.1 and 1.6 kg) for less vigorous vines such as pinot noir. Less than 3 pounds (1.4 kg) indicates the need for more nitrogen, especially if leaves are showing light green. More than 4 pounds (1.8 kg) means that the vines may be growing too much wood. In this case, eliminate fertilization until pruning weights drop.

At 6- to 8-foot (1.8–2.4 m) spacings, properly fertilized mature vines will cover about 90 percent of the trellis with dark green leaves in mid-August. Many growers who see less growth think that nitrogen fertilization will correct the problem, but that's not necessarily so. The problem may be overcropping. If overcropped, highly fruitful French-American hybrids eventually lose vine size. Reduced vine size leads to even more fruitfulness. This causes yet more vine stress and even smaller vines. As long as overcropping is happening, extra nitrogen will only cause more problems than it solves.

Proper fertilization of grapes with nitrogen, such as is achieved with moderate applications of good compost, supplies the right level of nutrients in the berries for wine yeasts to eventually grow on.

Too much nitrogen produces free amino acids in the grape juice, which is a cause of hydrogen sulfide production in the wines. This is usually a consequence of using highly soluble commercial nitrogen fertilizers like ammonium sulfate, urea, or nitrates, or fresh manure in excess.

Making Compost

You don't have to make a hot compost pile to get good fertilizer for grapes. A large pile of leaves mixed with other plant matter will slowly and coolly decay over a few years by itself until it turns into a rich humus. It's likely to be low in nitrogen, so you may want to supplement it with some horse manure: 10 parts old humus to 1 part horse manure, mixed together and applied around the vines. Applied by themselves, fresh manures give too much nitrogen to the vines, causing excessive vegetative growth that's slow to mature, and reducing the quality of the fruit crop. Old, well-rotted manure is good, but it may or may not have had most of its nitrogen leached. Go sparingly with rotted manure until you know that you're not overfertilizing. With vines, underfertilization is much preferable to overfertilization.

Some people make a large bin and toss in all the plant matter from their property. They take rotted material from the bottom continually, and add material to the top continually. It should take a couple of years for top material to reach the bottom, at which point it has been transformed from trash to humus, the first step toward the megachange to wine.

With good compost, you don't have to worry about whether you have phosphorus, potash, manganese, zinc, or any other mineral. It contains everything the vines will need, including all the trace elements. Using compost fertilizers solves a host of problems at once, and in my view it is so far superior to commercial fertilizers (which contain only nitrogen, potassium, and phosphorus and tend to kill off earthworms) that I strongly recommend it for home vineyardists.

If you intend to use commercial fertilizers, despite my recommendation, you'll need a soil test (which can be arranged through your local county extension service) to get recommendations for rates of fertilizer to apply.

Table 14: Leaf Deficiency Symptoms of Four Trace Elements Important to Quality Grape Production

ELEMENT	MILD SYMPTOMS	SEVERE SYMPTOMS	LOCATION OF MOST SEVERELY AFFECTED LEAVES	CORRECTIVE MEASURES
Potassium	Yellowing between veins and on margins	Leaf scorch from margins inward	Midportion of shoot	Dust soil under vines with wood ashes or add ashes to compost.
Magnesium	Yellowing between veins does not extend to margins on some leaves.	Increasing yellowing with rusty blotches and dead spots on leaves	Base of shoot	Add dolomitic limestone to compost or dig in 1 pound (0.5 kg) under each vine.
Manganese	Yellowing between veins in an intermittent pattern	Same as mild, only getting worse	Base of shoot	Add compost made with manure to soil under vines.
Iron	Yellowing extends to the veins.	Yellowed areas become intensely creamy white, then die.	Shoot tips	Add compost made with manure to soil under vines.

Source: *New York State College of Agriculture and Life Sciences, Cornell University*

TENDING GRAPE CROPS

As we've discussed, all flower clusters are picked off vines in their first year. In the second year, very vigorous and fruitful vines may be allowed to ripen a few clusters, just so you can taste the berries. In the third year, a light crop may be had, and you can make your first batch of wine, which will probably be less than half of what you'll get when the vines reach maturity. Four-year-old vines are capable of producing a crop, but if you allow more than one cluster per shoot, you'll have trouble reaching good sugar levels.

About eight weeks after bloom, you'll see the grapes start to change color. This point is called *véraison*, and it is the beginning of the ripening process. From here until harvest, your job will be to keep the clusters hanging airily in their redoubts under the leaves. On trips to the vineyard, pull away any dense foliage that's crowding the grape clusters and place it in a better position. Pull off any dead leaves that might be near a bunch. Repositioning rather than detaching green leaves that are crowding bunches is best. The leaves that arise nearest the bunch produce the most sugar for the bunch if positioned well to intercept light.

Grapes ripen best and give the highest-quality wine when they get lots of air circulation and light, even including direct sunlight. It was thought (and taught) for many years that direct sun would scald the grapes and lessen quality, but new research shows that added light means a reduction in the vegetative compounds that give off-flavors (like a canned asparagus taste) to wines. Not only that, but grape bunches in top positions where there's more air and light will ripen first, while bunches lower, in the dense shade of the canopy, will ripen last.

DETERMINING RIPENESS

From véraison onward, sugar and acid levels in the grapes can be measured and plotted so that you can see the moment of perfect ripeness approaching and be ready for the day when it arrives.

The concept of perfect ripeness needs some explaining. Some say perfect red grapes give the following readings: 22 Brix, 0.75 acid, and a pH of about 3.4. That's like saying the perfect poker hand is a royal flush. You don't see it very often. Sometimes you're dealt a pair of fours, sometimes a full house.

There are three factors — sugar, acid, and pH — that can be tracked weekly after véraison and that will reach optimum levels when the grapes are ready to harvest for winemaking. For years I made wine without measuring these factors. Some wine was excellent. Some was poured out as undrinkable. For consistently good wine from grapes of optimum quality, I'd suggest getting the equipment necessary to make these tests. Taste the grapes as you test them weekly so that you can learn to associate certain tastes with certain changes in the measured factors. Eventually, you would like to be able to walk into the vineyard, taste the grapes, and decide whether to harvest. As far as I know, nobody interested in producing great wine does that. They're too interested in knowing the numbers.

The factors to be measured are Brix, titratable acidity, and pH.

Brix

Also known as degrees Balling, Brix is really the percentage of sugar in the grape juice. Sugar's presence raises the specific gravity of grape juice above 1.000, which is the specific gravity of distilled water. Therefore, we can use a hydrometer that measures Brix to ascertain the sugar content. These are found at most winemaking supply shops (see appendix 3). Some hydrometers are Baumé hydrometers. Don't use a Baumé, or you'll have to do cumbersome conversions.

Two separate 100-berry samples, each crushed, sieved, and measured with a hydrometer, with their specific gravities then averaged, will give an accuracy of plus or minus 1 degree Brix for the grapes in the whole vineyard. Five 100-berry samples will give an accuracy of plus or minus half a degree.

For analysis of ripeness, take sample berries from the middle of the bunch.

The berries should be selected from the middle of the bunches, taken randomly from vines of the same variety, avoiding end vines and obviously diseased or stunted vines.

The samples should be lightly crushed and the juice sieved to remove any free-floating particles, which would interfere with the reading. Pour the juice into a glass tube, such as a graduated flask, that will accommodate the hydrometer. Swirl the hydrometer in the juice to rid the glass of any air bubbles that could throw off the reading. Table 15 converts specific gravity to degrees Brix. This table also shows potential alcohol.

It gives you an idea of the final alcohol level if the grapes are fermented to dryness — that is, if all sugar is converted to alcohol. The actual final alcohol may differ slightly, but not by much. Winemakers' supply stores also have tables for conversion of specific gravity to Brix.

Hydrometers usually come calibrated at 59°F (15°C), meaning that any deviation from that temperature will expand or contract the liquid, throwing the reading off. Take the temperature of the grape juice and use table 16 to make conversions.

Over the years, scientific experiments have shown that there are optimum Brix readings for ripe grapes of various varieties in varying climates that give wine of the highest possible quality. Don't worry if your grapes don't reach these sugar levels when your measurements say harvest time has arrived. It is possible to add sugar in order to bring up the alcohol level — although sugar additions add nothing to the taste of wines. American and French-American hybrids in the East are best at 19 to 23 Brix, with the optimum of 21 to 22 Brix. In cooler areas or when the weather hasn't cooperated, they may often be below the minimum Brix and may need additional sugar for balance in the final wine. For vinifera, the optimum Brix is between 22 and 24.

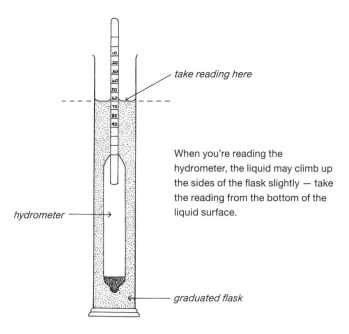

take reading here

When you're reading the hydrometer, the liquid may climb up the sides of the flask slightly — take the reading from the bottom of the liquid surface.

hydrometer

graduated flask

Table 15: Hydrometer Readings/Brix Equivalents

SPECIFIC GRAVITY	BRIX	PERCENTAGE POTENTIAL ALCOHOL	SPECIFIC GRAVITY	BRIX	PERCENTAGE POTENTIAL ALCOHOL
1.040	10.4	5.4	1.090	22.0	12.7
1.045	11.6	6.1	1.095	23.1	13.4
1.050	12.8	6.8	1.100	24.2	14.2
1.055	14.0	7.6	1.105	25.3	15.0
1.060	15.2	8.3	1.110	26.4	*
1.065	16.4	9.0	1.115	27.5	
1.070	17.6	9.7	1.115	27.5	
1.075	18.7	10.4	1.120	28.5	
1.080	19.8	11.1	1.125	29.6	
1.085	20.9	11.9	1.130	30.6	

*At about this point, the alcohol concentration becomes sufficient to kill the remaining yeast, and any residual sugar will stay unfermented.

Table 16: Correcting Hydrometer Readings Based on Temperature

TEMPERATURE OF THE LIQUID (FAHRENHEIT)	SPECIFIC GRAVITY WILL BE RAISED OR LOWERED BY	BRIX READING WILL NEED TO BE RAISED OR LOWERED BY
41°	−0.002	−0.05
50°	−0.001	−0.25
59°	—	—
68°	+0.001	+0.25
77°	+0.002	+0.50
86°	+0.003	+0.75
95°	+0.005	+1.25
106°	+0.007	+1.75

Titratable Acidity

Acids give crispness, brightness, and thirst-quenching qualities to wines and are essential components of the balance in a fine wine. Most of the acid will be tartaric, and some will be malic, with some tiny amounts of other kinds, such as citric and succinic. Grape acids protect the must from the growth of spoilage organisms.

Just as sugar has an optimum level around 22 Brix, so acid has arguable optimum levels of 0.60 to 0.80 percent for reds and 0.65 to 0.85 percent for whites. Harvest is indicated when the acid comes closest to these optimums at the same time that sugar comes closest to its optimums. In many cases, the optimums will not be reached, so later in this section I'll be giving rules of thumb for judging readiness for harvest.

Titratable acidity (TA) is a measure of total acid in the grape juice expressed as the tartaric acid content. Tartaric is a sharply sour acid with by far the largest effect on taste, while malic acid is softer, with a less-pronounced effect. The procedure for determining titratable acidity isn't complicated, but it must be done carefully. TA test kits are available from most home winemaking suppliers (see appendix 3). If you live in a town where there's a wine laboratory, such as North East, Pennsylvania, or St. Helena, California, you can have juice tested for a nominal cost.

Determining titratable acidity involves neutralizing a predetermined amount of juice with an accurately measured standard alkaline solution. The point of neutralization is confirmed by use of an indicator, usually phenolphthalein.

Your apparatus will include two 20 mL syringes, one for juice and one for alkaline solution. These should not be used interchangeably, so mark them if they're not differentiated in your kit. You'll also need a beaker that should be kept with the kit and used for no other purpose.

Your reagents will be a high-accuracy 0.1 normal (deci-normal) solution of sodium hydroxide, which is the alkaline neutralizing agent. You'll also need distilled water, although Dr. John McGrew says he uses tap water that he measures with his indicator kit to make sure it isn't either acid or alkaline. (I'd stick with distilled water.) Your kit will also have a bottle of phenolphthalein solution.

Using one of the syringes, draw up 15 mL of juice and squirt it into the beaker. Then add from three to five drops of phenolphthalein solution — follow your kit's instructions for the proper number of drops. Using the other syringe, take up 20 mL of the sodium hydroxide solution and add it drop by drop, swirling the liquid in the beaker to mix it thoroughly. Continue the drops of sodium hydroxide one by one until you first see a pink color in white juice or a blue-gray-black color in red juice, which doesn't disappear when the liquid is swirled. This is the *end point*. When the addition of more sodium hydroxide doesn't change the color further, you've overshot the end point. The color appears only when the acid is neutralized. Some practice will soon make you as expert as you need to be.

When the end point is reached, note the number of milliliters of sodium hydroxide solution used. Divide that number by 2. This gives you the tartaric acid concentration in parts per thousand (ppt), or tenths of a percent, equivalent to grams per 100 milliliters. For instance, if you've used 10 mL of sodium hydroxide solution, that will be 10 ÷ 2 = 5 ppt of tartaric acid, or TA of 0.50 percent (five-tenths of 1 percent, usually shown without the percent sign, or 0.50 grams/100 mL). Our optimum acid of 0.70 for white wine would thus have required 14 mL of sodium hydroxide solution; an acid reading of 1.00 would have required 20 mL, and so forth.

Obviously, very dark red juice or wine is going to create end-point identification problems, since it's hard to see a color change occur in a dark red liquid. The answer is to add five volumes (75 mL) of distilled water to the 15 mL of juice in the beaker. The water will reduce the color, but not the total amount of acid in the beaker, which will require the same amount of sodium hydroxide to neutralize as the pure juice. This is more of a problem when finding TA for wine, since it's not hard to get a clear juice even from red grapes, as long as you don't squeeze the skins enough to break the color sacs. White juice from red grapes will turn pink when the end point is reached.

Most winemakers do the TA test twice, then average the results. If the results of the two tests differ by more than 0.05 percent, something has gone awry, and you should start again with new juice. The same grape berries used for determining sugar content should be used for TA, since these are randomly picked from the whole plot and will give the most accurate results.

At this point, you will know the Brix and the TA of your grapes.

pH

As you probably remember from high school chemistry, pH is a measure of the number of free hydrogen ions (H+) in a solution. The pH is related to TA but differs from it in significant ways, and the pH of grape juice may or may not correlate with the amount of tartaric acid. As with our other measurements, there are optimums: pH 3.1 or 3.2 for white grape juice, and 3.4 for red.

You can buy pH papers designed to test juice, but most are hardly accurate enough for fine winemaking. We need to know pH to 0.1, which means the use of a pH meter. These cost somewhat more than a hand refractometer. If you don't want to buy one, I'd suggest talking to the chemistry teacher at your local high school about going in after school hours to test juice with one of the department's pH meters. Colleges have them as well. And most towns have commercial laboratories that do chemical analysis and will probably charge a minimal amount, if anything at all, for plunking their pH meter's measuring rod into some juice. Make sure that the meter gives readings with an accuracy of plus or minus 0.1. If you have access to one that gives an accuracy of only plus or minus 0.15, which many do, run several measurements and see if they differ. If they do, average them. Use clear, strained juice, as solid particles in the juice will distort the reading.

Even when TA is within a good range, pH can run high: above 3.3 for whites and 3.5 for reds. High-pH juice can lead to wine defects from spoilage organisms. If the pH is high, your grapes may be overripe, or your soil may have too much available potassium in it. High soil potassium is directly linked to high pH in the juice. Such juice can be given extra tartaric acid and malic acid during winemaking. The pH of finished wine will be higher than that of the juice, as some acid is reduced and some precipitated, while still more is changed during fermentation to less acid substances.

With an accurate pH reading, you now have the three factors you'll need to determine when to harvest.

Brix: TA Ratio Measures Ripeness

The balance between sweetness and acidity is a basic concept in judging the quality of fruits and other foods, and grapes and wine are no exceptions. When connoisseurs speak of "balanced" wine, that balance of sweetness and acidity is most of what they're talking about, even if they aren't aware of the chemistry involved.

The *ratio* of Brix to TA is a better indicator of ripeness and quality than sweetness or tartness alone. Researchers at UC Davis have found that wines are most in balance when the Brix:TA ratio is between 30:1 and 35:1. So let's say your grapes are ripening. You've been taking weekly measurements of Brix and TA since véraison, and you see these values changing toward the moment of perfection when harvest is indicated. Let's say your grapes are at 16 Brix and 1.10 acid. The Brix:TA ratio is about 15:1 — nowhere near the harvesting point. But now let's say your grapes have developed to 22 Brix and 0.75 TA. The ratio is now about 30:1, and you can start harvesting at any time. Keep plotting this ratio from véraison, doing it more frequently as the grapes near the 30:1 ratio. You can let them hang after they reach 30:1, but don't let them go beyond 35:1 unless you're making botrytized or sweet dessert wine (see page 117).

Letting grapes hang is good practice. The numbers may show that your grapes are ripe, but they may not be mature. For instance, a heat wave during the final stages of ripening may drive the sugars to 23 Brix while the acid is dropping, and yet the grapes haven't had the chance to develop mature flavors. Great years are generally ones of moderate, steady temperatures that allow the fruit a long "hang time." They'll reach ripeness, and the Brix, TA, and pH will hold steady, allowing the development of mature flavors.

During ripening, the sugar levels go up and the acid levels come down. At some point they will reach a ratio of 30:1, and that's your cue to harvest. However, especially in cold, eastern regions where high acidity is a problem, they may only get to a 25:1 ratio and stay there. Now check the pH. If it's approaching 3.4 to 3.5, harvest and crush before the pH goes above those numbers, no matter what the Brix and TA are doing. The pH reading thus gives a check against total reliance on the Brix:TA ratio.

A Better Measure of Ripeness

There is another, probably even more accurate, measure of harvestability, and it is especially good to use in high-potassium soils where there's a danger of high pH. Since you have readings for Brix, TA, and pH each week, it takes only a moment on the calculator to get this alternative measure, which is Brix times pH^2. That is, you multiply the pH by itself, and then multiply the product by the Brix. Harvest grapes for white wines when this number gets as close as possible to 200, and grapes for red wines when this number approaches 260. Examples for each are shown on page 116.

HARVEST AS A FUNCTION OF SUGAR/ACID RATIO

Harvest in this range

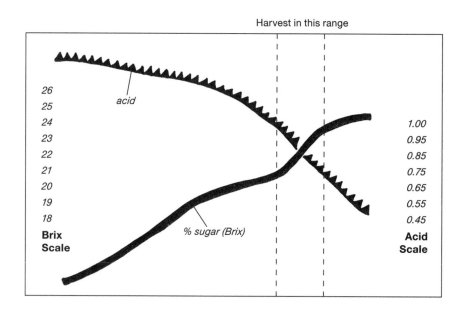

White

Brix = 20
pH = 3.3

Calculation: $20 \times (3.3 \times 3.3) = 217.80$

A calculation of 217.80 is not bad for a white. If the number has been rising steadily, harvest. It will only go higher.

Red

Brix = 19
pH = 3.5

Calculation: $19 \times (3.5 \times 3.5) = 232.75$

Again, not bad for a red. If the number has been rising steadily, check again tomorrow. Don't let the pH go any higher than 3.5, however, before harvesting.

HARVESTING BOTRYTIZED GRAPES

Given all these measurements, you should have no trouble knowing just when to harvest. You may, however, want to wait no matter what the scientific recommendations are, because you want to make a high-sugar, late-picked wine or are waiting for botrytis rot to do its thing. You should pick botrytized white grapes when the pH reaches 3.2, no matter what the other measurements are. Within three days of reaching 3.2, the pH of such grapes will take off and shoot up to 3.6 to 3.8, which is way too high. The grapes will turn to mush, and you'll lose the harvest. Also be aware that botrytized grapes are hard to ferment and often "stick" — that is, they stop fermenting. They are also prone to quick oxidation, as are all late-picked grapes.

Ravat 51 presents a different picture, however. In the Finger Lakes, this variety will reach 25 Brix with acid levels still up around 1.2 to 1.3. Even at 30 Brix, this variety will have acid levels of 1.0, with a good pH. In the cold portions of the East, this is the variety to grow if you want to utilize the benefits of botrytis.

Keep measuring. Don't let the pH go above 3.3 with whites or 3.5 with reds. Harvest when the Brix:TA ratio is as close as possible to 30:1 to 35:1, and when Brix $\times$ pH^2 is as close as possible to 200 for white and 260 for reds.

WEATHER AS A HARVEST FACTOR

Weather is an increasingly important factor as you approach harvest. If your grapes are slightly less than optimum, but the weather forecast calls for three days of drenching rain, get the grapes in. Rain just before harvest can swell berries, cracking them, diluting the flavor factors, and allowing openings for spoilage microorganisms. Weather must be factored into your harvest decision, but it's always a judgment call. Sometimes in rainy years the acid will always be too high, the sugar too low, and the flavor factors poor. In France in such years they used to make nonvintage wine, but this happens less and less these days; even the great châteaus now vintage-date their poor wines.

Some years will be better than others. That's what sharpens the home winemaker's ability to be philosophical. Measure, check, watch the weather, taste the grapes, and harvest when you've got as many of these ducks in a row as possible.

HARVESTING

When picking, cut the clusters off with shears, and look them over for small green shot berries, rotten or diseased fruit, and trash and dead leaves, and pick these out. Lay the grapes carefully in boxes. A word about these boxes: Commercial growers use plastic containers that hold about 40 pounds (18.1 kg) of grapes each and stack on top of one another without crushing the grapes beneath. These are ideal, but in a small vineyard, sturdy cardboard boxes that are clean and dry are fine, as long as you don't set them on top of one another. The last thing you want to do is crush or split any grapes before you're ready to, as unwanted molds and yeasts could colonize them.

Soon, the leaves will start to turn shades of light green, yellow, and red as they approach leaf fall and dormancy. Any late mildew should be checked. Your cover crop will turn brown after frosts. Leaves will drop. Now's the time to check the past season's shoots to see if the canes have properly matured. Most shoots, especially those from the renewal area, should be brown almost all the way, if not all the way, to their tips. Unripened cane will not overwinter. But let it go. You'll take care of winterkill when you prune the vineyard in the late winter or early spring. From now on, your attention is going to the grapes that will soon be wine. The plants have kept their part of the bargain and have delivered to you a harvest of sweet fruit. Taste it and relish it fresh. Of all juices, grape is the sweetest of nature's nectars.

PART 3

MAKING THE WINE

God makes wine. Only the ungrateful or the purblind can fail to see that sugar in the grape and yeast on the skins is a divine idea, not a human one.
— *Father Robert Capon*, The Supper of the Lamb

There are three ways to make wine: dumb luck, by recipe, and from know-how. It's possible to make great wine by dumb luck or recipe, but not consistently. Only by understanding what's going on in the vineyard, measuring several factors, and using careful skills such as cleanliness and timing can you make the best possible wine year after year. As Tom Cottrell, enologist at the Geneva, New York, Experiment Station, said, "Using a recipe may produce 'safe' wine, but cannot optimize or bring to excellence any wine with characteristics that lie beyond the scope of the recipes. Great wine produced by recipe is truly great luck."

When I moved from the East Coast to California, my dumb luck held, and within a month of landing in the wine country, I'd joined a group of three local guys, all to become close friends, who were home winemakers. We made wine together for a dozen years, and our best vintage was probably the 1990.

Here's what we put on the label:

```
1990 Cabernet Sauvignon
Sonoma Mountain 'Steiner Vineyard'


TA 0.65                    Alcohol 13.5%

pH 3.65                    Total SO₂
                              82
```

It is just these measurements that you'll need to know in order to maximize the quality of your homemade wines, and we'll be discussing what they mean for winemaking later in this section. Now, however, it's back to the vineyard, where our grapes are picked and lie in boxes ready to be taken in for crushing.

CRUSH IMMEDIATELY AFTER PICKING

Time, for the moment, becomes of the essence, as the grapes should be taken to your winemaking area and crushed into a fermentable slurry or pressed into juice as soon as possible. Immediately is ideal. If it's a hot day and you must hold the grapes for any length of time, get them out of the sun into a cool place. Don't try to cool them by hosing them with cold water. That'll cool them, but it will also immediately reduce the quality of the grapes by producing conditions for bad mold spores and off-flavored yeasts to multiply, and by washing away the microscopic spider nests and other goodies that contribute their *je ne sais quoi* to the finished wine. Have everything ready for the crush before you pick, and see how fast you can produce crushed grapes. The shorter the time from vine to crusher, the higher the quality of the wine.

Many home winemakers in the East get shipments of "fresh" California grapes. The packers stuff 40 pounds (18.1 kg) into boxes and nail on the lids, crushing many of the berries. Then they're refrigerated (a condition that the worst molds favor), shipped east, and days or even a week or more later carted home in the back of a hot station wagon. By the time they're crushed, many of the grapes are little vinegar pots, and it's almost impossible to make quality wine from them. Flash-frozen chunks of mashed grapes are now being sold and shipped around the country. These make a much better wine, but not up to the quality of wine from fresh-picked grapes, since freezing reduces total acidity and elevates pH — not desirable in California grapes.

As soon as the fruit is picked, it's likely to draw fruit flies, especially *Drosophila melanogaster*, the little fly with the giant chromosomes that geneticists are so fond of fiddling with. So it's important to get the fruit to the crusher quickly. From this point until the wine is safely bottled away, make every effort to keep fruit flies off the grapes and out of the must. These flies, because they're always walking around on split and decaying fruit of all kinds, carry acetobacter bacteria, the ones that turn alcohol into acetic acid (vinegar). This chemical transformation can take place only in the presence of air, which is why winemakers keep their developing wines away from air except in the first stages of the process.

- -

WINEMAKING PROCESS SIMPLIFIED

PREPARING THE MUST (DAY 1)

Red Wine

Stem and crush grapes into fermentation vat.

White or Pink Wine

Stem and crush grapes. If pressing immediately, press juice into fermentation vat or into carboys filled two-thirds full.

Then

- Test TA, Brix, and pH.
- Add potassium metabisulfite if necessary.
- Adjust sugar, TA, and potassium metabisulfite, if necessary.
- Press whites left on skins after 8–16 hours, transferring juice into fermentation vat or into carboys filled two-thirds full.

- On the second day, add yeast.

PRIMARY FERMENTATION (3–26 DAYS)

- Punch down cap twice a day during this period.
- Add malolactic starter culture just as primary fermentation begins to slow.
- When fermentation slows, test Brix; it should be reduced by two-thirds.

TRANSFER TO CARBOYS

Red Wine

Press and transfer juice to carboys filled to shoulder. Attach air locks.

White or Pink Wine

Transfer vatted whites to carboys filled to shoulder. Attach air locks. Whites in carboys can be given an optional racking 5 days after primary fermentation ends to increase freshness.

SECONDARY FERMENTATION (1 WEEK–2 MONTHS)

• Secondary fermentation ends when all bubbling ceases.

FIRST RACKING

• Rack into clean carboys filled to within an inch of the cork. Add oak chips, if desired. Or rack into an oak barrel at this time.

AGING (2–3 MONTHS)

• Cold-stabilize during this period.

SECOND RACKING

• Rack wine again. Top up.

AGING (3–4 MONTHS)

• Keep the wine in a cool, dark space.

FINISHING

• Rack again. Test pH, TA, residual sugar, and percentage of alcohol.
• Bottle the wine or top up carboys, or barrel and bottle at leisure.

DECISIONS OF THE FIRST FEW DAYS

Crushing immediately after picking means being ready to crush before you pick. Let's quickly go over what's going to happen during the first few days after picking, to give you an overall idea of the process. You're going to bring in the picked grapes and make some important decisions: whether to take the berries off the stems; whether to do a light pressing of whole or crushed grapes to capture the finest juice; whether to have the juice ferment in a vat, barrel, or glass carboy. In any case, you're going to end up with a container of grape juice, with or without stems and crushed skins. Now you'll read Brix, TA, and pH. From these you'll know whether to add sugar to increase final alcohol, and whether to adjust the acidity. Also from these readings you'll figure the amount of potassium metabisulfite to add to the must, if you decide to add any at all. Then you'll cover the container and forget the juice until the next day, when you'll add the yeast.

From crushing through the end of the primary fermentation a few days later, the must can be exposed to air without harm, although you'll cover the vat with cloth to keep out fruit flies. In fact, you'll be punching down the cap that forms on your fermenting must, to get some air into it and keep the must homogenized. White wines are much more prone to oxidation than reds, but even so, some air contact is important when the primary fermentation is going on. As Tom Cottrell says, although "oxidation paranoia is a relatively sane state" for the winemaker and the wine, "at the beginning of the life of the wine, some oxygen is actually helpful. By causing early browning of some phenolic compounds that subsequently precipitate when the wine ferments, the final wine is lighter and more resistant to oxidative browning in its later life. Having made clean, light chardonnays from oxidized musts that looked like lentil soup, I can assure you that even severe early browning of juice is not necessarily bad."

After the primary fermentation, when the furious action of the yeast on the sugar starts to settle down and wine has emerged from the grape juice, there will be time enough for oxidation paranoia.

Process only one grape variety at a time. Dumping several kinds of grapes in the hopper at once leads to mediocre wine in most cases. The exception would be when you're including some teinturier grapes for added color. Otherwise, I'd strongly recommend vinifying each grape variety separately, and blending much later in the process — just before bottling. It's a matter of control.

Blending pure variety types later gives you microfine-tuning capabilities that are impossible once everything's dumped together in the fermentation vat.

Now let's go back and look at the first day's procedures in more detail.

Stemming and Crushing

First, what kind of grapes do you have? And what kind of wine do you have in mind? The answers to these questions determine how you're going to handle the grapes you've just picked.

Most likely you'll have either red or white grapes. Pink grapes like Gewürztraminer and Catawba are usually handled like whites, although you may want to vinify them like reds after you possess enough winemaking skill to try knowledgeable experiments.

Red Grapes

Since you've already picked the trash off the bunches in the vineyard, it's possible to toss them in the vat without stemming them. They can then be mashed to a pulp with feet, hands, or a pestle of some nonporous material like stainless steel, porcelain, or plastic. With any such pestle, cleanliness is important. Wash in hot ammonia water (about 1 part ammonia to 5 parts water) and rinse *thoroughly* before using. You don't want to add any bacteria, mold spores, or material that could harbor decay microorganisms. Personally, I think feet do the best job. My wife scrubs her legs and feet until they're squeaky clean, and then from the shower she goes right into clean socks. These she strips off one by one as she steps into the vat of grapes. Given the size of our vats, the juice and pulp reach above her knees, and she treads in place until the grapes have been crushed and are all off the stems. This is not a bad time to put on some music and pass around some wine that's good for gulping. Treading about 150 pounds (68 kg) of grapes in a 30-gallon (114 L) vat of some kind (we'll discuss which "kinds" a little further on) shouldn't take more than 10 minutes. Make the most of them.

Leaving the stems in the must will give you more bitter principles, such as phenols and tannin, and some herbaceousness, too. These may be to your taste, and they will help the wine age the way a big red is supposed to. Many vintners stem the bunches by hand, but that's too much work for me. I think red wine benefits from some stems, so here's what I do: After the grapes are crushed, I go through the slurry with my (thoroughly washed and rinsed) arms and hands and remove most of the stems, which are floating free. I'd say that about 1 of every 10 original stems remains in the must after I'm finished. Doing this also gives me a chance to detach and squeeze open any berries still clinging to the stems, or, if the berries are underripe or mummified and cling tightly, to discard them with the stems.

Many winemakers have a stemmer-crusher, especially those who do any volume of wine, such as 50 gallons (190 L) or more a year. Small versions of these sit on top of your vat and do the stemming and crushing at the turn of a crank or, in some models, at the flick of a switch. While I like the hand-done (or foot-done) approach just for the tradition and fun of it, I'd invest in a stemmer-crusher if I made more than two barrels a year.

Allowing pulp, skins, some stems, and juice to ferment leads to a big, deeply colored red wine. This is because so much of the flavor and color is in the skins, and it's extracted into the wine during the primary fermentation. The juice is then pressed out after the primary.

A lighter, fresher red wine can be made by stemming and crushing the grapes right into a wine press and immediately pressing out the juice. Because the skins don't stew in the must during the primary fermentation, very little color and little of the subtle flavors of the grape suffuse into the juice, which will probably be a shade of pink, or in the case of De Chaunac, light orange. The resulting wine will be light, fruity, fresh, and drinkable next year. It won't age for more than another year before starting to lose quality. Such wine can be delightful, but it is almost always ordinary. Great reds, however, come from lots of skin and some stem contact in the fermenting must.

White and Pink Grapes

To get all the flavor and subtlety you can from a good, ripe chardonnay, seyval blanc, or other white that can yield big wines, stem and crush by hand or foot, or use the stemmer-crusher, and allow the juice to sit on the skins for 12 to 16 hours before being pressed, to pick up extra flavor. The benefits of soaking whites on the skins for about 12 hours go beyond enriching flavor. Susan Freas, a graduate student in enology at Penn State, described an experiment in which her department crushed three batches each of seyval blanc, Vidal 256, chardonnay, and riesling. One batch was immediately fermented. A second was left on the skins for 8 hours, and a third batch sat on the skins for 16 hours. These batches were then fermented and the resulting wines evaluated. With 16 hours of skin contact, all the varieties gave a greater yield of juice (due to the softening and enzymatic breakdown of cells in skins and pulp) and higher sugar, color, and flavor components, with lower acid levels, than wines from batches with less skin contact time or none at all.

If possible, the juice and skins should be kept between 55° and 65°F (13–18°C). At higher temperatures, there's a greater chance of oxidative browning and production of bitter phenols.

Winemakers seeking a light, clean, fresh, and fruity white wine stem and crush the grapes and immediately press out the juice. All the juice can be pressed out at once, or you can make two grades of wine. The finest and lightest grade comes from grapes that are stemmed and then put uncrushed into the wine press for squeezing. A light to medium pressure is applied. The juice that comes from this light squeezing will be very clear and fine and will make an exceedingly light and pleasant wine. This "first-run" juice is fermented separately from the juice that runs from harder pressure. At the second pressing, don't press too hard — just enough to get the bulk of the juice out. Some winemakers who are running both reds and whites toss the white's solids into the red's fermenting vats, which, counterintuitively, can intensify the color of the red wine and add a little more complexity to the flavor. It's not necessary, though.

Cleanliness

Everything that contacts the crushed grapes or must should be thoroughly clean, and rinsed with a sterilizing solution. I usually wash everything with hot ammonia water — never soap. Rinsing well is imperative, since you don't want even a molecule of ammonia in the wine. Most winemakers use a sterilizing solution of sodium bisulfate or potassium metabisulfite, rather than ammonia (see the sidebar on page 127).

The air is swarming with all manner of bacteria and spores, so you can't be antiseptic. Just make sure that everything is clean. And that includes the room you're in. The image of mold-encrusted walls in a dank wine cellar may seem romantic, but that isn't the way it is in the winemaking room, unless you want all that dankness to add its ugly bouquet to your wine.

A Sterilizing Solution for Winemaking Equipment

You can use either potassium metabisulfite or sodium bisulfate to sterilize winemaking equipment. Two ounces (56 g) of the white sulfite powder
dissolved in 1 gallon (3.8 L) of water makes a strong solution. This solution
should be used as a final rinse, as further washing would allow the surfaces
of the equipment to be recolonized immediately by yeast and mold spores,
and bacteria. Stainless steel is an exception, however; it *should* be rinsed,
as sulfite may pit its surface if left standing. Keep the sulfite solution tightly
stoppered. The sulfite solution will give off a smell like burning kitchen
matches, which is the characteristic smell of sulfur dioxide gas. Ventilate
the room where you're using it, since the sulfur dioxide is poisonous in large
concentrations.

Choosing a Primary Fermentation Vat

At this point, you have a vat of juice, or juice and pulp, or juice, pulp, and
stems, depending on how you've crushed the grapes. The best vat for the first
few days of primary fermentation is an open-topped barrel or cylinder. Here's
a rundown of possibilities, with their pros and cons, from the most to the least
recommended.

- **Stainless steel drum.** Ideal. These are easy to clean, nonporous, and in
  all ways superior. You'll find a supplier for them listed in appendix 3.
  They come in many sizes, but a 55-gallon (208 L) drum lets you ferment a little or a lot.

- **Food-grade plastic vats.** Also ideal. These are 4 by 4-foot (1.2 × 1.2 m)
  tubs with flat lips around the top, made of food-grade plastic, that
  slip into wooden frames. They hold about 1,000 pounds (454 kg) of
  grapes — which will make about 100 gallons (380 L) of wine. Easily
  found in California's wine country, where these commercial tubs are
  used for transporting grapes from the field to the crusher at large
  wineries, they may be hard to come by in other areas.

- **A large vitreous crock.** As long as the inside surface is not cracked, revealing the porous crockery underneath, these are excellent. It's sometimes difficult to find them in sizes large enough to hold the amount of juice you're vatting, and they do get heavy when they're large. I use a 15-gallon (57 L) crock for 10-gallon (38 L) batches.

- **Fresh whiskey barrels.** These come from the distilleries bunged, clean, and smelling strongly of whiskey. Their insides will have been burned to charcoal before the whiskey was put in, and the charcoal can help absorb some impurities, and possibly some flavor or color constituents, from the must. I've used these with excellent results to vat 40 gallons (150 L). You must cut out or knock in one end of the barrel, then rinse with clean water before putting in the grapes. This is an expensive route, since you can vat only one primary fermentation in them. After that, they're impossible to clean well enough to store for future vattings. They do make great planters.

- **Five-gallon (19 L) glass carboys.** While glass is always excellent, due to its nonporous nature, these carboys are less than optimum for reds due to the small neck, which makes it difficult to punch down the cap of bubbles, spent yeast, and grape detritus that rises during the primary. It's also difficult to introduce air into the must, which would help disperse odors and gases during the rapid fermentation of the first few days. They're good for fermenting white juice, however, as they prevent overoxidation. I keep the top stoppered with a loose wad of sterile cotton that allows gases to escape. Two or three times a day I remove the cotton, put my (washed) hand over the opening, tip the carboy, and shake it to mix down the cap. Then I blow a puff of fresh air into the carboy for luck, wipe off the rim with a paper towel moistened with the sulfite sterilizing solution, and replace the stopper with fresh cotton.

Stretch a towel or other covering over your primary fermentation vat, keeping it in place with a heavy board if necessary.

- **Plastic garbage cans.** Some winemakers use large plastic garbage cans purchased especially for the purpose of vatting wine during the primary. I don't recommend them at all. Plasticizers and plastic flavors can leach into the fermenting must.

The primary fermentation will be vigorous and rapid, and the bubbles and cap will rise as much as a third above the level of the must. Therefore, never fill your container — whether drum, barrel, or carboy — more than two-thirds full for the primary.

When the must is made and vatted into your container of choice, cover the vat with a clean towel kept stretched tight across the top of the vat; you can secure the towel in place by laying a board across it. This arrangement lets gases out and air in and keeps the must secure from fruit flies. Remove the towel only when adding sulfite, taking juice to measure pH, adding sugar, or adjusting the total acidity in low-acid musts — all operations done this first day.

For some reason, musts and wines don't like being disturbed. "Don't mess with it" is surely engraved over the lintel of heaven's chai. (*Chai* is the French word denoting a building that holds barrels of stored wine.) This rule becomes more important after the primary fermentation, when the wine is set aside to finish working, and more important still when the wine is resting in carboys before bottling. The less you do to wine, the better. The steps listed in this book are the minimum needed, I think, to produce fine wine. And doing the minimum is not only thrifty but benefits the wine.

Adding Sulfite to the Must

As soon as the grapes are crushed and vatted, they are susceptible to unwanted yeast and microorganisms growth and to oxidation. The grape skins are abloom with wild yeasts, which will immediately start to reproduce in the sweet must. In some wine-growing regions of the world, especially Europe, winemakers will sometimes allow these wild yeasts to go ahead and ferment the must, and some winemakers feel that the wine will be more natural if it ferments using the yeast that nature grew on the skins. This is fine for advanced winemakers with lots of analytical tools to keep tabs on things, but for home winemakers, I think this is wrong, for several reasons.

It's wrong first because wild yeasts are unpredictable. Some wild strains found on the grape skins may indeed make acceptable wine, but many will stop working and die off at low (4 to 6 percent) alcohol concentrations, well before the fermentation has proceeded to dryness. Others may produce huge amounts of volatile acids, which give a vinegary taste to the wine. Others introduce bitter tastes into the wine. And the worst of them form hydrogen sulfide gas, which makes the wine smell like rotten eggs. In wine-growing regions that have been fermenting grapes for thousands of years, selected yeast strains abound. The best yeasts are used, and the spent yeast is poured out, or fed to pigs, where billions of still-live spores enter the air, just waiting to colonize next year's grape crop. The wild yeasts present in America are not these selected strains, although research shows them building up in the wine regions of California.

So winemakers have taken to using potassium metabisulfite to kill off or stun into stupefaction all yeasts and microorganisms in the must as soon as it's pressed. The sulfur dioxide (SO_2) that's released by the sulfite into the juice both prevents oxidation and cleans the juice of unwanted organisms. The sulfite is added to the juice as soon as it's crushed and is then allowed to sit for about a day, at which point the desired wine yeast is added.

Wine Yeasts Can Tolerate Sulfite

The yeasts we use today have been selected for complete fermentation, meaning they can still work and exist in alcohol concentrations up to about 15 percent or more and in SO_2 concentrations that kill or stop wild yeasts from working. The best of them are also resistant to the formation of hydrogen sulfide. They form compact lees, or dregs, when they settle (a bad yeast settles lightly and clouds the wine as soon as you try to move it for racking; such a wine can be difficult to clear later in the winemaking process).

How Much to Add

Adding sulfite takes precision. You should understand exactly how much you need to add so that you don't oversulfite the wine. I once ruined 10 gallons (38 L) of the most beautiful chardonnay by misplacing a decimal point and adding 10 times more sulfite than I should have. Once it's in, there's no way to get it out. Since sulfite can be harmful to humans, we want to add as little as possible. Some commercial winemakers use the Walthari method, in which no sulfite is used. But that method involves keeping everything under carbon dioxide, including a special airproof bottling machine. The only way to do away with sulfite in the home situation is to take your chances with the wild yeasts, hoping that your addition of a selected yeast will overpower the wild ones and the increasing alcohol levels will keep them off. And this may be the answer if you are allergic to or sensitive to sulfite and the sulfur dioxide it produces. There are rare individuals who are violently allergic to sulfite, and others who get headaches, flushed feelings, or other low-grade reactions to just a glass or two of wine. Most people, however, are not allergic to sulfite at all, and if the amounts are kept to a minimum, it won't be noticed by or harm the drinker, as generations who have used wine as a healthful beverage can attest. The problem with commercial wines is that winemakers tend to go overboard with the sulfite. The FDA allows up to 350 ppm (parts per million) of sulfite in wine. In California, the Wine Institute proposes an upper limit of 175 ppm in reds and 225 ppm in whites. Even these amounts will grossly oversulfur a wine.

Even 100 ppm can be detected by a sensitive nose. I remember sitting with one of the most respected winemakers in the Napa Valley. I'd tasted his sauvignon blanc the day before and smelled sulfur in the nose — the faint aroma of sulfurous match fumes. During our discussion of sulfur, he pulled out a bottle of the same vintage of sauvignon blanc I'd wrinkled my nose at and poured out glasses to show how clean the smell was, even at the 100 to 150 ppm sulfite he was using. It smelled like sulfur to me, and I told him so. He sniffed at it and said that his very trained nose could detect no sulfur. It was then that I formulated my theory that sulfur can burn out well-used noses to the point that it makes itself undetectable.

Wines made using the recommendations in this book will not smell like sulfur dioxide. Besides the problem of sulfur smell, too much SO_2 can destroy tannins and flavor constituents in the must. You'll notice that when you clean up a red wine spill with a cloth soaked in sulfite solution: it immediately bleaches out the color. It does this in the must, too.

"A general recommendation is to add 50 ppm total SO_2 at crush," says Tom Cottrell, "but if you've got a high pH, that may not be enough. Conversely, if you've got a low pH, that may be too much."

I'm going to recommend that you add 50 ppm of potassium metabisulfite (sodium bisulfate can add a bitter taste) to the must. When potassium metabisulfite is added to a liquid, it dissociates, releasing sulfur dioxide, a gas that dissolves in the liquid. Fifty ppm is enough to kill spoilage microorganisms, act as an antioxidant, and stun wild yeasts, so that tomorrow when you add your strain of yeast, it can take over without challenge. It's also low enough so that the red will be able to undergo malolactic fermentation at the end of the primary, when you may decide to add a malolactic culture to the wine. At concentrations higher than 50 ppm, malolactic fermentation is inhibited by the SO_2.

Be aware, however, that this figure of 50 ppm is for a must with a pH in the ideal range of 3.2 for whites and 3.5 for reds. At pH 2.8, 15 ppm may be perfectly adequate, as more sulfur dioxide stays in active form at lower pHs. As the pH rises to 3.3, 25 ppm can be adequate. At 3.5, 50 ppm is enough. But at pH 3.6, you will have to use 75 ppm, and at pH 3.8, it will take 100 ppm of sulfite to achieve the desired effect.

At pH 3.5, more than half of the potassium metabisulfite will quickly *combine* with organic molecules in the musts and be rendered unfit for active duty. About 40 percent will be *free* bisulfites and other salts, and a small percentage will be *active* SO_2. At lower pHs, the percentage of active SO_2 is higher. At higher pHs, almost all additions of potassium metabisulfite are turned into unavailable compounds, so more is needed to get enough active SO_2 into the must to gain its benefits.

Whites, because they need more antioxidant, and because they are not usually inoculated with malolactic starter, take about 70 ppm at a pH of 3.4, as do reds immediately pressed into juice.

Scientists have discovered a lot about sulfur dioxide in wine, but most of what they've learned is applicable only to the commercial winemaker who can measure molecular, free, combined, and total SO_2 in a wine. For the home winemaker at the crush stage, it's enough to shoot for the 50 ppm for reds and 70 ppm for whites, adjustable as the pH deviates from the optimums (see table 17). Most winemakers add more sulfite later in the winemaking process, and we'll address further additions when we get there.

When dealing with badly overripe grapes or botrytized berries, some winemakers recommend adding up to 150 ppm of total SO_2 to achieve the sterilizing effect. That's just too much. I'm assuming, however, that you've got grapes at the peak of ripeness in wonderfully sound condition, having just picked them from your vineyard. In such a case, 50 ppm for reds and 70 ppm for whites is sufficient. If the whole idea of adding this chemical to your wine bothers you, add at least 25 ppm at crush and 25 ppm before bottling at mid-range pHs. Or add none at all and trust to luck.

Table 17: pH Effect on Sulfite Additions

pH OF MUST	TOTAL S$_{O2}$ NEEDED FOR EQUAL STERILIZING POWER	CAMPDEN TABLETS TO ADD PER GALLON OF MUST
Red Wines		
2.8	15 ppm	⅓ tablet
2.9	20 ppm	½ tablet
3.0	25 ppm	½ tablet
3.1	30 ppm	⅔ tablet
3.2	40 ppm	⅔ tablet
3.3	50 ppm	1 tablet
3.4	50 ppm	1 tablet
3.5	50 ppm	1 tablet
3.6	60 ppm	1⅓ tablets
3.7	70 ppm	1½ tablets
3.8	100 ppm	2 tablets
White Wines		
2.8	20 ppm	½ tablet
3.0	40 ppm	⅔ tablet
3.2	60 ppm	1⅓ tablets
3.4	70 ppm	1½ tablets
3.6	80 ppm	1⅔ tablets
3.8	120 ppm	2½ tablets

Note: *For those who can't measure pH, figure underripe and tart grapes at pH 3.0, ripe grapes at pH 3.2 to 3.6, and overripe grapes at pH 3.8.*

Tablets vs. Crystals

To get the desired amount of sulfite in the wine, you can use Campden tablets, available from any wine suppliers (see appendix 3), or pure loose crystals of potassium metabisulfite. Campden tablets have the virtue of being premeasured doses — each tablet contains 0.44 gram of sulfite and will bring 1 gallon (3.8 L) of must to about 50 ppm total SO_2, which is what we're after for a must of about pH 3.5. Five tablets treat 5 gallons (19 L), and so on. The tablets must be crushed, added to some of the juice, and stirred until totally dissolved. I usually dissolve them in a little warm tap water because the must is so murky that I can't see if there are any undissolved particles. Once dissolved, in juice or water, the dosed liquid is stirred thoroughly into the vat of must so that the sulfite is dispersed evenly through the whole vat. This is most important, so stir until you know it's thoroughly mixed in.

If you're using the potassium metabisulfite crystals, figure 2 grams to 5 gallons (19 L) of must. Dissolve them in a little warm water before adding to the must, and mix thoroughly, as with Campden tablets. Unless you have a very accurate scale, I'd strongly recommend sticking with premeasured Campden tablets for additions of sulfite to musts, and reserve the powdered form for making sterilizing solutions. That way you can hardly go wrong.

Adding Sugar to the Must

As a very rough approximation, the amount of alcohol in the finished wine will be a little more than half the Brix of the must. In many lackluster years, growers in the northern half of the country will find that Brix reaches only 17, 18, or 19 — or less if the weather has been disastrously cold and cloudy. The grapes just don't ripen. That's one reason why it's so important to choose the right variety, one that ripens well in your climate, for the backyard vineyard. Low-sugar grapes produce low-alcohol wines: A must of 17 Brix, for instance, will yield a dry wine of just a little more than 9 percent alcohol. Low-alcohol wines are soft, prone to wine disorders and to infections by organisms that would otherwise be discouraged by adequate alcohol content. It makes sense to add sugar to the must to produce wines of 12.5 percent alcohol — the optimum for a fine wine.

For the first few years that I made wine, I avoided adding sugar, or *chaptalizing*, as it's called in France, where there are laws against it. I thought that if the French eschewed the practice they had good reasons. And they do: Grape-growing areas of France are planted with vines that almost always reach sufficient sugar for an alcohol content of about 12 percent. Besides, I thought, white sugar is terrible, tooth-rotting, body-buzzing stuff, and I didn't want it in my wine.

I've since learned that although I may add sugar, I don't get it in the finished wine. It's entirely converted to alcohol by the yeasts — the self-same ethyl alcohol that they produce from the natural sugars in the grapes. There are no flavor components in pure sugar to affect the taste of the wine either way. All it does is raise alcohol toward desired levels.

Pure, white table sugar is perfect for this task. Wine yeasts are excellently equipped with the know-how to convert almost every molecule to alcohol. This sugar, sucrose, is cheap, and every bit as good as dextrose, fructose, and other kinds of sugar. In fact, it's superior to most and costs less. Exotic sugars may or may not be suited to the taste of your yeast. Grape sugar, or d-glucose, is ideal; so is fructose. Maltose, lactose, and others shouldn't be used. When sucrose, ordinary table sugar, is dissolved in water (which comprises most of the grape must, of course), it dissociates into d-glucose and d-fructose. Wine yeasts go right to work on it. (A lot of beer makers go wrong by adding sucrose to their malt. Beer yeasts have trouble converting sucrose to alcohol, and that's why so much homemade beer has an unpleasant, sweet aftertaste.)

Only pure white table sugar should be used. Brown sugar, "raw" sugar, or turbinado sugar all contain molasses, which will add nothing to a fine wine but a suspicious taste.

Of course, there's something to be said for a natural wine — one with only 11 percent alcohol made from a must with a Brix of 19. That way you can say, "This is the way it was that year — a little light on the sugar, but a nice year nevertheless." Eleven percent alcohol is a little light, but still enough to preserve and protect the wine. Anything less than 19 Brix, however, needs extra alcohol for balance as well as protection, and sugar should be added. My personal rule is to add sugar to any must under 20 Brix.

The Right Gravity

A must with a specific gravity of 1.088 contains 230 grams of soluble solids (sugar) per liter. The finished wine will contain 12.5 percent alcohol. This is what we're shooting for.

Table 18: Figuring Sugar Adjustment

SPECIFIC GRAVITY OF MUST	SUGAR IN THAT MUST (GRAMS/LITER)	BRIX
1.047	124	12.0
1.051	135	13.0
1.055	145	14.0
1.059	157	15.0
1.063	168	16.0
1.068	178	17.0
1.072	188	18.0
1.076	201	19.0
1.081	213	20.0

Note: *Remember to adjust the specific gravity for temperature variations from the norm (see table 14, page 107). And when figuring specific gravities between the above numbers, interpolate other numbers. For example, a must with the specific gravity of 1.065 would contain about 173 grams of sugar per liter, with a Brix of about 16.5.*

Now read the Brix of your must with the hydrometer. (The hand refractometer isn't accurate enough for this purpose.) Let's say that the reading is a specific gravity of 1.070. By consulting table 15 (page 111), which gives percentages of "potential alcohol," you'll see that this must will produce a wine with about 9.7 percent alcohol. Sugar should be added. Now consult table 18 (above) to convert specific gravity to grams of sugar per liter. A specific gravity of 1.070 means the must contains about 182 grams of sugar per liter. The must needs 48 grams per liter more sugar to bring it from 182 to 230. Now multiply 48 times the number of liters in your must to get the total grams of sugar to add. If you've got 60 liters, you'd add 2,880 grams. A thousand grams is a kilogram, equal to 2.2 pounds. Put another way, a pound equals 454 grams. Dividing 2,880 by 454 gives us 6.34 pounds of sugar.

To figure pounds of sugar to add to a must, use this formula:

x = grams sugar/liter (figured from the specific gravity of the must)
y = liters of must

$$\text{Pounds of sugar to add} = \frac{(230 - x)y}{454}$$

For example, assume the must has a specific gravity of 1.071, equivalent to 186 grams of sugar per liter, and that you have 20 liters of must.

$$\frac{(230 - 186)20}{454} = \frac{(44)20}{454} = \frac{880}{454} = 1.94 \text{ pounds of sugar}$$

Adding 1.94 pounds of sugar to this 20-liter must will raise the specific gravity to about 1.088, equivalent to about 230 grams/liter of sugar, which will yield a final alcohol content of 12.5 percent.

Adjusting Acidity

It's extremely important that the acid (titratable acid, or TA) content of a wine be at least 0.55 for reds and 0.65 for whites. Most home winemakers won't experience acid-deficient musts unless their grapes are overripe. Those who live in hot regions may, however, have acid-deficient grapes. Adjusting the acid up to appropriate levels should always be done in such cases. Low-acid wines don't live very long and are subject to wine disorders. Worse, they are flat and flabby, unbalanced, and short on thirst-quenching power. The reason why a cold glass of unsweetened lemonade seems to work better than plain water on a thirst is that the acid in the lemon juice gives that slightly sour edge that slakes a thirst.

Most of the acid in a must — usually somewhat over 50 percent — will be tartaric. About 30 to 35 percent will be malic, and the rest will be citric, with traces of a few other organic acids. Acid blend, available from most winemaking suppliers (see appendix 3), is a mixture of tartaric, malic, and citric acid in about those proportions. Malic acid is very sour, tartaric is milder, and citric is for balance. Because citric acid can be converted to vinegary acetic acid during fermentation, it's best not to use it for musts, and so many winemakers adjust acid using only tartaric acid. Incidentally, the whole point of doing a malolactic fermentation on your must is to change the very sour malic acid to lactic acid, which is smoother on the palate.

We're going to assume that you want to bring the acidity to an optimum 0.60 for reds and 0.70 for whites — figures slightly higher than the minimums mentioned on page 137. We know that 18 grams of tartaric acid will raise the TA of 5 gallons (19 L) of must by 0.10 percent. Thus it's easy to figure how much acid to add to your acid-deficient must.

Let's say that we have a red must with a TA of 0.53.
Desired TA = 0.60
Actual TA = 0.53
Difference = 0.07, or ⁷⁄₁₀ of 0.10 percent
⁷⁄₁₀ of 18 grams = 18 × 0.7 = 12.6 grams of tartaric acid per 5 gallons (19 L) of must

Let's do another example, this time for a white must that measures 0.58 TA. And let's say that we're vinifying 20 gallons (76 L).
Desired TA = 0.70
Actual TA = 0.58
Difference = 0.12
An increase of 0.12 = 18 × 1.2 = 21.6 grams per 5 gallons (19 L) of must
For 20 gallons of must, 21.6 × 4 = 86.4 grams of tartaric acid

It's much more common for northern home winemakers to run into high-acid grapes. Some commercial winemakers reduce the acidity of musts by adding alkaline substances such as calcium carbonate, or by adding low-acid grape juice concentrates to dilute the acidity. Both methods are a way to turn a promising wine into something mediocre and, in the case of using calcium carbonate, something undrinkable.

The two safe ways of reducing acid are (1) to inoculate the must with malolactic bacteria toward the end of the primary fermentation, so that a percentage of the malic acid is converted into lactic acid — a much milder acid on the tongue, and (2) to cold-stabilize the wine, which precipitates some tartaric acid out of the wine. We'll describe both these operations later, as we get there.

Other than using these methods, I'd let the natural acidity be. That may mean making wine with somewhat higher acidity than is perfect, but it will be a clean wine, unadulterated with chalk or concentrates.

Acid Adjustment and pH

A TA above 0.90 usually unbalances a wine, making it too acid to the taste. Some whites, such as Champagne-based wine or botrytized Ravat 51, can carry slightly higher acidities, but 0.90 is considered an upper limit for high-quality, balanced wine, white or red. One would think that high TA would correlate with the pH of a must or wine, as pH also measures acidity. But pH is the negative logarithm of positively charged hydrogen (H) ions, while TA measures the acid content of must or wine by weight. They do not correlate perfectly. In Washington State, for instance, growers often experience a grape crop with high acid *and* high pH.

Tartaric acid dissociates in a liquid into positive and negative H ions more easily than malic acid, which is why it is stronger to the taste. The free H ions are atomic mousetraps, just waiting for anything they can chemically grab to bump into them. This includes the human tongue, and it's their presence that the tongue interprets as sour — too sour and you spit it out fast.

pH SCALE

Increasing Acidity

- 1.0 — *Most acid*
- 2.0
- 3.0
- 4.0   ] *Range of wine pH*
- 5.0
- 6.0
- 7.0 *Neutral*
- 8.0
- 9.0
- 10.0
- 11.0
- 12.0
- 13.0
- 14.0 *Most alkaline*

Increasing Alkalinity

If you add tartaric acid to a low-acid must, you'll also beneficially decrease the pH by a hard-to-predict amount toward the acid side of the scale. Robert Byloff of Penn State tells of a poor-nosed, off-color wine of high pH (4.0) that was brought to pH 3.4 by the addition of tartaric acid and then was cold-stabilized. He claims it won a bronze medal at a national tasting.

TA correction with tartaric acid has a beneficial effect on high pH, bringing it down, but *the correction is always made to adjust the TA, not the pH*. If the TA is just right but the pH is a little high, a smart wine-maker would leave it alone. TA has

10 times more effect than pH on a wine's taste, so it's TA that's adjusted, and pH is left to fend for itself. Even though we don't adjust much for pH, that measurement is important to know for its effects on wine quality, and for the addition of the proper amount of sulfite. After adjusting with tartaric acid, the pH should be read again, as it will change.

Wines under pH 3.0 are hard to ferment, and ferment more slowly when they do start. They have dipped into the acid range where wine yeasts start to give up. Wines at pH 4.0 or more taste poor and flabby and lack character and fruitiness. They are also susceptible to the growth of wine spoilage organisms that like conditions tending toward the neutral. A pH of 3.5 stops almost all growth of bad microbes. For this reason, some wine scientists say that 3.5 should be the upper limit of any wine pH.

Here are some other effects of pH: As the pH rises above 3.5, wine color tends toward the violets and purples; below pH 3.5, toward reds and typical claret colors. Wine connoisseurs consider a ruby red color superior to shades of purple. And according to scientific tastings, they have every reason to correlate color with quality, since wines at pH 3.5 or lower consistently score higher in flavor categories than wines of higher pH. It's a color component, anthocyanin, that correlates most strongly with good flavors in red wine.

Also, as we've seen, lower pH helps potassium metabisulfite do its job, as more SO_2 is preserved in its free and active forms. At pH 4.0, almost all SO_2 is changed to bisulfate ions. A high-pH wine is also much more prone to oxidation, which reduces flavors and adds brownish colors to both red and white wines. Finally, reds with a pH of less than 3.3 tend to resist malolactic fermentation.

The pH of a must will go up as fermentation progresses. "Musts of pH 3.2 to 3.4 end up as 3.6 to 3.8 as wine," says Byloff, "so I'd say that 3.1 or 3.2 is the ideal must pH for whites, and the ideal for reds is something like 3.4."

We've already factored proper pH into our decision (made earlier in the day) to harvest, so most likely you'll have a must with a pH close to ideal, or at least as close to ideal as allowed by the other factors of Brix and TA. And yet it's good to check the pH of the prepared must, so you can be aware of all the important conditions as you replace the towel for the last time and head off for a well-deserved beer in front of the TV.

Harvest Day Summary

This, then, is harvest day:

1. Read the Brix, TA, and pH of a sample of vineyard grapes to decide to harvest.

2. Harvest.

3. Make the must.

4. Read the Brix, TA, and pH of the must.

5. Add potassium metabisulfite now if the TA is above 0.55.

6. Adjust the sugar, if necessary.

7. Adjust the TA with tartaric acid, if necessary.

8. Reread the pH after the addition of tartaric acid to get the final pH before fermentation.

9. Add potassium metabisulfite now if the TA was below 0.55 and has been adjusted.

10. Clean up all equipment and spills.

If, at this point, you've got a crock of whites soaking on the skins, plan to press out the juice 8 to 16 hours later, usually the next morning before work. What's getting up a couple of hours early compared to the thrill of a home-made chardonnay with character? Otherwise, you're off duty for 24 hours.

The bride is prepared for the bridegroom. Tomorrow, grape juice will be introduced to yeast. The courtship will start slowly for a day or two, then skyrocket into a fountain of sparkles. After this mad passion of first meeting, the yeast and grape juice will be no more, spent and exhausted from their wild revel. In their place will be grape juice transformed and yeast fulfilled: wine. If the wine is well made, the marriage will improve with age.

Pressing Whites for Fermentation

After 8 to 16 hours, whites that have been left on the skins should be pressed out. You'll want a grape press, because while you can squeeze the must by pouring it through cheesecloth and then pressing by hand, that's a long and messy procedure. Presses are usually wood, although occasionally one of stainless steel will pop up. No other materials will really do, and aren't likely to be found. A basket press is best for the home winemaker.

I find that extra hands make pressing go much easier. One person dips the must into the press's basket, which should always be lined with a fine-mesh nylon bag (sold by all winemaking suppliers; see appendix 3). It's a good idea to have two or three bags, and while one is being emptied of the pressed skins, called pomace, the other is in the basket being filled. Then it's nice to have someone on the crank or handle and someone else selecting music, watching out for spills, and helping as needed. You can, however, do all these things yourself. From long practice, let me encourage you to enlist at least one other person.

As you pour the must into the nylon bag, a lot of free juice will run out, down into the press's sluice, and into a waiting vat. The vat can be a carboy if you want to do the primary fermentation in glass to give white wines extra protection against oxidation, or an open-topped vessel of the types already described. Wide funnels, available at wine shops, get the juice into the carboy and not all over the floor. A wide funnel may be the most useful piece of equipment of all, this first week. In any case, the press needs to be placed on a table, or somewhere above the vat or carboy. For up to 50 gallons (190 L) of wine production, the smallest presses will do.

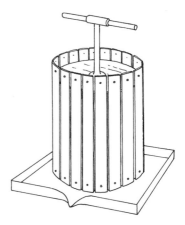

A basket press separates the grape juice from the pomace.

You can choose to save the free-run juice and vinify it separately, looking for an extra measure of quality. A white made from this juice will be lighter and fresher, but not necessarily more flavorful. I think a more well-rounded wine results when the free-run and pressed juices are vinified together. If the pressed must contains lots of solid particles, and you're looking for a light and delicate wine, you can let the must settle for another day and rack the juice off the muck before adding yeast.

When the nylon bag is about three-quarters full of juice and loose skins, fold the top over and start applying pressure. Firm squeezing is enough.

Pressing too hard adds the worst of what the skins have to offer, such as bitter principles, and the bitter contents of broken grape seeds. Just get most of the juice out and let it go at that. The pomace cakes are good for the compost pile. They'll also lure bees, yellow jackets, and other "sweet-toothed" insects.

Some European vintners use the pomace — there, called marc — to make a low-quality distilled drink called marc or grappa. Usually they dump sugar, water, and the pomace together and ferment it. It is nearly always a bad drink. In aristocratic ages, when the ordinary fellow had little of anything, marc was certainly better than no spirits at all. It's a personal test of macho to down a shot glass full of marc without a grimace. I say forget it. It will make better compost than beverage. In fact, Austrians are using ground grape marc in composting toilets — waterless toilets with a tank of rotting marc that digests human wastes to a clean, odorless state within a month. Also, the heat from a 5-cubic-meter block of marc will warm a small room or stable over a five-month winter, and the Austrians and French are investigating its uses as a fuel. These are better applications for it than making a beverage.

After pressing, clean the rim of the vat or carboy with a clean cloth or paper towel moistened with the sterilizing solution, and wash any spilled juice off the outside. Cover with towel and board, or cotton in case of the carboy, and then clean up the equipment and floor. Puddles of grape juice left lying around or splashed on surfaces will become nurseries for grape molds and fungi. The press should be given a final rinse of sterilizing solution, and the nylon bags should be made as clean as when you bought them, then air-dried and stored away.

Adding the Yeast

About a day — more or less, the hours aren't critical — after you add the sulfite, you add the yeast.

When the grapes come from the vineyard, the skins are colonized by any one of hundreds of possible yeasts. But researchers in Europe have found that these are mostly low-alcohol-tolerant strains such as *Kloeckera apiculata*. In fact, one scientist who microscopically identified yeast strains from vineyards in the north and south of Europe said that good, alcohol-tolerant wine yeasts "are inhabitants of wineries, not grapes on the vine."

Occasionally *Saccharomyces cerevisiae*, a true wine yeast, does occur on ripening grapes, but it can't be depended on to be there. Many home winemakers routinely use a popular strain of *S. cerevisiae*, known commercially as Montrachet 522, or just Montrachet, to ferment their musts.

Here I must add a word of caution. It appears that Montrachet 522 is implicated in production of hydrogen sulfide (H_2S). Although this yeast works fast, does a complete job of fermentation to dryness, and makes compact lees, hydrogen sulfide production is intolerable. There's some dispute on this. Dr. John McGrew at the USDA shook off the suggestion that Montrachet yeast causes H_2S. "It's more likely due to the lack of yeast nutrients in the must, or elemental sulfur left on the grape skins at harvest," he said. Similarly, Theo Rosenbrand, former winemaster at Sterling Vineyards in the Napa Valley, said, "I use Montrachet for all our wines, white or red."

On the other hand, Mike Grgich told me, "Montrachet does produce H_2S. I use Pasteur Institute yeast." That's a strain of *Saccharomyces bayanus*, known widely as Pasteur Champagne yeast. "I use Pasteur Champagne yeast from the Wine Lab [now Gusmer Enterprises; see appendix 3] for all my wines," said Arnold Tudal. And many others I've met agree that Montrachet, for all its virtues, is the single greatest reason for H_2S in wines. I've personally used Montrachet and made wines completely free of H_2S's awful smell, but then I've also had the H_2S problem in other batches using this yeast. I think the condition of the grapes has a lot to do with it; the fresher the grapes, the less likelihood of H_2S. But recently, after hearing a number of horror stories about Montrachet, I've sworn off in favor of Pasteur Champagne.

Types of Wine Yeast

There are many other commercial yeasts available to winemakers, and the subject of their subtle differences would take up a book in itself. Here's a summary of the most popular types:

- **Montrachet** (*Saccharomyces cerevisiae*). Most widely used yeast; numbered UC Davis 522. A vigorous strain with high SO_2 tolerance. Implicated in hydrogen sulfide production.

- **Pasteur Champagne** (*Saccharomyces bayanus*). A yeast developed by the Pasteur Institute and numbered UC Davis 595. Moderately vigorous with high SO_2 and alcohol tolerance. Used for all wine types, but especially for sparkling wines and stuck fermentations.

- **California Champagne** (*Saccharomyces bayanus*). Another strain of *bayanus*, number UC Davis 505. Slow to moderately vigorous with extremely rapid, compact precipitation of spent yeast lees. Facilitates riddling of bottle-fermented sparkling wine.

- **Epernay 2** (*Saccharomyces cerevisiae*). A slow-fermenting, general-purpose strain of *cerevisiae*, as opposed to Montrachet's fast fermentation. Used for reds, whites, and sparkling wine. Also known as Côte des Blancs.

- **Flor Sherry** (*Saccharomyces fermentati*). UC Davis 519. The culture needed to produce flor or fino-type sherries in hot, dry regions.

Most of these and many others are found at good winemaking supply shops, but if you can't find the one you want, there are a number of companies that specialize in wine yeasts, including these basic types. There's a list of mail-order suppliers in appendix 3.

Many growers of pinot noir recommend the use of Assmanshausen wine yeast for that variety. It's a slow-acting yeast and gives a long fermentation under cool conditions. Pinot noir can be left on the skins as long as two weeks with use of this yeast and fermentation temperatures in the low 60s or upper 50s Fahrenheit (12–18°C).

One study done by the Taylor Wine Company evaluated the length of fermentation and quality of seyval blanc, De Chaunac, and Vidal 256, each vinified with four yeasts: Pasteur Champagne, California Champagne, Montrachet 522, and Epernay 2. Epernay took 67 days to ferment to dryness, compared with 72 days for Pasteur Champagne and California Champagne, and even less for Montrachet. Montrachet and Epernay produced better-tasting Vidals than either Pasteur or California Champagne, but flavor differences among the other grapes and yeasts were not discernible.

If you're vinifying any species of *Vitis rotundifolia*, the muscadine grape, be aware that musts of this grape are usually deficient in natural available nitrogen, which yeast needs to work properly. In musts of other varieties, there's ordinarily enough nitrogen from proteins that the yeast breaks down. But muscadine musts should be given added yeast nutrients, available at most winemaking shops or any of the mail-order yeast suppliers in appendix 3.

The yeast usually comes in a freeze-dried powdered form and is dormant. Some winemakers will start the yeast in lukewarm water charged with a little sugar on harvest day so that the yeast is awake and beginning to work when it's added to the must the next day. It does get the fermentation off to a faster start, but the value of doing that is debatable, except when the air temperature is very warm and it's desirable to have wine yeast colonize the must as soon as possible to prevent spoilage by other organisms.

Usually, I simply dissolve the yeast in lukewarm water — *not hot water* — and pour it into the must, stirring it in thoroughly. Hot water can kill the yeast, so make sure the water temperature is less than 100°F (38°C). Yeast usually comes in packets, with a packet good for 5 gallons (19 L) of must. Bulk jars of yeast are available but are probably much more yeast than a home winemaker needs, and it's not a good idea to keep yeast for a year. Buy just what you need. If you do add from a jar, figure about 1 tablespoon (14 g) per 5 gallons (19 L), since even one yeast cell will, in time, multiply enough to colonize the must.

Yeast and Stuck Fermentation

Sometimes the fermentation will stick before the yeast has entirely converted the sugar to alcohol — that is, fermentation will just stop. This is often due to a shortage of yeast nutrients. Most winemakers in this strait will add some more wine yeast, plus some yeast nutrient, and hope that the must starts working again. A light aeration by racking will help the new yeast charge get going.

THE PRIMARY FERMENTATION

Now the must is charged with yeast. There's no turning back. Your grape juice is on its way to becoming wine. Within 12 to 24 hours, the must will start to bubble; by 36 to 48 hours, it will be fizzing strongly; at 70 to 80 hours, the process will peak, and then the bubbling will slow down and taper off. Exactly how long all this will take is determined primarily by the temperature. At 50 to 55°F (10–12°C), it can take several weeks for the primary fermentation to finish; at 85 to 90°F (29–32°C), the must can rush to a violent completion in three days.

Punching Down the Cap

Once fermentation starts, you should punch down the cap at least twice a day. The cap comprises the skins and other material that floats on the fermenting must. I wash my left hand and arm, then reach into the vat and swirl the cap down into the wine, breaking it up and making sure that liquid covers it all. This adds some air to the must, which helps the yeast work and carries off any odorous gases. Keeping the cap punched down also prevents bad bacteria or molds from colonizing the skins that float on top. White wine has less of a cap, since there are no skins, but needs stirring of the surface scum twice a day too.

This is a very important step and shouldn't be shirked. I shirked it on one of my first batches of red simply because I didn't know I was supposed to do it. After five days of primary fermentation, the cap looked very unsavory, and the wine eventually tasted the same way. Keeping some air in the must during the primary also reduces the chance of hydrogen sulfide production. Finally, keeping the skins mixed into the must elicits the most color and flavor extractives from them.

Fermentation Temperature

The art of winemaking comes into play now, as the winemaker determines how long the skins will remain in the working must, and how long the primary fermentation will take. In commercial wineries, the temperature is often controlled: I've seen stainless steel tanks wrapped with hoses, through which flows water of predetermined temperature, to cool down warm-weather fermentations or warm them on cold days. I've seen whole rooms of vats that are temperature controlled. The furious fermentation of a primary creates *heat*, and at the gallonages vinified commercially, enormous heat, which must be controlled. Small batches such as 5 to 40 gallons (19–150 L) heat up only a little. We home winemakers are pretty much limited to temperatures we can find around the house. Many basements stay at about 60°F (16°C), if they're well insulated from the first floor. Check the temperature there if you've got a clean place to put your vat. When I lived in Pennsylvania, I used to use my living room. To keep the temperature of red musts up, I placed the vat near a hot-air vent — but *not* so that the air could blow directly on the vat. Whites were sheltered in a corner near the bookcases, where the stone walls kept temperatures down. Some people use a porch, garage, or other place subject to outside ambient air temperatures. But these places are exposed to large temperature swings between days that may reach 80°F (27°C), and nights that could get down in the 50s Fahrenheit (teens, in Celsius). A steady temperature is much preferable to wild swings. The latter can result in a stuck fermentation as the yeast — alternately pushed toward action in the daytime and dormancy at night — gives up.

As a general rule, Tom Cottrell says, "the lower 80s [high 20s, in Celsius] is a happy place to be for fermenting reds. At higher temperatures, you can get off flavors. If the temperature is much cooler, you get less color extraction." The general rule for whites is a range from 55 to 65°F (12–18°C), although chardonnay will be excellent at temperatures in the 65 to 75°F (18–23°C) range.

Skin Contact Time

At this point, your intention — what kind of wine you want to make — comes into play. If you're going for a big, intense red, you'll want more skin contact time; light, fruity reds will take less contact time. A lot of winemaking involves creating conditions and letting natural processes work, but the decision of wine style is yours alone, and contact time with the skins is one of the points in the process that allows your art to flow in. If it's your first time with reds, shoot for about five days on the skins, depending on how fast your fermentation is proceeding. If the air temperature in your fermenting area is only in the low 70s Fahrenheit (20s, in Celsius), don't fret. That temperature will do fine for reds, too, although the fermentation may take a little longer. As you're about to see, winemakers do their fermentations at all kinds of temperatures and skin contact times, and end up with wines to their taste.

Dr. John McGrew, for instance, talks about how he achieves a fruity red that can be drunk early, while more "important" reds are aging in the bottle. "If you want some reds to drink early and don't mind reducing the ultimate quality a bit, let the must ferment until just a third of the sugar is gone. [If you started at 21 Brix, that would mean when the must is reduced by fermentation to 14 Brix, as measured with the hydrometer.] Then press the must to take the wine off the skins and finish fermenting the wine with no more skin contact. You'll get softer and earlier wines using this technique."

"For excellent fruitiness in whites," he adds, "I stem and crush, add the sulfite, let it sit on the skins overnight, then press the juice out lightly and let it settle for 24 hours. Then I rack off the lighter juice, leaving the thick solids behind. I add the yeast to this lighter juice."

This early racking is unusual, but it adds to the freshness and fruitiness by getting rid of solid particles quickly. As is so often the case in winemaking, opinions differ widely: I know of one California winemaker who leaves his white wine on the gross lees for *nine months*. And he stirs it up every two weeks! More commonly when making whites, vintners count it a virtue to get the wine off the lees quickly.

To extract full flavor from reds like cabernet sauvignon or zinfandel, which have so much to give, long skin contact times are called for. I know one winemaker who keeps his Cabernet on the skins for six days at a fermentation temperature of about 80°F (27°C). He feels this extracts all the color and flavor he needs. Arnold Tudal in the Napa Valley fermented his cabernet sauvignon at cooler temperatures, 70 to 75°F (21–24°C), but left the wine on the skins for 11 days. Still others have told me of leaving it on the skins for two weeks at 55°F (13°C). Tom Cottrell says he believes most wine will have too much tannin with that long a skin contact time, especially if there are stems in the must. Tudal's wine, however, is not overly tannic, although it is very big and bursting with flavor and color intensity. Long skin contact time is common in Bordeaux and Burgundy. The fermentation of big reds at very cool temperatures, such as 55 to 60°F (13–16°C), is undergoing a vogue now in California, but one risks stuck fermentations at those levels. One home winemaker told me that he had made a zinfandel fermented at 60°F (16°C) and it took two months to work down to 1.2 Brix, and then it stopped working. Although it still had this residual sugar, he bottled it, and, of course, it started working again in the bottle. "It started pushing all the corks out," he said. "I thought about wiring them on, but the wine was in regular bottles, not Champagne bottles that can stand pressure, and I had visions of bottles exploding in the cellar." He finally stood the bottles up, removed the corks, plugged the tops with cotton, and let them stand this way for two days to let the residual sugar finish fermenting. Then he put the corks back in. But the spent yeast from this last fermentation kept that wine cloudy forever. So, it's important to make sure that your wines ferment at high enough temperatures to keep the yeast from quitting on you. I think Tom Cottrell's figures of about 65°F (18°C) for whites and 80°F (27°C) for reds are about right.

A word here about Maréchal Foch. If it's fermented on the skins, it often develops musky, metallic flavors. Some people like Foch that way, but I find the flavors less than subtle. Foch can be handled like chardonnay — crushed and allowed to sit on the skins overnight, then pressed out and fermented — to make a strawberry-colored "nouveau" that's ready to drink in a few months and is quite delicious.

Extended Maceration

Maceration means allowing the skins to sit and soak in the must. An extended maceration means just that — allowing them to sit in the must for an extended period of time.

My winemaking buddies in California and I started doing extended macerations on our cabernet sauvignons in 1988, and the result was a revelation. Even coming out of the press, the new wine had none of that gritty, hard taste or texture. It was smooth and fruity. The next two vintages — 1989 and 1990 — were incredibly good. And they've only gotten better since. One of my friends says ours is the only California wine she likes, and one of my winemaking buddies who owns a wine shop says that on those rare occasions when his customers get to taste our homemade stuff, they plead with him to sell them some. But of course we never do. We save those great wines for ourselves.

The extended time on the skins has several beneficial effects. Enzymes in the grapes and the yeast have plenty of time to disassemble the cells in the skins, allowing everything that the skins have in the sway of color, flavor, and fragrance to enter the wine. When we pressed our reds after just five days or so of fermentation, the skins were thick and hard to press, still containing lots of unbroken cells. After an extended maceration of three weeks, the skins are so spent that they press down easily and are like thin little slips of paper, even after a rather soft pressing.

The extended skin contact time also has the effect of allowing short-chain tannins to link up, forming long-chain polymers. These polymeric tannins are not as hard and bitter as the short-chain tannins. One of the functions of aging a wine is to give the tannins time to soften. Extended maceration allows that to happen to some extent before bottling, so the wines, while still tannic, are more drinkable sooner than wines pressed within a week or two of the start of fermentation.

How long should an extended maceration go? We let ours go 22 to 24 days. Some commercial winemakers in California allow the maceration to go for 28 days, which is about the outer limit. The commercial wineries, however, usually do the extended maceration at cooler temperatures. We do ours at ambient air temperatures, which means warm days and cool nights in coastal California at crush time.

Here's how we do it:

After the primary fermentation begins to slow and the fizz becomes light instead of rolling and boiling, we cover our fermenting vats with clear plastic taped down around the outside of the fermenter with duct tape. This keeps out fruit flies. We punch a small hole in the top of the cover near an edge to allow the carbon dioxide to escape. And of course we have to remove half the taped cover twice a day, or more often if we can, to punch the cap down.

When the fizzing really slows or the fermentation is complete (sometimes a strong yeast under warm temperatures will finish fermenting all the sugar in a week), we get a tank of carbon dioxide. Most towns have businesses that sell tanks of gases like oxygen and carbon dioxide; you return the tank when you're finished, so you're really only paying for the gas inside. We attach a piece of clear plastic tubing, such as you use for siphoning wine, to the nozzle on the tank and run it into the fermenting vat through the hole in the plastic cover. Then we add carbon dioxide gas under the plastic, but not into the must. The gas, since it's heavier than air, will float on top of the must, protecting it from air contact. We do this after every punchdown, and as we near the end of the maceration, we turn on the tank just a hair, so a minute amount of gas is flowing into the fermenting vat constantly.

After anywhere from 20 to 28 days, the cap of skins and detritus will fall and disappear under the wine. When the cap falls through, we know it's time to press. Sink a glass into that new wine and taste it. I bet you'll be very pleasantly surprised.

Malolactic Fermentation

When the primary fermentation starts to slow down, you may choose to add a culture of *Oenococcus oeni* bacteria (formerly known as *Leuconostoc*) to red musts. This causes a malolactic fermentation. The culture has one effect — it converts malic acid in the wine to lactic acid. This reduces the perceived sourness of the wine on the palate, along with reducing the acidity of the must, with a concomitant rise in the pH. Adding the culture is always called for when acid levels in reds are high (over TA 0.70). If you've adjusted the TA with tartaric acid, you wouldn't need to induce a malolactic fermentation. Cultures are obtainable from winemaking supply shops. Winemakers in the West tend to use a strain developed at UC Davis, available from Gusmer Enterprises (see appendix 3), while winemakers in the east tend to use PSU-1. Either strain will work wherever the wine is made. Putting white wines through a malolactic would reduce the acid considerably, possibly leaving the wine flabby, although full-malolactic, barrel-fermented, full lees–contact chardonnays have become popular at some California wineries.

Incidentally, once a barrel has held a wine undergoing malolactic fermentation, enough leuonostoc will lurk in the wood to cause a malolactic reaction in future young wines put in it.

There's a notion in France that new wine starts to ferment again, after sitting overwinter, due to rising spring temperatures. Winemakers there are actually noticing a naturally occurring malolactic fermentation, which can start all by itself in young wine when it gets warmer in the spring. Adding malolactic culture at the end of primary will head off this spring spritzing, which can push corks out if you've already bottled the wine, or at least make wine *pétillant* — prickly with tiny gas bubbles. To prevent this, I never bottle any wine until it's at least six months old, and preferably a year. If it's going to undergo a spontaneous malolactic fermentation in the spring, it will happen while the wine is still in the carboys or barrel and the gas can escape through the airlocks with which they're fitted.

After adding the malolactic culture, this special conversion of malic to lactic acid should be entirely completed within 10 days.

Pressing the Must

If the Brix of a red wine must has dropped by about two-thirds, or the specific gravity is between 1.030 and 1.040, you can press the wine off the skins and into carboys for further, slower fermentation to complete dryness (the secondary fermentation).

With whites, when two-thirds of the sugar has fermented or the specific gravity is about 1.010, transfer the wine into clean carboys with airlocks, racking it off the gross lees.

After your first few batches, you'll get a feel for how the length of the primary fermentation and temperature affect the final wine.

Once the bubbling in the primary vat slows down and you've determined by hydrometer that about two-thirds of the sugar is gone, the primary is over. The new wine — for it's qualified to be called wine now — is more exposed to air than it was when billows of carbon dioxide were coming off it. At this point it's necessary to transfer it to glass or barrel to keep it away from air for the rest of the fermentation (unless you follow the steps for an extended maceration; see page 150). Vinegar-producing organisms need air to survive, and they'll start working if the new wine is allowed to contact air for any length of time.

Reds with skins can be pressed out now, again, unless you're going for an extended maceration. As you're dipping the must out of the vat into the basket of the grape press, don't stir up the bottom of the vat. The bottom will contain a thick layer of grape seeds and spent yeast called the gross lees. Once your dipper starts to contain an abundance of grape seeds, stop and discard the rest. It should be only about a tenth of the vat or less, depending on how much gunk is down there. Only pressed-out new wine should go into the secondary fermentation vessels (carboys or a barrel). For whites, you've already pressed the skins, but try not to transfer the thick gunk on the bottom of the vat. Again, you should leave only a tenth or less of the vat's contents of spent yeast and solids that could impart off flavors to the wine. If your primary was done in a carboy, siphon it into clean carboys or a barrel, leaving the gross lees behind. A large siphon hose of high-quality clear plastic, available from all winemaking suppliers, can be used. A big funnel helps to catch splashes, even during siphoning.

THE SECONDARY FERMENTATION

The secondary fermentation can be done in 5-gallon (19 L) glass carboys or in an oak barrel. Some winemakers employ a combination of these, finishing the secondary in glass, and then, when the wine is completely fermented and relatively clean, racking it into an oak barrel for six months to a year. I recommend allowing the fermentation to finish before putting the wine into barrels. Here's why:

Barrels are used primarily to impart oak flavors to a wine. That can be just as easily achieved — or even more easily achieved — after the fermentation's finished. The secondary fermentation deposits lots of sediment, and this is far easier to deal with in glass. Consider: After the wine has spent a month in carboys, you decide to siphon (rack) it off the deposits into clean carboys. You can see the deposits (lees) in the bottom, easily distinguishable from the clearer wine above. In a barrel, you can't see the demarcation between the wine and the lees at all. So let the secondary fermentation finish in glass. When the wine is finished working, then put it in a barrel if you desire. You can add oak flavors to wine in glass carboys, too, avoiding barrels altogether. We'll consider this in detail when we discuss oak and barrels, but let's first describe how to set up your new wine in carboys.

USING AN AIRLOCK

1.

Fill the airlock with enough sulfite solution that each chamber is a little less than half full.

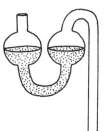

2.

When fitted to a carboy with fermenting wine, the carbon dioxide from fermentation forces itself through the first chamber and bubbles through the second.

3.

If you see the sulfite solution being drawn back toward the bottle, then fermentation has stopped and a slight vacuum has formed in the bottle. Immediately top up the carboy.

TYPES OF AIRLOCKS

cork to fit a 5-gallon (19 L) carboy; hole accommodates an airlock

two-piece plastic airlock

one-piece glass airlock

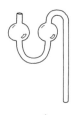

one-piece plastic airlock

New Wine

New wine, indeed. Although it's just past the primary, it is wine. Sample it as you would castor oil — just get a quick impression of the taste. It will be awful. Even Romanée-Conti is awful at this stage — replete with yeast, living and dead; full of all kinds of fresh volatile compounds produced in the fermentation; possibly laced with *Leuconostoc* bacteria. In France, in November, the new wine is sold as *vin nouveau*. When it's *really* vin nouveau (and not the filtered jug Beaujolais the French are happy to ship to people who think it's important to taste the new vintage before someone else does), it can be quite rough. I remember ordering vin nouveau in Angers and getting a raw, chalky-looking mixture of yeast and wine that gave me the sulfur burps for a day.

The new wine is a baby, by yeast out of grape juice. Just like a human baby, who's all squawks and bubbles and elimination at first but develops into a remarkable creature, so too will the new wine develop over time and with experience.

Using Airlocks

Five-gallon (19 L) carboys are familiar to anyone who's seen a water fountain with a large bottle of water upside down on top. So, if you have a friend in the bottled water business, now's the time to draw on that friendship. Most of us, however, will buy our carboys at the winemaker's shop. Choose glass carboys over plastic ones, as the acids and alcohol in the wine may leach unwanted compounds from plastic.

Because it's so important to keep air off the wine from now on, the carboys are stoppered with a cork that has a hole in it. An airlock will fit into the hole and allow CO_2 and other gases from the fermenting wine to pass out, but no outside air to pass back in. There are many types of airlocks. The most common are illustrated below. My favorite, for aesthetic reasons, is the one-piece glass airlock. It is very breakable and costly though, so mostly I use the plastic one-piece airlock.

Fill the carboys to the shoulder so there's plenty of room for foam in the bottle. Never let the foam reach the bottom of the cork, or it will go up through the airlock, and even out of the airlock all over the floor, where it will draw fruit flies and encourage molds to form. Then fit the airlock into the

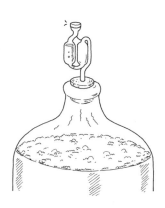

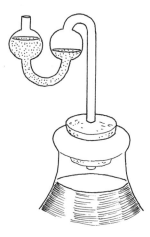

When filling a carboy for primary or secondary fermentation, fill only to the shoulder; this leaves room for foam. Foam should never reach or enter the airlock.

When topping up a carboy after fermentation, bring the wine into the lower neck, about an inch from the bottom of the cork.

carboy, filling it with sterilizing sulfite solution, as shown in the illustrations above. If wine does bubble into the airlock, clean and replace the airlock and lower the level of wine in the carboy.

The secondary fermentation should proceed in a room with relatively cool temperatures — from 60 to 70°F (16–21°C). Try to keep the carboys away from cold drafts. I threw a blanket over my bottles when I lived in Pennsylvania, so autumn was characterized at our house by a blanket in a corner of the living room from which protruded a group of airlocks burbling a gaseous rondo.

When the secondary fermentation ends completely, the space in the bottle may form a slight vacuum, which pulls the sterilizing solution in the airlock back toward the wine. Don't let this vacuum make the airlock work in reverse, pulling air (and drops of solution) into the bottle. The way to prevent this problem is to watch the secondary very carefully. After anywhere from a few days to a month or two, the bubbles through the airlock will slow from many a minute to just a few a day. A few days after that, all bubbling should have stopped. As soon as you're sure the bubbling has stopped for good, rack the wine off the lees into a clean carboy and stopper it with an airlock that's been well washed and recharged with sulfite solution. This time, fill the carboy with wine to within an inch (2.5 cm) of the bottom of the cork. This will leave only a minute amount of air in the bottle, which can be removed by giving the carboy a little shake. Some of the gases dissolved in the wine will come off, the airlock will give a few bubbles, and then all will be quiet and ready for aging.

Cleaning the Carboys

All carboys should be scrupulously clean. I remove spots from the inside by pouring a handful or two of clean sand into the bottle, then adding about 3 inches (7.6 cm) of hot ammonia water (about 1 part ammonia to 5 parts water). Stoppering the end with one hand and grasping the bottom of the bottle with the other, I swirl the sand-ammonia mixture throughout the bottle so that it scours the sides and bottom. Then I pour out the contents, fill with 3 inches (7.6 cm) or so of clean water, swirl again, pour it out, and fill, swirl, and pour twice more until I'm sure that the carboy is *clean* with a capital K.

I also wash the corks and airlocks with ammonia and hot water and rinse them in a similarly fanatic manner. After filling a carboy with wine, I wipe the rim and down inside the neck a little bit with a paper towel moistened with sterilizing solution. Then I put in the clean cork. I put the cork in first, add sterilizing solution to the airlock, then fit it down into the cork. That's easier than trying to get the right amount of solution into the airlock after it's in place on the bottle.

THE FIRST RACKING

Many winemakers add more sulfite to the wine at the first racking. If you've added the minimum that I recommended before, you could add half a Campden tablet per gallon (3.8 L) — or two to three tablets per 5 gallons (19 L), which would give you another 20 to 30 ppm sulfur dioxide in the wine. Many claim that this cleans and helps preserve wines, especially those that will eventually be laid down when aging. Since I have a bug about adding any more chemicals to my wine than I absolutely have to, I seldom add sulfite at this stage, so far with no apparent ill effects to any of my wines, even those that have reached ripe old ages of a dozen years or more.

Because the length of the secondary fermentation and the establishment of a clearly defined lees can take anywhere from 1 to 10 weeks, it's hard to give any rules for the timing of the first racking. Suffice it to say that it should be done when the fermentation has proceeded to dryness and bubbling stops. Almost always this will be before Christmas.

After the first racking, the amount of wine you have will be reduced by the amount of lees you've discarded. I've found that, as a general rule, you can expect to get two fully filled carboys from three secondary-fermentation carboys filled to the shoulder. If you need more wine to top up a bottle, use a sound and similar wine from the store or from your own stores of homemade wine. Racking involves having extra carboys on hand — you need only one extra if you clean the one you just emptied and use it for the next bottle you

- -

RACKING THE WINE

1. When carrying a carboy to your racking setup, handle carefully to avoid dispersing the lees back into the wine.

lees (sediment)

2. When siphoning, make sure the higher bottle is entirely above the lower bottle for positive suction. Siphon down as close to the sediment as you can before it starts to get sucked into the siphon.

Sometimes it's hard to see the end of the siphon in the murky wine, but it will usually curve to the side of the bottle, where it looks like this. Avoid stirring up the lees when jiggling the siphon to find the end.

have to rack. Over the years I've collected about four or five extras. They come in handy and, rather than cleaning as I go, I can clean the used carboys of their lees at my leisure, after I've finished racking.

Often you'll find that when you fill your carboys or barrel, there will be less than a carboy left over. This is where 1-gallon (3.8 L) glass jugs, like the kind used for apple cider, come in handy. You'll find that your wine shop will have stoppers with holes that will fit the gallon jugs and will accept airlocks. Having several gallon jugs of young wine available is very helpful when topping up carboys. In no case do you want to allow a carboy of wine that's finished fermenting to be partially filled, unless you're interested in watching strange and ugly cultures of microscopic organisms grow on your wine.

COLD STABILIZATION

Winemaking in cold-winter areas has some advantages, especially regarding cold stabilization. The basement receives the new, fully filled carboys. They go down anywhere from late October to December, depending on how long the secondary takes. The typical basement is in the low 50s Fahrenheit (low teens, in Celsius) at that time of year but by January can get down to the lower 40s or 30s (about 5–0°C), where it will stay until late February. This cold period has a beneficial effect on the wine. Not only do suspended solids settle, leaving a relatively clear wine after this two- to three-month period, but the wine is cold-stabilized, too. Cold stabilization precipitates bitartrate — cream of tartar or tartaric acid — out of the wine, and crystals of the compound settle to the bottom, putting a hard crust over the lees. This greatly simplifies the next racking, which should be done in March, or two to three months after the first racking.

The lees at the first racking are loose and prone to billow up into the wine, and they are easily sucked up into the siphon hose. At the second racking, after cold stabilization, the lees are fairly well sealed and don't billow. I still use care, though.

If you don't have a basement that naturally gets down into the low to mid-30s (0–5°C) for two months, I'd suggest investing in an old refrigerator that will hold a carboy when the shelving is removed. About two to three weeks in a refrigerator set for about 32°F (0°C) should be enough to precipitate out the potassium bitartrate. If you're doing larger batches that make this method impractical, and there's no nook or corner of your house that gets down to the right temperature, you might consider asking the owner of a walk-in refrigerator to let you store your bottles in there. If you don't know anyone with a walk-in, or don't want to bother, forget about cold stabilization. The potassium bitartrate in solution doesn't harm the wine — it doesn't *need* to be precipitated. If wine that hasn't been cold-stabilized is later bottled, and then cooled to near freezing, the crystals will precipitate out in the bottle. It's not a defect, and it doesn't affect the taste. Many an experienced wine drinker has occasionally noticed crystals in the bottom of a glass when finishing up certain wines, especially big reds from small wineries. Cold stabilization has these benefits, however: It gets rid of the crystals, which is nice in a cosmetic sense. And it reduces the acidity slightly and softens the wine. This latter benefit is the chief one.

Before going on to more aging and, finally, bottling the wine, we must go back to the end of the secondary fermentation and talk about oak and the use of barrels.

USING BARRELS

I must admit that the idea of an ancient barrel filled with gorgeous home-made wine tucked away in a corner of the cellar is romantic. Romantic, yes; practical, no.

The chief purpose of barrel aging is to add subtle oak flavors to a wine. Long-term aging in a new barrel — particularly a new American white oak barrel — will leave a wine absolutely stinking of wood. Unless you want to have your wine taste and smell like a sawmill, oak aging will take anywhere from a few months to a year, depending on the age of the barrel.

French oak barrels from Nevers, Limousin, or the Centre region of France are the finest money can buy, and I've seen them used by many home wine-makers. These barrels are very expensive, but worth it if money isn't the object.

There's really not that much difference between American white oak and the oaks used in France. The difference is that French coopers expose the wood to the elements for many months. The sun, rains, frosts, and snows leach the heavy, oaky volatiles from the wood. Then the wood is made into barrels that are capable of imparting delicate nuances of oak to a wine.

For years, American white oak barrels were not so leached and could over-oak a wine in a matter of a few weeks. But in recent years some coopers, in Wisconsin and Arkansas especially, have been treating their American oak barrels with more care, and the results are excellent. I fully endorse the use of American oak barrels if — and it's a big *if* — they have been properly aged and cured, not kiln-dried. Check with your wine shop to make sure you're getting a properly cured American oak barrel.

Barrel aging fine-tunes the taste of wine, imposing light oak flavors that make up what the wine doesn't deliver. It will take experience to determine exactly how much oak to give red wines and chardonnays, but the general rules given below will get you started.

I routinely oak my red wines. Chardonnays, among whites, can benefit from a little oaking, unless you're going to make sparkling wine. Reds handled like whites and whites themselves, other than chardonnays, usually don't benefit from oaking. And chardonnays need less oak flavor than red wines do to round them out. And many wine-savvy folks think it's an abomination for chardonnay to see any oak at all.

Beaulieu Vineyard in the Napa Valley uses American white oak barrels. The company ages its lesser reds in new oak barrels — that is, their most ordinary wine goes in first, when the oak is new and harshest. After this, they refill the barrels with their Rutherford wines, which are of better quality. When the Rutherfords are done, their Reserve wines go in. By this time, the barrels have held several wines and impart only nuances of wood flavor to the wine. Their Reserves can stay in the barrel for a year without getting over-oaky. Surprisingly, they don't top up their barrels during this time. *Topping up* means taking out the bung and filling any air space that's present with a sound and similar wine. While Beaulieu may not top up its barrels, I'm going to recommend that you do. That air space is too easily colonized by aceto-bacter bacteria, and their vinegary presence can spoil a wine.

A FRAME FOR HOLDING A WINE BARREL

2 × 8

2 × 4

Cut out the arch where the barrel will rest with a chain saw or saber saw.

siphon in

siphon out

The frame in use

When you go to buy a barrel, you may be asked which toast you prefer. The toast refers to the amount of charring done to the inside of the barrel when it's assembled at the cooperage. A fire of sawn barrel staves is built on the floor and the barrel set over it. The inner wood accepts a light, medium, or heavy toast (char), depending on how long the wood is exposed to the fire. The barrel end, called the head, is toasted separately and can also have a light, medium, or heavy toast.

Rather than get into the nuances of toast, I recommend a light toast, for both the head and the body of the barrel, for a white or lighter red wine, and a medium toast, for the head and the barrel, for most full-bodied reds. With a heavy toast, you're playing with fire. Delicate whites are probably best fermented and held in glass carboys without seeing any wood during their *elevage*, as the French call the in-house aging process.

Barrels come in many sizes. The smaller the barrel, the greater the wood-to-wine ratio. That is, more wood will be in contact with any given amount of wine. Wine will therefore extract more wood flavors and need less aging time in smaller barrels. Barrels are heavy and difficult to move when filled with wine, so consider where you're going to store the barrel, and fill it in place. Also think now about getting the wine out of the barrel, later on. The

CONVERTING AN OLD BARREL TO PLANTERS

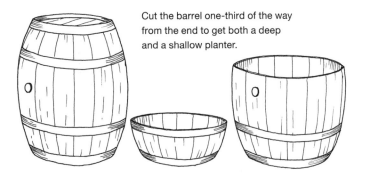

Cut the barrel one-third of the way from the end to get both a deep and a shallow planter.

best way is to siphon it out, but if your barrel is on the floor, it's going to be very difficult to siphon. I have built a frame, from scrap wood, that holds the barrel a few feet above the ground, high enough that I can siphon the wine into 5-gallon (19 L) carboys when the aging is through. To siphon wine from carboys *into* the barrel, you'll have to set the carboys on a high table, or even on a box on a high table, but that's not hard to rig up.

Obviously, the size of the frame will depend on the size of the barrel. I've used 15-gallon (57 L), 20-gallon (76 L), 30-gallon (114 L), 40-gallon (151 L), and 55-gallon (208 L) barrels, and I'd say that a 30-gallon (114 L) barrel is the minimum. Smaller ones tend to leak, and they can put too much wood on the wine. A 60-gallon (227 L) barrel is most common, and is ideal.

The barrel size you choose will depend on the amount of wine you're making. Since only wine that's finished working will go in the barrel, make sure that you take the reductions from wasted lees into account when estimating barrel size, or you may have to add a lot of store-bought wine to top it up. Buy the barrel just before using it. It will take a few days to prepare the barrel (see page 164), but then, once it's ready, fill it. Don't let it sit around wet and unused, or the moist wood could become colonized with mold.

Let me add here that I would not use any old barrel that's been used before, unless it's yours and it's been handled properly. Using old barrels is dangerous. Any off smell in a barrel will be transferred to the wine, and a barrel that's been emptied and not refilled immediately can become colonized with all kinds of bad microorganisms in a few days. Old barrels make great planters, especially when cut one-third of the way from an end. That way you get two planters — one shallow and one deep.

Table 19: Using Washing Soda to Leach a New Barrel

BARREL SIZE	AMOUNT OF WASHING SODA TO USE
50 gallons (189 L)	1 cup (224 g)
40 gallons (151 L)	¾ cup (168 g)
25 gallons (95 L)	½ cup (112 g)
20 gallons (76 L)	⅓ cup (75 g)
15 gallons (57 L)	5 tablespoons (70 g)
10 gallons (38 L)	3 tablespoons (42 g)

Local winemaking supply shops usually carry barrels, and there are commercial cooperages in many places (see appendix 3.) New barrels — French or American — must be prepared before filling them with wine, or they will sprout leaks. First, fill the barrel with water (hot or cold) and put in the bung. Turn the barrel so the bung and hole are in contact with the water. The moisture swells the wood, closing the gaps between the staves. The leaking should stop within three days. If it doesn't you may have a leaker. Leaking can be a big problem in barrels. Make sure, when you're buying a barrel, that if it turns out to be a leaker you can return it for a sound one.

When the leaking has stopped, pour out this water and fill the barrel halfway with hot water. Measure out washing soda (soda ash) according to table 19. Dissolve the washing soda in the least amount of water possible, then add to the half-full barrel. Bung the barrel securely.

Roll the barrel back and forth vigorously, sloshing the solution inside over all parts. Do this for at least a half hour. The washing soda will be leaching harsh, intense oak components from the wood. Then fill the barrel the rest of the way with hot water, rebung, and allow the barrel to stand for 24 hours.

Empty the barrel and fill halfway with cold water. Bung it, then roll it back and forth vigorously for 5 to 10 minutes. Roll it from side to side and end to end. Empty and repeat this rinsing three times. Empty for the final time.

Now your barrel is ready for use. Immediately fill it with wine (see page 165).

Filling the Barrel

Siphon wine from the carboys into the barrel, with the bung hole at the very top. Fill not to the point that wine squishes out when the bung is inserted, but to just before that point. You want as little air as possible in the barrel. If some wine does squish out and run down the barrel, remove a little wine from the barrel and clean up the spill with sulfite sterilizing solution. If you don't have quite enough wine to fill the barrel, top up with a sound and similar wine.

Insert the bung snugly, then turn the barrel slightly so the bung and hole are covered by wine inside. If it's a wooden bung, knock it in with a sharp blow from a wooden stick. The silicone bung can be seated by hand pressure, and removed by hand, too. To remove a wooden bung, turn the barrel so the bung is at the top, use a wooden stick, and knock the bung from side to side, firmly but gently so you don't shatter any wood. The bung will slowly work its way out with this technique. I always clean up the bung with sterilizing solution, then rinse it, before reinserting it.

For the purposes of oaking, I'd allow a wine from six months to a year in a new barrel prepared the way I have outlined. Taste the wine at the end of that time. It should have just a nice hint of oak. If you think the oak flavor is too strong, cut down on the time for the next batch. If not strong enough, allow an extra couple of weeks. Oak should be a nuance, not a major factor, so err on the side of caution and don't over-oak your wine.

A barrel that's been used before can hold wine for up to two years if it's held several batches of wine.

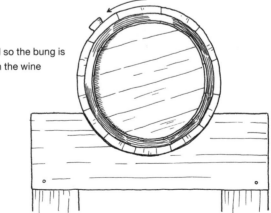

Turn the barrel so the bung is in contact with the wine when storing.

Storing a Barrel When Not in Use

Barrels can be stored empty after a sulfur wick is burned in them, but not for long. If the staves dry out, they can warp, and the barrel can be damaged. To prevent this from happening, store empty barrels filled with a sulfite sanitizing solution.

Immediately after emptying a barrel of wine, rinse it by filling it one-fourth full with cold water, bunging, rolling, and emptying. Repeat at least three times.

Fill the rinsed barrel halfway with cold water. Measure out sodium bisulfate or potassium metabisulfite and citric acid in the proportions given in table 20. Dissolve the sulfite and citric acid in water and then add it to the water in the barrel. Mix thoroughly by bunging the barrel and rolling it for 5 to 10 minutes. Then fill the barrel completely with cold water, bung it securely, and place it in storage.

Top up the barrel every month with cold water. If the barrel will continue in storage after a year, repeat the above steps to clean it and refill with fresh sanitizing solution.

When you're ready to use a barrel stored with sanitizing solution for wine, rinse it several times with cold water, rolling it vigorously each time, before filling.

Table 20: Sanitizing a Barrel for Storage

BARREL SIZE	AMOUNT OF SULFITE TO USE	AMOUNT OF CITRIC ACID TO USE
50 gallons (189 L)	1½ cups (399 g)	1 cup (224 g)
40 gallons (151 L)	1 cup (224 g)	¾ cup (168 g)
25 gallons (95 L)	¾ cup (168 g)	½ cup (112 g)
20 gallons (76 L)	⅔ cup (149 g)	⅓ cup (75 g)
15 gallons (57 L)	½ cup (112 g)	5 tablespoons (70 g)
10 gallons (38 L)	⅓ cup (75 g)	3 tablespoons (42 g)

Topping Up

"The major failure of home winemakers, in my opinion," says Earle Presten of St. Helena, "is they get all enthusiastic about the excitement of the crush, but forget about the racking and topping up during the aging period." I agree with him. Rackings are necessary, and so is topping up.

A big temptation is to open up a barrel or carboy, siphon a little wine out for sampling, and then replace the airlock or bung without topping up. Air is the enemy of wine, and I've personally spoiled at least 50 gallons (189 L) over the years by not topping up. With 2 to 3 inches (5–8 cm) of air space in the carboy, everything will look okay at first, but one day the wine will have a whitish skin on it, and then I know I've blown it. The whitish skin is acetobacter bacteria happily turning my wine into vinegar. It means the wine is spoiled. It won't even make very good vinegar. All you can do is pour it out.

If you want to have a little wine for tasting, fill a couple of gallon (3.8 L) jugs with new wine and put on airlocks. Taste from these. If one of these develops acetobacter, you've lost only a gallon. Keep everything else topped up.

Oak Chips in Glass Containers

I promised to discuss adding oak without using a barrel. I learned the technique from Dr. John McGrew, who gave up using barrels ("they leak"). The idea is to use oak chips or pieces of oak in glass carboys. Oak chips are available from most winemaking supply stores, and they're perfectly good to use. Use the commercial chips, a few grams per gallon (3.8 L), for a few weeks.

The Importance of Oak

Oaking is important. It's your chance to add an extra, intriguing, quality taste to the wine, but it should not be overly obvious. Neither should it be undetectable. Try some good California chardonnays or a Beaulieu Rutherford if you want to taste commercial oaking to give you a benchmark to shoot for. Good red Bordeaux are also oaked, usually with great finesse, and you can sample some for benchmark oak flavors, too.

FURTHER RACKING AND AGING

After oaking, if you're not using a barrel for aging, siphon the wine into clean glass carboys for further aging. You'll be automatically racking the wine at this point. When siphoning finished wine, place the end of the siphon hose under the surface of the wine in the bottle that's being filled, so the stream doesn't bubble into the wine already in the bottle. Bubbling incorporates air into the wine, and while some air was good for the wine during the primary fermentation, it will only reduce quality and oxidize the wine now. Try to get as little air as possible into the wine when racking. This is especially critical with whites. Rather than stoppering the carboys with a solid cork, I reattach airlocks. If the wine undergoes a natural malolactic fermentation, or otherwise decides to give off gas, the airlock will allow the gas to escape. I clean up the corks and airlocks and give the airlocks a fresh charge of sulfite sterilizing solution. Then I put the carboys in the cellar and pretty much forget about them for a while, until I'm ready to bottle the wine.

You could bottle the wine now, but I don't recommend it. The wine will be only about six months old at this point. It may taste fairly decent, but it'll get better if it has any aging potential at all. A light red wine or fresh white, drunk as a nouveau, could be bottled now, but even these will benefit from a total of a year in storage.

The wine will probably be a bit cloudy — not much, but less than perfectly clear. Nothing makes homemade wine more suspicious-looking than a cast or cloudiness. The cloudiness is most likely caused by particles of spent yeast, which, if bottled, will add off flavors to the wine as the dead cells slowly disintegrate. The cloudiness will usually settle by itself, or it can be removed in the step that comes just before bottling — a step called *fining*, which we'll discuss on page 172.

How Much Aging?

How long to age the wine before bottling? It's up to you, really, but here are the considerations that will lead to a rational decision:

- **Full-bodied reds.** I'd say let them age for at least a year, even two, before bottling. Drinking them too young is like eating the cookie dough before you bake it into cookies. The dough may be irresistible to the young, but the wiser person knows that there's no comparison with the baked cookies. During the storage time, the wine will settle down. Flavors will mingle and meld. Harsh and bitter constituents will disappear. Off flavors and young tastes will age gracefully into smoothness. The cloudiness of the young wine may entirely settle out, and you may not have to fine the wine at all. Right now I have 20 gallons (76 L) of four-year-old cabernet franc that's still not bottled. It's a crystal-clear ruby red, and still improving, although I think it won't improve much more. I guess I should go down there and bottle it. Four years is a bit long, I admit, but I get a perverse satisfaction out of not drinking all my wine young. The point is that aging in bulk makes a smoother wine than aging in the bottle. Wine, for some reason, ages faster in a small bottle than in a 5-gallon (19 L) carboy — probably because the greater bulk in the carboys is less subject to temperature fluctuations than wine in small bottles. After the third racking, I'd give a big red wine *at least* a year in the carboys, or in the cask, if you're using an old one with little flavor to impart.

- **Light reds.** A year would be nice, but six months will do. They'll be at their freshest and most drinkable at one to two years old.

- **Full-flavored whites.** I'm thinking primarily here of Chardonnay. From six months to a year after the third racking is minimum.

- **Light, fruity whites.** From three to six months aging after the third racking is enough.

Storage Conditions for Aging

Storage conditions should be cool — from 50 to 60°F (10–16°C) is ideal. Nothing ages a wine more quickly than high temperatures, which, at 80°F (27°C), can age a wine twice as fast as at 50°F (10°C). An absence of molds and grungy conditions in general helps prevent anything from sneaking its way into the wine and spoiling it. The storage room should be *dark*. Exposure to light, especially to sunlight, reduces wine quality quickly. This will give you reason to remember to turn off the cellar light. Wine bottles are smoky or dark tinted to keep light from the wine. Try to provide the same conditions in your storage cellar. Finally, find a storage area where there are no vibrations to jostle the wine and where the temperature doesn't fluctuate over short periods. I won't say not to talk too loud, but a quiet place away from hustle and bustle makes for better aging. Wine is delicate stuff. We've heard about wine that's "travel sick." Bouncing around in train, car, or plane upsets wine. I always let wine that's traveled sit in my cellar for a month before opening it.

The perfect place for storage is a root cellar or part of an underground cellar insulated from the temperature swings and activities of the rest of the room. At least keep the aging wine in a cool, dark place.

WINE DISORDERS

Wine disorders do happen, but the only ones I've had experience with are acetobacter and hydrogen sulfide. If you keep air away from your wine and keep your containers topped up, you should not experience the awful, slow vinegarization of what was otherwise a promising wine. Acetobacter, by the way, has a hard time establishing itself in wines over 12 percent alcohol, although severe air contact will eventually allow it to grow. That's one good reason for adding sugar to low-sugar musts.

The rotten-egg smell of hydrogen sulfide gas in your wine, or the chemically related smells of garlic or asparagus, means disaster has struck. I've read of many ways to rid a wine of H_2S, but they all involve adding poisonous substances like copper sulfate. I wouldn't serve a wine containing such compounds. If a racking with good aeration — that is, allowing the stream of wine to splash down into the filling bottle, bubbling air into itself — doesn't solve the problem, discard the wine.

There are other wine disorders, but if your air security is good, you shouldn't see them. One disease, called ropiness, or oiliness, which turns the wine into a thick, ropy mass, is caused by a lactic bacterium that doesn't need air to thrive. It also spells the end of the wine. It's never happened to me or anyone I know who makes wine, so don't worry about it. If it develops, think of yourself as one in a million, and pour out the wine.

It can happen that, after bottling, anaerobic bacteria turn an odd bottle. This "bottle sickness" will probably be confined to that bottle, and the rest of your wine will most likely be all right.

In California, you hear a lot about brettanomyces, usually called brett — a yeast organism that can impart a mousey or metallic flavor to wine. It occurs naturally in the vineyard and on grapes, but it is very sensitive to sulfur dioxide, so if you follow the recommendations for the use of potassium metabisulfite (see pages 129–134), you shouldn't have a problem with it. If you do notice an unpleasant metallic or mousey (you know what an old drawer where mice have lived smells like?) aroma, it's more than likely brett. Once it's established in a barrel, it's best to discard the barrel. A thorough cleaning with ammonia and sterilizing solution will rid a glass carboy of it.

It can happen that certain bacteria or mold organisms can be lodged in the crevices of corks used to stopper the finished bottles of wine. If these organisms grow in the cork, they can also enter the wine, giving it a pronounced musty smell, like old, decaying cardboard. Such a wine is called "corked." Dispose of that bottle and try another. Usually only a few corks in a batch — or more typically none at all — will harbor organisms that will spoil the smell of wine. Dipping corks in a sterilizing solution and then giving them a clean water rinse before corking your wine bottles can help reduce any problems with corked wines. The use of artificial plastic corks prevents the problem from arising, but I don't know anyone who really likes those plastic corks.

FILTERING

Filtering, by the way, can be done in the home winery. It takes the place of *fining* the wine — clearing it by adding a fining agent. It also removes substances that will deposit out in the bottle. And because filter pads have holes only a few microns wide, it can remove quality right along with all these things. I'm not an advocate of filtering wines, but if you're interested, small-scale filtering equipment, hoses, and pumps can be purchased.

FINING

Given the carboy storage times I've recommended, most well-made red wine will fall brilliantly clear and can be bottled with no fining. Occasionally, however, a wine — especially a white — will have a slight haze or cloudiness that refuses to settle out. If you must clear a wine, fining does less harm to the wine than filtering.

Many agents are used to clear wine. Ox blood was once common and is still used in Burgundy, France. Gelatin and isinglass are still used occasionally. Bentonite from Wyoming — a very fine, pure clay — is most commonly used in North America to clear white wines of haze. While the clay works well, it leaves a large, fluffy lees, and you can lose an awful lot of wine in the fining process.

Egg white fining is used to reduce tannins as well as cloudiness in red wine. The procedure is very simple. Carefully separate one fresh egg white, with *no* trace of yellow yolk. Beat the white gently. One egg white is enough for about 10 gallons (38 L) of wine. Pour half the beaten white into the 5-gallon (19 L) carboy and stir it in gently and thoroughly with a *clean* rod or stick. Try not to incorporate too much air into the wine. Replace the cork and airlock. Within 10 days the wine should fall clear. If it hasn't, your wine will remain cloudy. If it tastes good, throw a big party and make wine punch. If it doesn't taste good, it's probably a candidate for the drainpipe. As soon as the wine clears, rack it off the lees, and bottle it.

Since fining reduces tannins and can remove the subtle highlights from a wine, I never do it unless a wine has an objectionable haze. I'd estimate that 95 percent of the wines I've made have fallen perfectly clear of their own accord.

BLENDING

After a sufficient storage period and fining, if necessary, bottle the wine. The only additional operation may be blending. Most often the home winemaker will bottle examples of 100 percent varietals, but blending two or more wines can be the last fine-tuning in your quest for a truly fine wine.

Fine Bordeaux wines are usually blends of cabernet sauvignon, merlot, cabernet franc, Malbec, and occasionally petit verdot. Varying proportions of these wines are blended to achieve stunning balances among the wine's components. In California, more and more winemakers are blending merlot with cabernet sauvignon to soften the wines. In the east, vintners have found that a 50-50 mixture of Maréchal Foch and Cascade makes a good wine. Commercial blending experts always set a goal for blending. So should the home winemaker. If you have no clear goal in mind, don't blend.

To that I'd add another rule: unless the blend is better than any component in it, don't blend. And finally, blend similar wines: robust reds with robust reds, light whites with light whites, and so on.

Some of the goals achievable by blending:

- **Color correction.** Since my Chancellor grapes in Pennsylvania sometimes lacked color, I planted several Colobel vines among them. These are teinturier grapes, rich in color, that add depth to the color of the Chancellor. Alicante Bouschet is a variety used similarly for color in California. Only a small percentage of one of these is needed in the blend to enrich a poorly colored wine.

- **Acidity reduction.** It's possible to reduce the acidity of an over-acid wine by blending in a neutral, low-acid wine of similar type. You may not have these available from the home vineyard, however. If the wine is severely acidic, consider diluting it with a similar California jug wine just to make it drinkable, or with distilled water.

- **Tannin reduction.** Winemakers use merlot to soften cabernets because merlot is lower in tannins than cabernets. Too much tannin can pucker the mouth and render a wine undrinkable until age changes the tannins in the bottle. New grape tannins are short-chain molecules. Over time, these tannin molecules link together to form long-chain polymers that are much softer in the mouth than new tannins. These polymers also incorporate color, flavor, and aroma compounds in the wine called anthocyanins, enhancing those qualities. This is what happens when big, tannic Bordeaux age into soft, complex maturity. Heavily tannic wines can be made drinkable earlier by the addition of some low-tannin wine of otherwise similar characteristics, and of course by decanting the wine the day before you drink it.

- **Oak reduction.** You may, despite your best efforts, over-oak a wine. By adding a similar wine that's not over-oaked, or not oaked at all, you can reduce the oakiness to the proper level.

- **Body improvement.** I'm not sure improving body is a reasonable goal. *Body* refers to the fullness of flavors and feel in the mouth. Trying to improve a wine with low body by adding one of high body will probably produce a mediocre wine of medium body. In most cases I'd think the full-bodied wine should be kept as a treasure and not blended. In rare cases, the blend could be better than either, and blending would be a good idea. Chambourcin adds body to a blend, for instance, while by itself it may be of inferior quality.

Unless you have one of these clear-cut goals in mind, blending probably won't improve the wines involved.

Blend small batches at a time, and gather some friends or family knowledgeable about wine to help you. In blending, several opinions can guide you in deciding whether to blend, and, if so, in what proportions. It's really trial and error until you feel that the blend is an improvement upon all of the individual wines used in it. If you decide to blend, use a clean carboy and siphon the appropriate proportions into it from the containers of the pure varietals. Be careful not to bubble too much air into the wine: keep the end of the siphon hose beneath the surface of the wine in the filling bottle. I'd plan to bottle the wine immediately after blending to avoid further aeration.

FINAL MEASUREMENTS BEFORE BOTTLING

At bottling, it's a good idea to take the following final measurements for your records, or for the label if you choose: pH, titratable acidity, residual sugar, and alcohol. Of course you've already taken the pH and TA, but aging, fining, racking, and other handling can change these figures to some degree. Kits are available to measure final SO_2, but you may want to simply list the total of all sulfite additions you've made.

Alcohol Content of Finished Wine

At the end of the primary fermentation, the Brix was down to somewhere around 8. This remaining sugar was slowly fermented to alcohol during the secondary. When the fresh-crushed must was all sugar and no alcohol, its specific gravity was about 1.080. As alcohol started forming and sugar began disappearing, the specific gravity started dropping.

Pure ethyl alcohol has a specific gravity of less than 1.000. Pure water has a specific gravity of 1.000 and is the standard on which the scale is based. Water with dissolved sugar has a specific gravity higher than 1.000. At the end of the primary, the specific gravity gets down to 1.030 or thereabouts. During the secondary, it drops to 1.000, and then keeps dropping. Finished wine has a specific gravity of less than 1.000, with the actual number depending on the alcohol content.

"Complete dryness" means that all the sugar has been converted to alcohol. Figure the alcohol content of your finished wine from table 15 (page 111).

Testing Residual Sugar

An accurate way to determine if your wine has any residual sugar after it has completely finished fermenting is to use a urine glucose measurement kit, such as those used by diabetics. Kits can be purchased in any drugstore and go by trade names such as Dextrocheck and Clinitest. They will show residual sugar up to a few percent very accurately. Less than 1 percent residual sugar usually adds a little softness to a wine and is desirable. Amounts in the order of 2 to 3 percent will make a wine taste sweet, and could be due to sugar left after the alcohol content rose high enough to kill off the yeast, or to a fermentation that stuck toward the end. Most wine yeast are killed off at about 15 to 16 percent alcohol by volume. Therefore, if you've got a wine with 11 or 12 percent alcohol and 3 percent residual sugar, the fermentation stuck. You should try to restart it (see the directions on page 146). If your wine shows 16 percent alcohol and 3 percent sugar, you undoubtedly started with grapes of high Brix; your wine will remain sweet. Some extraordinary wines — Port, Sauternes, Auslese — are made with residual sugar left on purpose, either because the grapes had very high Brix or, in the case of Port, because brandy was added before all the sugar was converted to alcohol. Such sweet wines make excellent after-dinner or dessert wines.

Your label could then contain all of the following:

- Brix

- pH

- TA

- Residual sugar

- Total SO_2

- Percent alcohol

More than this even the most dedicated oenophile won't ask.

BOTTLING

There are wine bottles, and then there are wine bottles. The most common types are illustrated on page 177.

I use Bordeaux bottles for reds and Burgundy bottles for whites, as tall German white wine bottles can be hard to stack on their sides. Never use screw cap bottles or oddly shaped bottles that may take odd-sized corks. Bottles definitely run in grades of quality. The highest grade has an extra heft from the additional glass used. Both high-quality Bordeaux and Burgundy bottles have an indentation called the punt on the bottom that some say holds sediment when the wine is being decanted, but I've never noticed that it works very well for that purpose. I think the punt is an artifact of the manufacturing process for high-quality wine bottles. I have found that bottles with indentations on the bottom are usually of higher quality than those without. All bottles should be dark shades of green. The best Burgundy bottles are "dead-leaf green," which is a more brownish yellow-green than others. This bottle color is beginning to be used in the United States and is more available to home winemakers.

One can, of course, buy wine bottles. I never do. I save nice bottles that I buy from the store and I have a deal going with several restaurants that I patronize. The restaurant owners are amenable to putting aside good-quality bottles for me to pick up. Now if I only could wangle the owners into getting the dishwashers to rinse them for me, I could save myself some work.

- -

WINE BOTTLE TYPES

high
shoulders

sloping
shoulders

best to find
high-quality
burgundy
bottles colored
dead-leaf
green

thick glass and
deep indentation
denote quality

Bordeaux   **German &**   **Burgundy**
                  Alsatian

Pre-cleaning Bottles

Probably the most time-saving thing you can do in all of winemaking is to clean out bottles when you get them and never let bottles sit around with wine residues in them. I clean them, plug them with pieces of paper towels to keep airborne dust and debris out, and store them in a dry place until I need them. Then they will need minimal scrubbing. Very cruddy bottles can be cleaned up and used, but they're a lot of work to clean. Any bottles that don't yield their deposits quickly should be discarded.

Cleaning Again at Bottling

I wash my bottles before filling them with wine, whether or not they're clean, in an ammonia solution (about 1 part ammonia to 5 parts water), using a bottle brush available at winemaking supply shops. Then I rinse the bottles three times to make sure all the ammonia is gone and they smell sweet and fresh. Usually the labels soak off — especially European wine labels — during the washing. American labels are made with sterner stuff, and I've soaked some American bottles for a half hour and still had to scrub them off. One of those copper wire scrubby pads for pots and pans works well on labels.

After the final rinse, I set the bottles on a table, then cover them with a towel. Figure that you'll need 5 bottles for each gallon (3.8 L) of wine — so if you are bottling one 5-gallon (19 L) carboy, have at least 25 bottles on hand.

Filling the Bottles

It helps to have a couple of people bottling, but it can be done alone. I place a clean towel or newspaper on the floor and set five bottles on it. I set the carboy on a table above. Using a siphon hose, I get the siphon going and fill the bottles to a point in the neck that will be about a half inch (1.3 cm) below the bottom of the cork when it's inserted (see the illustration on page 179). A little practice will make you expert in this.

Some winemaking supply shops sell a stainless steel device that fits on the end of the siphon hose and dispenses wine when it's pressed on the rim of the bottle, then closes when the hand pressure is released. This keeps wine from dribbling all over when you are filling the bottles, but a deft hand with a kink in the siphon hose accomplishes the same thing. And there are bottle fillers that have three spigots and give a correct fill automatically, but these are expensive. When filling, I try to be very careful not to froth and overaerate the wine. I run it relatively slowly down the inside of the bottle, adjusting the rate of flow by how hard I'm kinking the siphon hose. I check to make sure the level is correct in the neck, and when my five bottles are filled, I put them under the towel. I take out five more and fill them, return them under the towel, and so on until the carboy is finished. I don't say *emptied* because most often there will be a deposit in the bottom of the carboy. Take care not to suck up any deposits into the wine. Ordinarily, you'll lose a little wine that gets stirred up with the deposits in the very bottom, but that's better than bottling muck.

Now you have a couple dozen bottles under the towel ready for corking.

CORKING

Corks should be of excellent quality. Don't pinch pennies. Look for long, straight corks. I use #9 corks, a little larger than the #8s used by many wine-makers. The longer the corks and the fewer dark pits in them, the higher the quality. They should never be tapered, but always straight. Synthetic polyethylene corks are available, but why go synthetic when real corks do the job? The synthetics don't breathe the way real cork does, allowing the wine inside a minimal interaction with the world outside.

The dry corks will be larger than the hole you have to put them in. Just before filling your first bottles, bring a pot of water to a boil and drop in about 30 or so corks — enough for the 25 bottles you're likely to get from one carboy, plus extras in case a few corks don't seat properly and you have to recork. Cover with a lid so the corks are steamed. After boiling for 5 minutes, the corks will be ready to use, having absorbed some water and become pliable. Some say the heat makes corks crumbly and reduces their life, but I've never noticed that. Mine have lasted for years with no problems. The alternative is to soak them for several hours in a 1 percent solution of sulfite in cold water. Soaking corks isn't as easy as it sounds, since corks obstinately float. Put them in a jar, fill to the top with solution, keeping the corks under the water with one hand, then clamp on the top and turn it upside down.

You can't pound the corks into the bottles with a mallet. Believe me, I've tried, early on in my winemaking career. What's needed is a nifty piece of equipment called a hand corker. I have one made by Sanbri, a French firm, and it continues to serve me through the years. It has a chamber into which you place the cork. A piston is adjusted so that the top of the inserted cork is flush with the rim of the bottle's neck. The chamber is closed by bringing the handles together, and the cork is squeezed by hand pressure. Holding the handles closed with one hand and positioning the corker over the bottle, the other hand works a lever that drives the piston forward, driving the cork into the neck of the bottle. Practice on some empty bottles until you get the hang of it. It takes a little practice to get a feel for doing it correctly every time, but it's nothing you won't learn quickly. If you

top of cork flush with rim of bottle

Fill to line, so that there is ½" (13 mm) of air space when cork is in place.

seat a cork poorly, pull it with a corkscrew or cork puller and reinsert a new one. Lever-action corkers on stands are available, but they are expensive and may be overkill for small batches of wine.

I take the bottles out from under the towel one by one and immediately cork them. When all are corked, I rinse them under cool water in the sink. They should be taken to the cellar at once and laid on their sides. Laying the bottles on their sides allows the corks to touch wine. The cork cells will swell, making a perfect closure. Very rarely, a cork will leak, but this usually stops within a day, and only a few drops are lost. If a cork continues to leak, take the bottle upstairs and recork it.

If you've got the energy, repeat this scenario for the next 5-gallon (19 L) jug. I find that 10 gallons (38 L) — 50 bottles — a day is about my limit if I'm working alone. If I have 100 bottles to do, I save the second 50 for another day. If you're working with help, you'll find you'll bottle until all the wine is bottled or you've drunk enough wine that you're unable to bottle any more.

When you're sure that all your corks are secure and the bottles have dried off, you can bring them up for labeling and capsuling.

LABELING

I used to make all my labels by hand: cutting out the paper, using India ink and brush and pen, doing a little drawing on each one. They looked fine, but it was a lot of work. Over the years, I've decided to use pressure-sensitive labels — white, 4 × 1.5 inches (10 × 3.8 cm), easily obtainable at any office supply house. On these go the measurements we discussed before: pH, Brix, residual sugar, alcohol, total SO_2, plus the variety of grape, the year, and our names. They are unceremoniously written out and slapped on the bottles, from which they peel easily before the next washing.

I've grown to like the no-nonsense look of these labels for my everyday wine. If I'm going to make a bottle into a gift, then I get fancy just for that one bottle. I find a quality paper, usually buff or cream-colored (any color will do as long as it harmonizes with the bottle color). Then I carefully draw a picture of my conception of a beautiful wine label, including a sketch and data about the wine. If it's a special occasion, or for a special person, I'll refer to it on the label.

I've done dozens, each different, for friends. They make beautiful personalized gifts. Many home winemakers sketch their labels and have them set up at a copy store, where you can even do color. The labels below were set up on my home computer.

Attaching the Labels

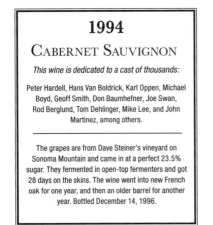

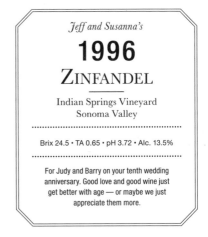

The easiest way to attach a plain paper label to a bottle of wine is with a glue stick. These are sold in most stationery stores. They're like a tube of lipstick, except that they contain a white pasty glue instead of lip gloss. Run a strip of this down all edges of the label, lay the label on the bottle, then smooth down first one edge, then another, keeping a gentle tension so the label doesn't buckle. For very fancy gift bottles, I'll put the year or a special greeting on a small label that flies above the large one. I even made a tiny booklet once to describe the way we made a particularly interesting wine and hung it by a gold thread around the neck. That one was for a wedding.

Label making can go too far. Two San Franciscans were arrested once for faking labels of 1975 Château Mouton-Rothschild, attaching them to Bordeaux bottles full of ordinary California red, and trying to sell them at the "bargain" rate of $250 a case to liquor dealers. Their "special consignment" of Mouton led to special confinement after the federal agents got hold of them. Perhaps it was fitting that they chose the 1975 Mouton to fake: it carried a reproduction of a purple, orange, and green work by Andy Warhol.

Faking appearances in the wine world is not limited to the illegitimate. I once purchased a bottle of 1963 J. W. Burmester Vintage Port at the Sherry-Lehmann wine store in New York City. I asked the salesman not to wipe off the bottle, for it was a crusty, dusty old bottle that appealed to me as much for its cobwebby-looking outside as for the rich port I knew was inside. The salesman said not to worry. "It won't come off. They spray it with something. People seem to like the bottles looking like that," he assured me.

Foil Capsules

Foil capsules on the top don't add a thing to the quality of the wine in reality, but, psychologically, I'd guess they're good for several quality points. They dress up the bottles immensely, and I always use them on gift bottles. Red foil for reds; gold foil for whites. Most winemakers' supply shops sell them. To put them on, I run three stripes of the glue stick from the lip of the rim as far down the neck as the capsule will go, spaced evenly around the neck. Drop the capsule over the neck and twist it on tight with a wringing motion. With all the bells and whistles attached, my fanciest gift bottles look like the one shown here. Of course, the wine inside the bottle should be at least as good and fancy as the gussied-up outside, or the bottle will promise more than the wine can deliver. Electric power foilers are available, but they are costly.

foil capsule

1991

Jeff's 1991 MERLOT

PH 3.6
TA 0.72
ALC 13.4

BOTTLED AT
HIS WINU.
IN STUART

MAKING SPARKLING WINE

Take the name "Champagne" out of your lexicon. What people in the Champagne region of northern France make is Champagne. Every other sparkling wine in the world, even in France, is just sparkling wine. And that includes the libations of America's home winemakers who attempt this vinous feat. I myself have made sparkling wine at home — still have some bottles tucked away in my wine cellar — and it is excellent. If you think a bottle of your own still wine will impress your friends, wait until you pull out a cold bottle of your own sparkling wine! So no, we can't make Champagne, but we can make killer sparkling wine.

In writing this section, I interviewed Tom Tiburzi, a friend who's the director of winemaking at Domaine Chandon, the sparkling wine house in Yountville in Napa County.

"What's the first thing I should tell people who want to make sparkling wine at home?" I asked him.

"Don't," was his reply. He meant it as a sort of joke, but he also was issuing a caution. It's entirely possible to do it, but, as Tom said, "don't skip any steps." To make a successful batch of your own sparkling wine, you need to be diligent and careful. You will find all the steps you need below.

Choosing a Style

We begin by deciding on a style. Brut — which means that the finished wine will have fewer than 12 grams of sugar per liter — is a popular style for a good reason. It is not overly sweet and has a refreshing acidity. Sparkling wine in general, and brut in particular, goes with just about every kind of food, from roast beef to the lightest fish.

Choosing Grapes and Yeast

Although any grape variety can be made into sparkling wine, chardonnay and pinot noir are the most commonly used grapes in France and California. In cold regions where chardonnay and pinot noir would freeze out over the winter, riesling is a good substitute, and you could experiment with some of the new hybrids listed in table 2 (page 26). And you may be able to find both Chardonnay and pinot noir in regions as cold as USDA plant hardiness zone 6. I made a fine still chardonnay in Pennsylvania (zone 6), and Dr. Frank made pinot noir in the Finger Lakes region of upstate New York. Of course, the best riesling in the United States comes from the Finger Lakes and from Michigan. So wherever you are, it may be possible for you to find one of these classic sparkling wine varieties growing near you.

I'd recommend using white grapes for your first batch, unless you are shooting for a sparkling rosé, for the color of red grapes is in the skins, and great care and very light pressure during the press must be used to get white juice from red grapes — and then, only from red grapes whose interiors are colorless. Many sparkling winemakers who want to use pinot noir simply use the free-run juice — that is, the juice that runs from the grapes crushed by their own weight. As a home winemaker, you probably won't have enough red grapes to get them to split under their own weight.

Make sure that before you harvest or buy your grapes, you have the proper yeast for the fermentation on hand. A slow fermentation can yield off aromas and flavors, so you want a quick, clean fermentation. Prise de Mousse (*Saccharomyces bayanus*) is a good choice of yeast to use for sparkling wine, and it is widely used in Champagne. Look for pelletized Prise de Mousse; in this form, the yeast reside in porous little pellets but seldom escape through the tiny holes, which greatly simplifies the job of riddling the wine later to get rid of the spent yeast at disgorgement, a task that we'll get into later.

You may also want to put your base wine through a malolactic fermentation at the end of the primary fermentation (see page 151), so have this bacterial culture at hand. Ask your supplier for a dry malolactic culture for a high-acid, low-pH sparkling wine. Tell them that you want to avoid any malolactic culture that will produce "buttery" flavors.

Making the Base Wine

"The base wine for a sparkler is not the same as a regular still wine," Tiburzi says. So you don't start the process by making a still chardonnay or pinot noir in the same manner as you would make a still wine. The base wine for a sparkler will, after it's made, have substantially less alcohol and substantially more acid. This base wine will later be charged up with yeast and sugar, raising the final alcohol and residual sugar. If you started with a regular still wine whose grapes were picked at from 23 to 25 Brix, your final alcohol would be far too high; the wine would prickle the nose and taste "hot." Besides, Tiburzi points out, if you used regular still wine whose grapes were picked dead ripe to make a sparkler, the flavors would be out of balance. "You want the grape flavors to be delicate and subtle, because the flavor of the wine will be amped by the bubbles," he said.

To get grapes with higher acids and lower sugars, you pick them before they're fully ripe, when the sugar is between 18 and 20 Brix and the acid level is between 7 and 10 grams per liter (usually expressed as 0.7 to 1.0 gram/100 mL), or even a little higher. The TA should be about 1.0; if you have your juice tested for the relative amounts of tartaric and malic acids, ideally that 1.0 TA will be split as 0.8 gram tartaric acid and 0.2 gram malic acid. If your malic acid content is up around 0.4 to 0.5 gram, it's especially important to put the must through malolactic fermentation; otherwise, the aggressive acidity of the malic may render the wine too sharp.

Pressing

Don't run the grape clusters through a stemmer-crusher. Use a basket press instead. Load your plastic press bag with whole clusters. The press bag is the plastic mesh bag that goes into the basket press and which you squeeze to get just the juice, leaving skins, seeds, and stems in the bag.

Press very gently for both white and red grapes. Overpressing extracts tannins and other phenolics, which are unpleasant in a delicate sparkler, as well as color from the red skins. It's better to leave some juice behind in the press bag rather than trying to get it all out. The sweetness of freshly pressed grape juice masks the astringency of phenolic compounds, so when tasting your fresh juice, allow the sweetness to fall off your palate, and any astringency will then be revealed. For sparkling wine, astringency is harsh and most unwelcome. Light and easy pressing is the rule here.

Browning and Adding Sulfites

Okay, so now you have your fresh grape juice. As we learned when making still wines, it's good practice to stun or kill off the wild yeasts that colonized the grape skins by adding potassium metabisulfite (sulfites, for short) in the form of Campden tablets. Before adding sulfites, though, be sure that the juice has oxidized to a brown color. Don't worry — these brown compounds will settle out with the yeast and grape solids after the primary fermentation. If you add sulfites before browning, the brown compounds may form in the bottle, spoiling appearance and increasing the risk of gushing by giving the dissolved carbon dioxide gas in the sparkling wine landing sites, so to speak, that allow it to come out of solution.

Once the juice has browned, it's time to add the sulfites. This step is exceptionally important for high-acid wines destined to become sparklers, because certain wild yeasts can create off aromas and flavors. First check the pH, TA, and Brix of the grape juice, and then add the proper amount of Campden tablets, as dictated by the pH, following the guidelines in table 17.

The pH of the grape juice before fermentation should be between 3.0 and 3.4 at most. When you cold-stabilize your wine later (see page 187), many of the positive potassium ions will precipitate out, leaving tartaric acid and negative radicals such as hydroxide to predominate in the juice. These negative radicals will lower the pH, making the final wine taste more acidic. The effect of cold stabilization is to lower the pH about two-tenths of a percent — lowering a pH of 3.4 to 3.2, for example.

Adding Yeast

The day after pressing and adding sulfite, your must will be ready for the addition of the yeast. It's added as with any still wine. Some winemakers start the yeast in a cup of fresh grape juice on crush day, before they add the Campden tablets, so it's up and running the next day, but I just add the dry yeast to the must the day after crush and stir it in. It will take a day or two to get going, but soon the primary fermentation will be roaring along.

Adding Malolactic Culture

Add the malolactic culture at the end of the primary fermentation, just after you rack the new wine off the gross lees. The bacteria should be dissolved in distilled water only, since city water contains bacteria-killing chlorine. The bacteria turn harsh malic acid into smoother lactic acid and operate best at temperatures from 60 to 75°F (16–24°C). If your base wine is in a place where temperatures fall lower than 60°F (16°C), the bacteria may stop working until temperatures rise again in the spring. The bacteria produce a fine fizzing of tiny bubbles, usually lasting a month or two. If the fizzing has stopped while the temperature is still above 60°F (16°C), the malolactic fermentation has ended in all likelihood. If you're not sure, let the base wine rest until things warm up in the spring and all bubbling is finished. During this rest, the wine should be positively kept away from any air contact and given only one racking over the winter. Keep the wine in glass carboys or steel barrels fitted with airlocks. You don't want the base wine to touch wood, as an oak barrel would impart harsh phenolics and unwanted oaky flavors.

When you're sure that the malolactic fermentation is finished, add enough Campden tablets to bring the wine to 25 to 30 parts per million (ppm) total sulfur. Since one tablet brings 1 gallon (3.8 L) of wine to 50 ppm, half a tablet per gallon of must will be about right.

Fining and Cold Stabilization

If your base wine is still hazy or cloudy after two rackings and several months of settling, you should fine it. Use bentonite clay according to the package directions. The haze should clear within a couple of weeks. If it doesn't, your wine will remain hazy. However, the bentonite — a clay that binds the proteins that make the wine hazy — will usually fall to the bottom as a rather fluffy lees, leaving the wine brilliantly clear.

Before you give the wine a final spring racking, there's one more step to take, and that is cold stabilization. Your new wine has potassium ions and free tartaric acid in it. At cold temperatures, these molecules form potassium bitartrate. If you place your carboys or steel barrels in a freezer held at about 20°F (−7°C) for a week or so, the bitartrate will precipitate out as a crust of crystals that will help hold those fluffy clay lees to the bottom, making the final racking easier. It will also reduce the acidity of the wine a little.

It's a good idea to test the pH and TA of the wine before you cold-stabilize. After this cold stabilization, test the pH again. If it's 3.3 or higher, make an acid adjustment using tartaric acid to bring it to 3.1 or less. If it's below 3.3, you don't need to do an acid adjustment.

The potassium bitartrate doesn't affect the wine's flavor, so you don't absolutely need to cold-stabilize it. But some people are disconcerted to find crystals of what looks like broken glass in their wine glasses — although you and I know they are harmless bitartrate. And if you don't have a walk-in freezer, surely you know someone — a restaurateur, maybe — who has one and would let you place your carboys in there for a week or two.

Procuring Bottles and Caps

Before you can think about bottling your new wine, you'll need to have bottles and caps at hand. Ordinary glass bottles will shatter under the pressures that build up during the in-bottle fermentation, so you'll need heavy glass American sparkling wine bottles, preferably green or some other dark color. You can save and reuse bottles or buy them from one of the home winemaking suppliers listed in appendix 3.

For each bottle, you will need a crown cap, like the old-fashioned ones used to cap soda pop bottles that didn't twist off. Nowadays there are crown caps made especially for American sparkling wine bottles; winemaking suppliers will have them. And you'll need a crown capping tool. Some are hand operated, some are stand-alone, and some can be screwed down to a bench for firm support. Again, winemaking suppliers will have them. Your capper will need a special bell, as the actual capping hood is called, for American bottles. Make sure you have the right one for your bottles and caps.

Some suppliers may also carry "bidules," which are small food-grade plastic cups. After a bottle has been filled with base wine, yeast, and sugar, you insert the bidule with the open end of the cup toward the inside of the bottle and the closed end of the cup at the top of the neck, but not protruding above it, because the crown cap will shortly clamp down, and you don't want the bidule to interfere with it. The purpose of the bidule is . . . well, we need to explain some things before we can understand the function of the bidule.

American sparkling
wine bottle

Putting the Sparkle in Sparkling Wine

So now you have both bottles and base wine, and it's time for the two to meet. You'll bottle the base wine with a charge of sugar and yeast and lay the bottles on their sides in a cool, dark place. The sugar and yeast produce a second fermentation in the bottles, giving you those sparkly stars that make the wine so special. After the second fermentation, the bottles will rest for at least one year. We'll get to specific instructions for the next steps in your winemaking adventure in a moment, but first, come with me as we take a journey down into a bottle of sparkling wine. This wine is resting, but not sleeping. Beautiful things are happening. We're going to plunge deeply into this bottle and its decomposing yeast. Pull on your rubber boots, for it can be a rather mucky trip, but at the end, we'll finish our journey with a glass of clean, tart, and toasty sparkling wine. It will not be just any bottle of bubbly, though. Our bottle will have spent enough time on the yeast — *en tirage*, as the French say — to become a truly great sparkling wine. How it gets there is a tale worth telling.

The In-Bottle Fermentation

When you first lay the bottle down, the yeast starts to work on the sugar that's been added. Sugar turns to alcohol and carbon dioxide, and this gas puts the contents of the bottle under about 80 pounds per square inch (552 kilopascals) or more of pressure — almost six times the pressure of the atmosphere measured at sea level. An ordinary wine bottle would explode at these pressures, hence the need for heavy, thick sparkling wine bottles.

The newly produced alcohol raises the existing alcohol content of the base wine a few percentage points — typically just 1 to 1.5 percent. The legal limit for sparkling wine alcohol content is 14 percent. So, you can see, that the base wine can't be too high in alcohol to begin with or the sparkler will end up knocking everyone for a loop. The carbon dioxide produced in the bottle can't escape, so it dissolves into the wine, to emerge later as the bubbles in your glass.

Even with the added alcohol of the secondary fermentation in the bottle, alcohol levels in most sparklers stay low. Roederer Estate in the cool western end of the Anderson Valley in Mendocino County produces L'Ermitage, its $45-a-bottle flagship sparkling wine, at a total alcohol of only 11.8 percent. Its pH is a very low 2.98, and it has enough residual sugar (1.2 percent) to ameliorate the puckery acidity of the wine. Winemaker Arnaud Weyrich says that while the high acid and low sugar of the grapes for the base wine are due to the foggy region, "very little of the flavors of the wine are due to the soils or the regional climate — there's nothing distinctively 'Anderson Valley' about it." Most of the flavors and aromas he's looking for come about in the bottle during and after the secondary fermentation.

It takes anywhere from a week to about three months for the yeast to ferment all the sugar in the bottle. Ideally it takes three to four weeks, as too rapid a fermentation in the bottle can stress the yeast, causing off flavors. The best way to prevent the secondary fermentation from being too fast or too slow is to not over- or under-inoculate with yeast and to maintain the temperature between 50 and 60°F (10–16°C).

En Tirage: Aging on the Yeast

After this secondary fermentation in the bottle, the yeast dies and falls to the bottom. Since the bottle is on its side, the yeast makes a long pool the length of the bottle, exposing a lot of surface to the wine. You'd think that the dead yeast would have finished their work at this point, but no. Their work has just begun.

Let's get miniature, like the crew in *Fantastic Voyage*, and stomp around in the pool of dead yeast. At our tiny size, the yeast cells are about the size of basketballs. Let's pick up one of these cells. Oof! It's heavy. The cell wall is hard. It's made of chitin — the same stuff that lobster and shrimp shells are made of — as well as mannoproteins (sugar-protein combinations) and lipids. Those lipids make up from 5 to 20 percent of the cell wall.

It's also kind of drippy — fluids are leaking out through holes developing in the cell wall. When it was alive, the interior of the cell had a nucleus and vacuoles filled with various compounds that functioned to support its life, all swimming in cytoplasm. But once it died, the material inside the cell fairly quickly disintegrated and became a soup of peptides, amino acids, and essential fatty acids. The super-long strands of RNA and DNA in the chromosomes fell apart into their constituent nucleotides, and these in turn began to fall apart into their precursors, nucleosides and phosphorus compounds. This soup of molecules is what's draining out of our dead yeast cell, whose walls are becoming increasingly porous. The soup floats away, entering the wine and affecting its flavor and aroma.

So the cell contents spill into the wine, but what about these hard shells? Do they have any effect on the flavor and aroma of the wine?

You bet they do. Probably even more than the cell contents. The chitin in those empty shells is a polysaccharide, a complex carbohydrate. The mannoproteins in the shell are a sugar-and-protein combination. And there are the essential fatty acids in the lipids. When the cell dies, the cell wall and the cytoplasmic membrane underneath it — think of the tissue-thin membrane between an eggshell and the white and yolk inside — release an array of enzymes designed by nature to break down each of these cell wall components into its constituents. The enzymes are catalysts that unlock the molecular bonds so they can disintegrate. The chitin falls apart into various forms of sugar, the protein falls apart into amino acids, and the fatty acids are taken by enzymes and introduced to alcohol, whereupon the two fall into a mad embrace and become esters. Esters are fabulously intense aromatic compounds that really start pumping up the aromas of the wines.

"Most autolysis [the scientific name for the self-destruction of the yeast cells] takes place in the first three years," says Tom Tiburzi. "But it takes five or six years for the yeast's cell walls to break down completely. The enzymes are active for that long a time. So 'late disgorged' wines [those that get left on the yeast the longest] get the maximum aroma and flavor factors from yeast autolysis. At five years, I see the toasty elements that have emerged integrate and harmoniously marry in the wine — toasted hazelnuts, bread, brioche, soy, and even hints of Vegemite." Vegemite — that's the pasty spread Australians like so much but most Americans can't stand.

While the yeast is falling apart, some oxidation is going on, too. During their three to four months of life, the yeast cells soaked up most of the oxygen in the wine to run their metabolisms. A little oxygen enters the wine via the crown cap seal during the second fermentation and tirage phase (as it does through the cork after disgorgement, when you extract the yeasty gunk from the bottle) and binds with fatty acids and other wine components to form aldehydes, and these give a subtle sherry-like or nutty flavor and aroma to the wine.

All these aroma compounds are volatile and could easily disintegrate except for the presence of large molecules that help preserve them. These macromolecules, as they're called, come from three sources: from the grapes in the form of polysaccharides; from botrytis — the noble rot, if any is present — in the form of glucans; and from fermentation and yeast cell walls in the form of mannoproteins. The mannoproteins are the most protective of aroma compounds and also help soften the astringency of tannins.

Wine chemists have tried to hasten the aging process by producing yeast autolysis products in the lab and adding them to sparkling wines, but these wines come out smelling and tasting oxidized and acidic, while wines allowed to age naturally on the yeast are judged as mature and finer, with more roundness and volume to the palate. You just can't hurry nature along when it comes to producing a fine bottle of sparkling wine.

Of all the compounds released into the wine by the yeast falling apart, it's the proteins crumbling into peptides and then into amino acids that contribute the most to aroma, flavor, and a rich mouthfeel. "It's likely that aminos and other autolysis breakdown products react with other substances in the wine to create greater complexity," Tiburzi says. Research backs Tiburzi up. Amino acids and nucleic acids have been shown to enhance flavors, particularly at the end of the palate. They yield sweetness — not sugariness, but rather the sweetness of fruit — when they bind with fatty acids. They modify esters, producing complexity in the nose. They are a natural fining agent, reducing yellow colors in whites without actual fining, which can strip wines of their polysaccharides. And they help to prevent the precipitation of potassium bitartrate crystals when the wines are cold.

About the bubbles in a glass of sparkling wine, or the mousse, as it's known: yeast autolysis has a great effect on it. One recent afternoon, I was working the harvest with David Munksgard, the winemaker at Iron Horse Vineyards, and Kristy Melton, an intern from UC Davis, who were delving into the subject of bubbles in a glass of sparkling wine. "As bubbles rise in the glass, they get larger," Munksgard said. "They get larger through commingling — bubbles touch and merge together into a larger bubble."

But he and Melton agreed that a fine mousse of small bubbles is what they're after. "With a short tirage, there's nothing in the wine to stop the bubbles from commingling, and so they get larger as they come together and rise," Melton said.

"But with a long tirage," Munksgard chimed in, "yeast autolysis produces fatty acids that coat the surface of the bubbles so they can't commingle. They stay small as they rise." Scientists have also discovered that proteins and glycoproteins also cling to the surface of the bubbles. As the bubbles rise, the flow of liquid around them pushes these large molecules to the underside of the bubbles, where they create a drag on the bubbles, preventing them from rising as fast as they otherwise would. The bottom line: all that stuff the disintegrating yeast put into the wine helps create persistent, small bubbles.

Munksgard poured a glass of Iron Horse's Brut Rosé. It had very fine bubbles and a showy cap of foam. "We measure the height of the cap and its duration," he said. "There's a tannin extracted from oak galls in France called tirage tannin. When you add that to a sparkling wine, it really enhances the height and duration of the cap."

So how long do Iron Horse's wines stay on the yeast before disgorgement? "It varies," Munksgard said. "We disgorge only when enough orders come in for us to make a new batch of finished wines, so we keep our wines on the yeast for as long as possible. But we find that we get optimum flavors and aromas when the wine is on the yeast for six years."

Arnaud Weyrich at Roederer Estate says he gets what he's looking for at about four to five years. Ludovic Dervin at Mumm Napa says "about five years." Bob Iantosca, winemaker at Gloria Ferrer, gives his Royal Cuvée five years and the flagship Carneros Cuvée eight years. Hugh Davies, president and winemaker at Schramsberg in Calistoga, says his current release J. Schram Rosé had seven years, while the regular J. Schram and the Schramsberg Reserve both got six years. And Eileen Crane at Domaine Carneros says that "at about five to five and a half years, the wine turns a corner — all the elements come together in a perfect balance. It smells wonderful, with toasty caramel notes. The physical characteristics are right. The yeast autolysis has maxed out."

Tiburzi uses autolysis as an essential creative tool to shape wine style, explaining that Domaine Chandon's Classic tier (its Brut Classic, Blanc de Noirs, and Chandon Rosé) is designed to show off fresh, vibrant fruit with complementary yeast autolysis contribution, and so it spends just a year or two on the yeast. The Reserve and Étoile tiers have three to five or more years on the yeast. "The fruit becomes elegantly subtle, surrendering to the rich, toasty autolytic aromas and flavors," he says.

Melton added that there's not much oxidation of the wine while it's on the yeast. "The yeast pretty much soaks up the oxygen," she said

"But after disgorgement," Munksgard added, "it's off to the oxidative races."

Disgorgement and Aging

After tirage, you need to get rid of the gunk — the spent yeast products — that would cloud the wine. And so you tilt the bottles bottom up and bump them several times a day so the gunk slides down toward the neck and collects at the crown cap. If you've used bidules, the small containers designed to hold that gunk, in your bottles, the gunk will collect in them. When the gunk seems fully settled, you pull the crown cap off a bottle, and the gunk and a

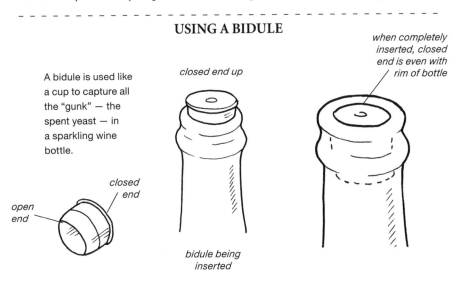

USING A BIDULE

A bidule is used like a cup to capture all the "gunk" — the spent yeast — in a sparkling wine bottle.

closed end up

when completely inserted, closed end is even with rim of bottle

open end

closed end

bidule being inserted

bit of wine splurt out. Then you top up the wine bottle, add a dosage of a very little bit of sugar, and reseal the bottle. This is disgorgement.

There seems to be disagreement among winemakers as to whether sparkling wines improve in the home wine cellar after disgorgement or just get more oxidized and flat. Almost all sparkling wineries rest their bottles for a few months after disgorgement to give the flavors of the dosage time to marry and for the shock of disgorgement to wane. But after that? I remember an executive of Laurent-Perrier telling me that there's absolutely no reason to age sparkling wine after disgorgement. But what about older vintage Champagnes, like the 1996 Krug now in release and similarly aged Bollingers?

Tiburzi says that the major oxidation contribution to these wines happens during the secondary fermentation and tirage phase. After disgorgement, more oxidation occurs. "A simple rule for holding wines after disgorgement is to match the time they have aged on the yeast with time in your wine cellar," he says. For example, if a wine has spent three years on the yeast, then it can keep for three years. The longer on the yeast, the longer it will hold; the same factors that allow sparklers to age on the yeast contribute to the wine's potential to hold after disgorgement. For very ageable sparklers, the limiting factor may be failure of the cork under the stress of dampness and pressure, allowing CO_2 to escape while oxygen intrudes.

Ludovic Dervin at Mumm Napa says that sparklers of good acidity can be aged up to 10 years in a good wine cellar. "But," he cautions, "many sparkling wines will be falling apart after 5 or 6 years at home if they don't have a good structure to begin with." Or if they aren't aged at a proper cellar temperature of 58°F (14°C), one might add.

Bob Iantosca at Gloria Ferrer agrees with Dervin. "Some sparkling wines are meant to be drunk as soon as you get them home," he says. "But others that have high acidity and low pH — even some phenolics that give grip — will evolve and change. Besides developing a sherry character from oxidation, home-cellared sparklers may show a silkier texture and bottle bouquet. It's no longer just about the fruit; other characteristics come into play."

"Some wines can go 20 to 30 years," says Hugh Davies at Schramsberg. "We recently opened a 1984 Schramsberg Blanc de Blancs that was a show-stopper. The chardonnay in that wine had high acid and low pH, and the fruit was sourced from cooler sites. It had turned no negative corners, and it showed caramelized apple and butter-brickle flavors." It had also spent 6 years on its yeast and was disgorged around 1991, so it was cellared for many additional years under ideal conditions.

The difference lies between vintage and nonvintage wines, claims Eileen Crane. "A vintage date on the bottle says to the consumer, this wine will age," she says. "And absolutely there will be development of flavors after home cellaring." But if the wine is nonvintage, then it's already a blend of newer and older vintages and needs no further aging.

Astute winemaker and marketer that she is, Crane has this tip for sparkling wine drinkers: "People think they have to drink up the whole bottle of sparkling wine right away, but if you cap the bottle with a sparkling wine closure, the wine will open up over five days in the fridge. You can enjoy a glass a day for a week. It won't go flat — it will keep its bubbles just fine."

Whether we're talking about the long process of making the base wine, storing the wine en tirage for years, aging it even more years at home, and then drinking it over a week, the rule with sparkling wine seems to be take it easy, take it slow, and the payoff will be all the greater.

I heard that same advice in a love song once upon a time.

So that's the story of your sparkling wine en tirage and afterward. But let's return to how we get to these stages in the life of a bottle of sparkling wine. First we have to add yeast and sugar to the base wine for the secondary fermentation in the bottle.

Charging the Base Wine with Sugar and Yeast

When the base wine has finished its fermentations, bottle up some of the wine as still wine; if you've made 10 gallons (38 L), two bottles of still wine will do. Crown-cap them. You'll need them later in the process, after the rest of the wine has finished its in-bottle second fermentation and become bubbly. Since these two bottles of still wine will look just like the bubbly bottles, label them so that you don't lose track of which is which. At disgorgement, when you blow the spent yeast out of the bottles, you'll lose some wine. You can use this still wine to bring the fill level back to where it should be, about an inch or so below the cork in the neck.

DV_{10} is one of the most widely used strains of yeast for this in-bottle fermentation (*methodé champenoise*) in the Champagne region. Famous for its ability to ferment under stressful conditions of low pH, high total SO_2, and low temperature, DV_{10} gives clean fermentations that preserve varietal fruit character while adding roundness. Its qualities make DV_{10} highly recommended for sparkling white wine varietals. The yeast gives best results at temperatures ranging from 50 to 85°F (10–29°C) and is tolerant of alcohol levels up to 18 percent — which, it's hoped, you will never reach. You can buy DV_{10} from many winemaking suppliers (see appendix 3); most will provide instructions for rehydrating and waking up the yeast so it's pawing at the starting gate when you add it with sugar to your base wine in the bottle.

You'll need yeast culture in an amount equivalent to about 3 percent of the base wine's volume. So if you are working with 10 gallons (38 L) of base wine, you'd prepare three-tenths of a gallon, or 2.4 pints (1.1 L), of reconstituted yeast.

For sugar, you'll need 3.27 ounces of sugar per gallon (or 24.4 grams per liter), which totals 32.7 ounces (928 g) for the 10 gallons (38 L) in our example.

Other additives to consider including in the charge for in-bottle fermentation are:

- **Yeast extract.** This feeds the yeast so the fermentation in the bottle proceeds positively, with no slowdowns or incomplete fermentations due to nutrient starvation. Add the yeast extract at the rate of 0.2 gram per gallon (3.8 L) of base wine, which would be 2 grams for 10 gallons (38 L) of base wine. You won't need yeast extract if the yeast culture already contains nutrients. But make sure that the yeast culture doesn't contain added vitamins, which give an off smell to sparkling wine.

- **Riddling aids.** Riddling is the process of by which you loosen the yeasty debris in the bottle and encourage it to collect into a plug that you can then remove. Riddling aids are adjuvants that help the gunk in the bottle to clump, making riddling easier. They aren't absolutely necessary, but they will make riddling easier. Using encapsulated yeast makes riddling easiest of all.

It's best to add yeast, sugar, and any other additives to the base wine before you bottle, for the obvious reason that you get an even distribution of these additions throughout the base wine rather than laboriously trying to dole out sugar and yeast in bottle-sized increments. But plan on bottling immediately after you make the additions, and stir them in thoroughly.

Bottling

Continuing to use our 10 gallons (38 L) of base wine as a model, you will need 48 bottles (four cases) to fill. But wait — isn't a gallon of wine five bottles? Yes, but remember, we already took two bottles' worth of base wine and capped them as still wine.

Fill the bottles just as you would for still wine (see page 179); a clean plastic hose (available at any winemaking supply shop) makes a perfect siphon. Next time you're in a wine shop, look at bottles of sparkling wine and make a mental note of how high in the neck they are filled. Leave roughly ¾ inch to 2 inches (2–5 cm) between the crown cap and the surface of the wine when the bottle is standing up. If you're using bidules, the wine should be below the open end of the bidule.

Crown-cap all the bottles immediately after you fill them.

Fermentation and Tirage

Lay the bottles on their sides in storage boxes or in a cool, dark cellar bin if you have one. If you've miscalculated and added too much sugar, you want the storage boxes or bins to contain the shards of flying glass when the bottles start exploding. The bottom line: Measure carefully and accurately.

The bottles should be kept at about 60°F (16°C); warmth is the enemy of fine sparkling wine, so find a storage area with a true underground cellar temperature.

Leave the bottles alone, untouched, for at least a year; two is better, and three or more is even better, as we've seen. You are making fine wine here, not that awful bulk stuff for which a large corporation makes a cheap base wine and artificially charges it with CO_2 (a process called the Charmat method) and sells it cheap.

Riddling

So . . . time passes and now you're ready to complete the process. The base wine is gone, having been transformed into delicious sparkling wine. Now to get the spent yeast gunk out of the bottle by riddling: turn the bottles upside down, give them a sharp shake regularly, and wait for the gunk to collect in the neck of the bottles.

If you bottled the wine with a riddling aid, two weeks should be sufficient to riddle the bottles. If you used an encapsulated yeast, a day or two should suffice. (This is why encapsulated yeast is such a great option for the home winemaker, and using it can make your task a lot easier.) Riddling can take up to a month if there's no riddling aid or encapsulated yeast.

Consider processing the bottles a half case at a time. You can easily cut two rows of 3½-inch-diameter (9 cm) holes (the width of the base of a sparkling wine bottle) into a 18 × 24-inch (46 × 61 cm) piece of plywood — three holes in each row — and set the plywood on a sturdy wooden box or plastic crate with a "Kick Me" sign on the side. This setup keeps the bottles firmly upside down, especially if you put a thick layer of crumpled-up heavy-duty aluminum foil in the bottom of the box. Slip the bottles into the holes in the plywood *sur pointe*, as the French have it, or neck down, and snug the crown caps down into the crumpled foil. The plywood will hold the base of each bottle firmly, and the foil will not allow the neck to wobble. Don't use a cardboard wine carton for riddling. Most carton manufacturers make the partitions very thin and short — too thin and short to hold up a bottle upside down without it flopping over.

- -

HOMEMADE RIDDLING BOX

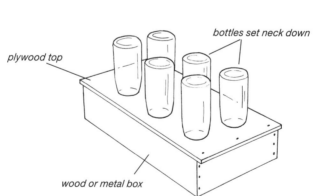

plywood top

bottles set neck down

wood or metal box

To riddle all 48 bottles at once, you'd have to make eight of these plywood bottle holders. Better to just do eight batches. But it's up to you.

Every time you pass the box with the upside-down bottles, give it a sharp little kick. This shakes the bottles enough to get the gunk moving toward the crown cap. After two weeks (or two days if you used encapsulated yeast), carefully pull a bottle straight up and inspect the neck with a flashlight. When all the gunk has reached the last ½ to ¾ inch (1–2 cm) of the neck, it's time for disgorgement.

Chilling the bottles before disgorgement is a necessity. It will greatly lessen the loss of pressure when you remove the cap. The bottles must remain neck down, so make room in the fridge and carefully transport the whole Kick Me setup into it. You can turn the thermostat to the coldest setting for overnight if you are planning to disgorge the bottles the next day. "Avoid jostling the bottles and re-suspending the sediment; this results in the need to re-riddle," Tiburzi cautions. If you end up needing to re-riddle a bottle, vigorously shake it to suspend all of the sediment, then lay the bottle on its side. Let the sediment compact for at least two weeks before attempting to riddle again.

Or, if you live in the wine country of northern California, just haul your grapes over to Rack & Riddle in Hopland, Mendocino County, where they will custom-crush the fruit, make the base wine, bottle, cellar, riddle, disgorge, and otherwise do all the hard work for you. But then, you'll be missing out on all the fun.

Calculating the Sugar Dosage

When making a brut-style sparkling wine, the aim is to balance the acidity with the sweetness. To that end, after disgorgement, you'll add enough sugar to reduce any acidic bite, but not enough for the wine to taste sweet. This addition is called the dosage (pronounced *doe-SAJ*).

Start by making a simple syrup by dissolving 650 grams (23 ounces) of ordinary white or quick-dissolving sugar in 1 liter of filtered water. Heating the water before adding the sugar will help it dissolve completely. Let this syrup cool to room temperature before using it, and make sure all the sugar is dissolved.

You will need to know the amount, if any, of residual sugar in your sparkling wine. You'll have to pop open one of your bottles of sparkling wine. Take out a sample, then recap the bottle and store it in the fridge (you'll need it later for testing and to top up bottles at disgorgement). You can take the sample to a chem lab for analysis, or you can test it yourself with a home test kit (see "Testing Residual Sugar" on page 175). If the wine shows no residual sugar and seems nicely balanced, you probably have between 0 and 0.5 gram per liter of residual sugar. That's a good default guess if everything seems squared away.

So, how much of this sweet syrup should you add to the wine to achieve the desired brut sugar level of 10 grams per liter? For a 750 mL bottle and using the simple syrup you've made, the rule is that for every 1 gram per liter (g/L) increase in sugar, you add 1.15 mL of the syrup. You will need a graduated cylinder or a pipette marked with milliliters to do this accurately. Thus, if you're shooting for a final sugar content of 10 g/L, which is brut, you'd add 10 × 1.15 mL of syrup, or 11.5 mL. (This takes into account the fact that the bottle is only three-quarters of a liter.)

However, you need to subtract from this amount the existing residual sugar in your wine. So if you've determined (or guessed) that your wine has 0.5 g/L of residual sugar, you will need to add just 11 mL of syrup. If testing shows that you have 1 g/L of residual sugar, you'll need to add just 10.5 mL to each bottle, and so on.

Before proceeding with disgorgement, it's good to do some testing to make sure you get the dosage right. Set six glasses in front of you and, using that bottle you took a sample from and then recapped, put 100 mL of the wine into each glass. Leave the first glass alone. Using a pipette, put 8 mL of the simple syrup in glass #2, 9 mL in glass #3, 10 mL in glass #4, 11 mL in glass #5, and 12 mL in glass #6. Taste each glass to see which one tastes best. Don't just go for the sweetness. Remember, you don't want your brut sparkling wine to taste sweet. You want balance and lightness. Let's say that you like the 10 mL per 100 mL wine best — this is equivalent to 10 g/L. Now fine-tune. If you fine tune, you'll need to open another bottle of your sparkling wine, which you may or may not want to do. This fine tuning step isn't absolutely necessary. Set up four clean glasses in front of you and put 100 mL wine in each. In glass #1, put in 9.5 mL syrup, then 10 mL in glass #2, 10.5 mL in glass #3, and 11 mL in glass #4. Taste through these and again select the one you like best. Whatever the number of milliliters (g/L) of syrup you put in that glass, use that number as your dosage.

Disgorgement

Because you will blow spent yeast and some wine out of the bottles as you disgorge them, you will need to add some liquid back to bring the bottles to the desired fill, or ullage, as winemakers call the space between the bottom of the cork or crown cap and the surface of the wine in the bottle. As we've discussed, the ideal ullage is between ¾ inch and 2 inches (25 cm). Use that test bottle in the fridge. If that's not enough wine to top up all the bottles, use still wine you've already set aside, or disgorge another one. Or use a bottle of commercial sparkling wine you've chilled. Just make sure it's at the quality level of the wine you're making.

Now for the disgorgement itself.

When you disgorge your wine, you'll be dealing with glass bottles under a great deal of pressure. The yeast and some wine will gush out of the bottle. The crown cap and bidule, if you use one, may bounce off nearby walls and tables and fly back at you. Bottles can break, though if you've used sound American sparkling wine bottles and followed the directions herein closely, it's not likely a bottle will rupture from the pressure. I suggest you wear gloves and protective goggles.

Disgorge in a place where the gushing gunk and wine can be easily washed down and cleaned up. Outside is best, but if you do it inside, consider the bathtub or deep sinks or tubs in a laundry room.

When you move your bottles from the refrigerator, be extra careful not to stir up the lees that have been riddled down to the neck. Here's where encapsulated yeast really helps by making this part of the job so much easier.

You will need a crown cap remover. There is a special tool called a disgorging key that allows you to keep your hand out of the way of the ejection when the crown cap comes off, but I have not seen them for sale in the United States, even online. However, you can also use a regular bottle opener that removes crown caps.

Bring your prepared sugar solution to the disgorgement area, along with a clean pipette for dispensing it. You'll also need a prepared sulfite solution: Dissolve half of a Campden tablet in a half gallon (1.9 L) of filtered water, which makes a 25 ppm solution, and have it at the ready.

You'll want to have all your bottles filled to the same level, so mark your desired fill line on the neck of an empty bottle. Then, as you top up your bottles after disgorgement, use the empty bottle's fill line as your guide.

It would be wise to practice on a few beer bottles before starting with your wine. When you're ready to disgorge the wine, with one hand gently lift a bottle straight up from the riddling rack, with its neck straight down. Hold the bottle opener in your other hand. Notice that a bubble of gas rests against the base of the bottle. Tilt the bottom of the bottle down until the bubble reaches the shoulder of the bottle, then pull off the crown cap and drop the bottle opener. As soon as the yeast gushes out, immediately put your thumb over the mouth of the bottle to hold in the gas, set the bottle upright, wait 10 to 15 seconds, and then slowly release your thumb.

Working quickly, fill your pipette with the sugar dosage you have previously determined. Insert the pipette into the neck of the bottle, and allow the dosage to slide down the inside surface of the bottle. This will keep fizzing and loss of carbon dioxide to a minimum. Again using the pipette, add just 3 mL of the sulfite solution to the bottle. Now top up the bottle with wine from that open bottle from the fridge, or with a sound and similar cold wine. Allow any fizzing to subside, wipe off the mouth of the bottle with a clean paper towel, and put on a crown cap. Make sure the cap is on securely, with the crimped edges flat against the glass.

This last addition of sugar will not ferment because the yeast in the bottle is entirely spent after a year en tirage. The tiny bit of sulfite you add will cut any chance that active wild yeast cells that may have entered the bottle during the disgorgement will start fermenting the dosage.

Store the wine in a cool, dark place; 60°F (16°C) is ideal. Lay the bottles on their sides (so you can spot any leakers). Now comes the hard part: Wait 100 days before you try a bottle. The wine will need that time to rest and come together. When you are ready to drink a bottle, chill it well. Place a dish towel over the crown cap and uncap it under the dish towel. This keeps wine from shooting all over the kitchen or dining room.

One last word of advice: Have fun.

CELLARING THE WINE

Wine will age in the bottle. Whites tend to peak within two or three years, then start a decline in quality. Light, fruity reds are usually good for a couple of years, but their freshness and fruit decline after that. Big reds can go for years, but it's the great one that will keep improving after a dozen years. All of which means that you're going to have to have a place to store carboys and bottles of many vintages. If you make just 100 bottles (20 gallons/76 L) of wine a year, you'll soon have hundreds of bottles of varying ages. We've discussed storage before, but let me give you a little more detail about what you'll need for the long haul.

Cellar Temperature

Of all the storage factors that adversely affect wine, high temperature is the most damaging. Storage at temperatures in the high 70s Fahrenheit (low to mid-20s, in Celsius) will dramatically shorten the life of wine, turning whites an ugly brownish color and reducing taste. This is called *maderization*, or oxidation, and is synonymous with a wine over the hill. Reds that age prematurely turn pale and flat, and their ruby red color changes to a brownish plum. Besides high temperatures, constantly fluctuating temperatures will also prematurely age the wine. Fluctuations also cause what's called the *bellows effect*. As the temperature changes, the wine inside the bottle expands and contracts, pumping air through the cork and causing oxidation.

The ideal temperature is a constant 58°F (14°C), which allows wine to age slowly and gracefully to perfection. Although you may not be able to arrange for a constant 58°F (14°C) (cooling units are not worth the cost for wine storage), remember that the limits are 50°F (10°C) minimum and 65°F (18°C) maximum, average yearly temperature. The normal seasonal rise and fall — averaging 10°F (6°C) annually 6 feet belowground, and only 1°F (0.6°C) 20 feet down — is slow enough that the wine rides along with it without damage. Below 50°F (10°C), maturation is delayed; above 65°F (18°C), it is hastened to the point of damage. The maturation of wine cannot be hurried without harming the quality. The best things take time.

An Insulated Storage Area

You can achieve temperatures like these in an ordinary cellar if you build an enclosure for a wine storage area that's insulated to R-50. Choose a corner of your basement farthest from the furnace or heat source. Because you'll probably be storing fine commercially made wine as well as your own, figure you'll need bins to hold about 800 bottles of wine (as long as you're going to do this, make it worthwhile). A bin 14 inches (36 cm) wide by 11 inches (28 cm) tall by 8 inches (20 cm) deep will hold 12 Bordeaux or Burgundy bottles, laid on their sides on top of one another.

The bins should be placed along two stone, block, or brick walls of the cellar, rather than on insulated walls, if you have enough room to accommodate the 70 or so bins that 800-plus bottles require. If each wall has 36 bins, for example (you build 6 bins across by 6 bins high), that'll give you 72 bins on the two walls, enough for 864 bottles. If you need extra room, you can use the insulated walls. This enclosed area will be excellent not only for wine, but also for storage of root crops like potatoes and fruits like apples and pears. Because it's entirely enclosed, a fresh air source is a good idea; if you have a casement window, open it the merest crack. Otherwise, 2-inch (5 cm) tubes set through the insulated walls, near the floor, will suffice for air exchange. It's comforting to have a room full of garden produce and wine snugged away in the basement, believe me.

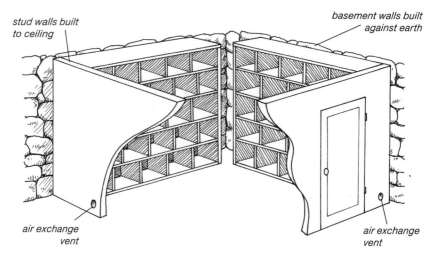

A BASEMENT WINE CELLAR

stud walls built to ceiling

basement walls built against earth

air exchange vent

air exchange vent

The interior walls are built of 2 × 4 studs and braces and insulated to R-50. The ceiling is also insulated to R-50. The foundation walls of stone, brick, or concrete touch outside earth and keep the temperature cool and constant in the wine cellar.

WINE ACCOUTREMENTS

Tasting the wine through all its developmental stages is the prerogative — nay, the duty — of the vintner. But actually *drinking* the wine, with no more cares about its production, comes only after bottle aging in the cellar. Then it ceases to mean anything but what wine always means to the consumer: a delectable drink, preferably taken with food.

Corkscrews

Which brings us to corkscrews. There are hundreds of devices on the market to get a cork out of a bottle, and most are worthless. Forget all the types with gears. Your arm is all the gearing you need. Find a corkscrew that is made from a round wire, not a square or flat one with any edge to cut the cork. The point of the corkscrew should follow the helix line of the turns, rather than point in toward the middle. It should have at least six, if not eight, turns around an empty space in the center. The popular Screwpull is such a cork-screw and does the job admirably.

I also like a cork puller. These have two prongs that are worked down on either side of the cork. With a pulling twist, the cork comes right out and is held by the prongs. Because the prongs don't pierce the cork but only grasp its sides, they don't destroy the cork, and it can be reinserted all the way into the bottle and taken out over and over again without damage. My favorite corkscrew is hand-forged (see the illustration), and my favorite commercial one is known as a "waiter's corkscrew." This device is superb.

Despite the best efforts, we all lose a cork once in a while. Some break off in the middle, leaving the bottom half plugging the neck. In such a case, I try to reinsert the corkscrew very gently, which usually doesn't work. If that fails, push the remainder of the cork into the bottle, use a nice lacquered chopstick to hold it away from the wine, and decant.

Or a cork may simply shred. The screw will pull out with a lot of crumbles, but most of the cork will remain seated around the edges. Just try to dig out as much as you can. If some cork goes into the bottle, oh well. Or the whole cork may suddenly slide into the bottle under the pressure of trying to insert the corkscrew or puller. In such a case, reach for the chopstick and decant. Any pieces of cork floating in the wine that's poured can also be fished out with the chopstick.

- -

TYPES OF CORKSCREWS

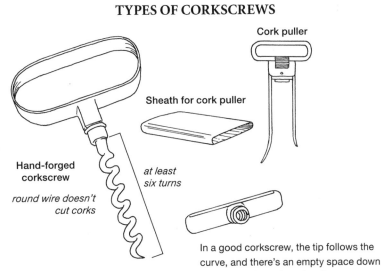

Cork puller

Sheath for cork puller

Hand-forged corkscrew

round wire doesn't cut corks

at least six turns

In a good corkscrew, the tip follows the curve, and there's an empty space down the center when viewed end on.

Wineglasses

Drinking Lafite — or your own good wine — from a jelly glass is abominable. Get some real wineglasses. They are designed to give you the greatest possible sensory experience of the wine.

For reds, get a tulip-shaped glass, at least 8 ounces (237 mL), with a rim that curves inward. For whites, a similar — if squatter, but just as generous — glass will do, especially one with a balloon shape. For sparkling wine, flutes are the real thing, with a slightly inward-curving rim and the shape that gives the most beautiful bubbles. Sparkling wine in other glasses tends to go flat quickly.

Baccarat makes the most expensive wineglasses, but the Riedel Company makes a range of high-quality glasses designed for individual kinds of wine. These are excellent.

TYPES OF WINEGLASSES

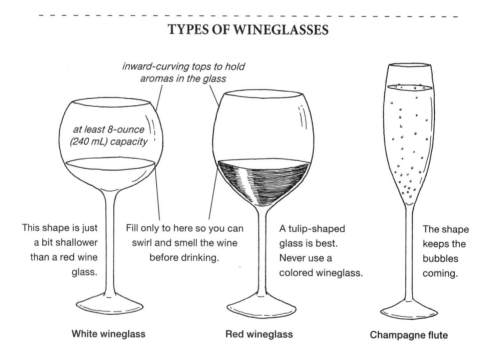

inward-curving tops to hold aromas in the glass

at least 8-ounce (240 mL) capacity

This shape is just a bit shallower than a red wine glass.

Fill only to here so you can swirl and smell the wine before drinking.

A tulip-shaped glass is best. Never use a colored wineglass.

The shape keeps the bubbles coming.

White wineglass   **Red wineglass**   **Champagne flute**

SENSORY EVALUATION OF WINE

The sensory evaluation of wine happens with first the *eyes*, then the *nose*, and then the senses of taste and feel in the *mouth*. Let's look at them in that order, even though the odor of wine is the most subtle and important sensory constituent, taste is of less importance, and the look of the wine is least important.

Clarity and Color

After pouring a couple of ounces of a wine into an 8- to 10-ounce (237–296 mL) glass, I first look for clarity. Any tartrate crystals will be seen now. Anything but a brilliantly clear wine makes me feel uneasy, even though a slight haze may mean nothing more than that the wine wasn't reduced in quality by fining. Then I look at the color. Some may look for a standard of excellence in wine color, but I just look at the color, simply drinking it in with my eyes. With no preconceptions, I know right away whether the color is pleasing. Muddy, brown, or purple colors just aren't as pretty as a deep ruby red or a strawy gold-white with a hint of green. The purity of the reds achieved in fine wines is astonishing. If you're fond of deep rubies and garnets in gemstones, as I am, a glass of fine red wine will have you practically ecstatic.

Looking at the Rim

Then, with reds, I evaluate the rim. I tilt the glass, causing the wine to thin out as it approaches the rim, allowing more light to pass through. At the rim, the wine is very thin, and colors change. I hold the glass above a white tablecloth or piece of paper to check the rim color. A red that simply thins out to a lighter tone but doesn't change color (hue) indicates a young wine.

If the rim shows bluish or purplish colors, that could be due to the grape variety, or it could mean that the grapes were not quite ripe when picked, or that the wine is young. If the red color thins out to a deep golden orange color, that means the wine is well aged and peaking. A brownish orange or brown plum rim means that the wine is declining and is probably past its peak.

LOOKING AT THE RIM

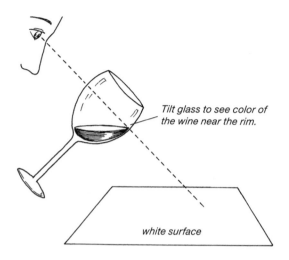

Tilt glass to see color of
the wine near the rim.

white surface

Legs

Then I swirl the wine in the glass to get a look at its legs. For many years I had read that the legs — the rivulets that form on the sides of the glass after the wine is swirled — were caused by the glycerin in the wine. I've since discovered that in reality they are formed because of the lower surface tension that alcohol causes. "Which is why you can get impressive legs with a glass of vodka," says Henry Finder of Loudonville, New York, who has investigated the phenomenon. A friend once gave me a bottle of St. Regis, "America's First Non-Alcoholic Wine." It's a sweetish, less-than-ordinary jug white from California, from which the alcohol has been removed by gentle heat. Because it contains no alcohol, it also has no legs.

the legs

The "Nose" of the Wine

The "nose" of the wine includes the *aroma* — which is the particular smell of the grape variety, such as the Welch's grape juice smell of Concord, or the hints of bell pepper in a cabernet sauvignon, or the smell of black raspberries in a petite sirah — and vinous smells, which are winey without any particular varietal characteristic. The nose also includes the *bouquet*, the odor of old leather, flowers, tobacco, honey, or other smells that arise after enough aging. The nose may show *off smells*. Some of the common defects in the nose are volatile acidity, or the smell of vinegar in small amounts; acetaldehyde, which smells like a nutty sherry; sulfur dioxide, which smells like the sulfurous odor of a burning kitchen match; mercaptan, which smells like a skunk; hydrogen sulfide, which smells like rotten eggs; sauerkraut odor, usually from a malolactic fermentation that proceeded in the bottle; and any other smell you choose not to like.

Oak will be another constituent of the nose. If excessive, it can detract from the sensory experience. When a wine, especially a red, is oaked just right, the nose gets a faint whiff of vanilla, rather than of a heavy wood.

When varietal aromas, a flowery bouquet, and a hint of vanilla oak mingle in harmony, the result is a great wine with enormous evocative power. We know that the sense of smell is linked closely with memory. A certain smell can bring back a moment more sharply and clearly in our minds than any other stimulus. You'll find that a great wine with a balanced nose is as sensual and pleasing an experience as you could ever expect from something to drink.

Retronasal Aroma

The direct aroma comes through the nose, but a richer aroma comes through the back of the nose when the wine is tasted. The wine is sipped and the sip is chewed to coat the mouth with it, and especially to work up aromas that will seep up the back of the nose and flood the olfactory organs. As Émile Peynaud said, "There are two types of aromas in wine, which are due to the same substances. There is the direct aroma, which comes through the nostrils, and the indirect aroma, or retronasal, when the wine is in the mouth. One can judge the quality of a wine by the intensity and persistence of the retronasal aroma."

When people speak of a wine's long or short finish, they are talking about the persistence of the retronasal aroma. A great wine will continue to unfold both aromas and flavors in the mouth for quite a long time, presenting facet after facet and nuance after nuance of both. The taster can find some new aspect of the flavor or a new aroma even after the sip has been swallowed, the lips smacked, and the sigh heaved.

Educating the Nose

If you are serious about being able to identify the smells in great wine by their proper terms, you can learn the skill at home with one of the new kits available. "Le Nez du Vin," for instance, contains 54 vials of pure essences of scents found in wine, packed in a folio-sized box with accompanying reference cards. They include tar, mercaptan, apricots, mushrooms, and 50 other smells. It's an expensive kit, however; you can find less expensive ones if you look around.

The Taste of Wine

Further sensory components are the four tastes: sweet, bitter, sour, and salty. If you run into salty, something terrible has happened — or you've broken into the cooking sherry. Residual sweetness, perhaps a slight bitterness or astringency from tannins, and a light acidity are all parts of a balanced wine. Any of them in excess, or missing, detracts from wine quality. For greatness, a wine needs all three in barely detectable amounts.

——— Table 21: Optimum Serving Temperatures ———

The temperatures noted below are "room temperatures," as *room* refers to the cellar in which they're kept. The only reason to chill a wine below 50°F (10°C) would be to kill the taste or mask the lack of one. The exception is Champagne, which is good served at 40 to 45°F (4–7°C). The lower temperature keeps the fizzing from proceeding too fast, and the wine will warm a bit as you drink it, so that the cold doesn't mask the taste.

TYPE OF WINE	OPTIMUM SERVING TEMPERATURE
Robust red wines	60–65°F (16–18°C)
Light red wines	55–60°F (13–16°C)
Robust white wines	55–60°F (13–16°C)
Light white wines	50–55°F (10–13°C)

Body

A final component of wine in the mouth is its body, texture, fullness, or mouthfeel — call it what you will. No one really completely understands what causes the body of a great wine, but you know it when it's there. Lesser wines feel thin, watery, unidimensional by contrast. A wine with good body fills the mouth with almost an oily characteristic, but not unpleasant the way oil would be. It tastes round, rather than flat, meaning that it has depth of body.

I have before me a piece of paper on which I made notes the night I drank a 57-year-old Bordeaux. It carried such an intense aroma and bouquet that it approached the smell of myrrh. I also found "almonds, beefsteak, frankincense, honey, and nuts." The taste was "velvety-smooth, concentrated, with a huge, elongated finish that yields new flavors all the way." The rim was a wide golden orange, and the color shone with rubies and garnets. My comments end with this question: "Will you be as young at 57 as this wine?"

I'd like to make a wine as good as that. Wouldn't you?

Let's do it.

Three bowls only do I serve for the temperate: one for health, which they empty first; the second for love and pleasure; and the third for sleep. When this bowl is drunk up, wise guests go home. The fourth bowl is ours no longer, but belongs to violence; the fifth to uproar; the sixth to drunken revel; the seventh to black eyes; the eighth is the policeman's; the ninth belongs to biliousness; and the tenth to madness and hurling the furniture.

— Eubulus (ca. 375 B.C.E.)

THE HOME WINEMAKER'S RECORD BOOK

The following information is helpful to have as reference when making wine in subsequent years. Copy these pages.

Year.......... Variety...................................

Number of vines...............................

Bud burst...

Weight of grapes..............................

```
················ SPRAYS ················
    Material        Date
   _____     _____
   _____     _____
   _____     _____
   _____     _____
   _____     _____
```

Full bloom............................. Volume of juice.................................

Véraison................................ Volume of wine.................................

Harvest date.......................... Volume of wine after all rackings....................

Brix at harvest....................... Sugar correction (adjusted Brix):....................

pH at harvest........................ Acid correction:.................................

TA at harvest........................

Crush SO_2.............................SO_2.......................... ....
  (Time/Date)   (ppm/Date)   (Adjusted acid/Adjusted pH)

Press whites..
                (Time/Date)

Primary fermentation...
            From (Date)   To (Date)

Press reds.................................Days on skins............Total SO$_2$ at end of primary........................
       (Time/Date)

Malolactic culture added...
             (Date/Type of Culture)

Racked to carboys....................Wine finishes working................................
       (Date)   (Date)

Further rackings (Dates)   SO$_2$ added(ppm)   Cold stabilization...................................

....

....

....   Fining..
                      (Fining Agent/Date)

Total SO$_2$ at bottling.................................   Oaking...

pH at bottling.................................   In cask from (date)   To (date)

TA at bottling.................................   Type of wood in cask................................

Residual sugar at bottling.............................   Bottling..

Alcohol by volume at bottling...........%   (Date)

    Chips...

.... REMARKS ··

FOR MORE INFORMATION

Alcohol and Tobacco Tax and Trade Bureau
www.ttb.gov

American Wine Society
888-297-9070
www.americanwinesociety.org
The society publishes many pamphlets covering all aspects of grape growing, vine selection, and winemaking. It also has hundreds of regional chapters that hold regular tastings. Among its publications are bibliographies of major wine reference works, books on specialized aspects of wine or grapes, and a journal.

Wine Appreciation Guild
800-231-9463
www.wineappreciation.com
The guild carries books, sources of supplies, wine storage racks, and information on many aspects of wine of interest to the home winemaker.

In addition, many states have a grape growers' association. Check with your USDA agricultural extension agent to find the name of the association that covers your area. These groups sometimes publish information and are a good way to find sources of vines and supplies.

Selected Periodicals

American Vineyard
www.americanvineyardmagazine.com
This monthly magazine carries agricultural articles aimed at larger growers but useful for the enthusiastic home vineyardist.

International Journal of Fruit Science
www.tandfonline.com/loi/wsfr20
This quarterly carries scientific articles and reports on small fruit growing and on viticulture. It reports on new technologies and innovative approaches to management of the vineyard.

Practical Winery & Vineyard Journal
415-453-9700
www.practicalwinery.com
A bimonthly magazine that is an excellent publication for the serious winemaker. Full of good how-to, it will serve as continuing education for readers of this book.

Wine & Vines
866-453-9701
www.winesandvines.com
The monthly magazine of the wine industry. The magazine also publishes an annual buyer's guide that is quite complete, listing every commercial winery in North America, plus all vineyard industry suppliers. Very helpful for anyone shopping for a home vineyard and wine operation.

Wine Business Monthly
800-895-9463
www.winebusiness.com/wbm
Read all about how people who actually make wine for a living do it. Fascinating stuff for the home winemaker.

Wine East
866-453-9701
www.winesandvines.com
A monthly insert in *Wine & Vines* that puts the emphasis on eastern wines, wineries, and the wine trade.

There are many other magazines, newsletters, and scientific journals devoted to all aspects of winemaking, grape growing, marketing, wine appreciation, and so forth. The ones listed above are solid sources for general information.

SELECTED BIBLIOGRAPHY

General Reference

Lichine, Alexis. *Alexis Lichine's New Encyclopedia of Wines & Spirits.* 3rd ed. New York: Alfred A. Knopf, 1982.

A very thorough, encyclopedic work brought up-to-date regularly by its editors, written for the wine buyer and those interested in the subject generally.

Robinson, Jancis, ed. *The Oxford Companion to Wine.* New York: Oxford University Press, 1994.

A huge, 1,088-page work that encompasses all aspects of wine, from soils to vines to the wines and their regions everywhere in the world. The contributors include the most erudite professionals in the business. Written intelligently, with style, and with strong opinions. Indispensable for all who love wine — professional or amateur.

Viticulture

Jackson, David, and Danny Schuster. *The Production of Grapes and Wine in Cool Climates.* Orinda, Calif.: The Wine Appreciation Guild, 1981.

Jackson and Schuster write about smaller-scale growing and winemaking "down under." But the information is still useful "up over."

Wagner, Philip M. *A Wine-Grower's Guide.* Rev. ed. New York: Alfred A. Knopf, 1965.

An excellent book on grape growing for the amateur, with a focus on French-American hybrids.

Weaver, Robert J. *Grape Growing.* New York: John Wiley & Sons, 1976.

Weaver covers the same material as Winkler et al. (below), but in a more concise and understandable way for the home grower. The book is designed as a freshman text for college courses in viticulture.

Winkler, A. J., J. A. Cook, W. M. Kliewer, and L. A. Lider. *General Viticulture.* Berkeley: University of California Press, 1974.

This is the premier viticultural textbook, but it is getting a bit dated. Its primary focus is on growing grapes in California, although other climates are covered.

Winemaking

Amerine, M. A., H. W. Berg, R. F. Kunkee, et al. *The Technology of Winemaking.* Westport, Conn.: AVI Publishing Co., 1980.

Even more detail on winemaking technology than *Table Wines* (below). Only for big producers or interested amateurs.

Amerine, M. A., and M. A. Joslyn. *Table Wines.* 2nd ed. Berkeley: University of California Press, 1970.

A monumental work for commercial wineries and graduate students in enology. Everything you'd ever want to know about the technology of winemaking, and more.

Jackson, D., and D. Schuster. *Grape Growing and Wine Making.* Orinda, Calif.: Altarinda Books, 1981.

Lundy, Desmond. *Leisure Winemaking.* Calgary, Alberta.: Detselig Enterprises Ltd., 1978.

A delightful book full of information on the chemistry involved in winemaking, written for the serious home winemaker. It was recommended to me by a commercial wine-maker who uses it to produce award-winning Napa Valley Cabernet Sauvignon.

Margalit, Yair. *Concepts in Wine Chemistry.* San Francisco: The Wine Appreciation Guild, 1997.

A new book on wine chemistry for those who really want to know what's going on in the must, molecule by molecule.

Wagner, Philip M. *Grapes into Wine.* New York: Alfred A. Knopf, 1976.

A paperback companion volume to Wagner's viticultural work.

Wine Tasting and Sensory Evaluation

Amerine, M. A., and E. G. Roessler. *Wines: Their Sensory Evaluation.* San Francisco: W. H. Freeman & Co., 1976.

An excellent, no-nonsense approach to wine tasting and techniques for judging wine quality.

SOURCES OF SUPPLIES

The best way to obtain winemaking supplies is to find a local dealer. Winemaking supplies are often sold in tandem with homebrew supplies, so check for homebrew suppliers as well. A number of suppliers now have their catalogs online.

If there are no local sources for vineyard hardware or winemaking equipment, I'd recommend looking up the following national suppliers.

Equipment and Ingredients

Beer & Wine Hobby

800-523-5423
www.beer-wine.com
Everything needed to make wine, brew beer, make cheese, and much, much more.

Brew & Wine Hobby

800-352-4238
www.brew-wine.com
Specializing in winemaking supplies and European juices.

E. C. Kraus

800-353-1906
www.eckraus.com
Since 1966 E. C. Kraus has provided winemaking supplies and service that puts its customers on the road to successful home winemaking.

Great Fermentations

888-463-2734
www.greatfermentations.com
Ingredients, yeasts, and equipment for the home winemaker.

Gusmer Enterprises, Inc.

866-213-1131
www.gusmerenterprises.com
Its catalog makes recommendations of specific yeasts for specific varieties, including French-American hybrids, which is very helpful. Formerly known as the Wine Lab.

Midwest Homebrewing and Winemaking Supplies

888-449-2739

www.midwestsupplies.com

Offers a full range of winemaking supplies, including bottles and crown caps for sparkling wines.

MoreWine!

800-823-0010

http://morewinemaking.com

Absolutely everything for small-scale winemaking, including DV_Ω yeast for sparkling wines.

Orchard Valley Supply, Inc.

888-755-0098

www.orchardvalleysupply.com

Vineyard hardware supply company with trellising equipment: "No vines . . . no wines . . . just everything in between."

Presque Isle Wine Cellars

814-725-1314

www.piwine.com

Almost everything for the grower and home winemaker; nice range of yeasts.

Prospero Equipment Corporation

800-953-3736

www.prosperoequipment.com

Pumps for racking your wines and transferring them from container to container; other accoutrements too, from presses to carboys to corks and cappers.

Quiedan Company

831-663-0770

www.quiedan.com

Designs and manufactures a complete line of trellis materials including a polyethylene slide grow tube, a variety of VSP line posts, lyre systems, Geneva double curtain system, several options for training stakes, grapestakes, crossarms, multi-part crossarms, pinch clips (miniature cross arms), wire forms (wrap clips), special fasteners, training clips, bud clips, wire tighteners, and all related products.

Scott Laboratories

707-765-6666

www.scottlab.com

Offers a wide range of yeasts (including encapsulated yeast), malolactic cultures, fining agents, riddling aids, and more, for still and sparkling wines.

South Hills Brewing Supply
412-937-0773
www.southhillsbrewing.com
Ingredients, yeasts, airlocks, and equipment for home winemakers.

TCW Equipment
707-963-9681
www.tcwequipment.com
Winemaking equipment, catering to small commercial operations.

Waterloo Container
888-539-3922
www.waterloocontainer.com
Wholesale wine bottles, corks, and capsules — just what you need to get set up.

Barrels

Although most winemaking shops carry barrels, it may be cheaper to order from the manufacturer. For French Nevers, Centre, or Limousin oak barrels, as well as American oak, try these sources.

Barrel Builders, Inc.
707-963-9963
www.barrelbuilders.com
Full line of wine barrels, including French Tonnellerie Marchive, Hungarian oak, and American oak barrels.

Seguin Moreau
info@seguin-moreau.fr
www.seguin-moreau.fr
Top-quality French oak barrels; they give you the toast you ask for, both in the barrel and on the head.

World Cooperage
707-255-5900
www.worldcooperage.com
American and French oak barrels.

SOURCES FOR GRAPEVINES

There are thousands of retail outlets for grapevines in the United States. The following is a representative sample of suppliers from coast to coast. Contact them to find out what varieties they are currently carrying.

Brigadoon Wine Company
541-998-2600
http://brigadoonwineco.com

Duarte Trees and Vines
800-472-3833
www.duartenursery.com

Grafted Grapevine Nursery
315-462-3288
www.graftedgrapevines.com

Hermann J. Wiemer Vineyard
800-371-7971
www.wiemer.com

Mahonia Vineyards & Nursery
503-585-8789
www.mahonianursery.com

Sunridge Nurseries
661-363-8463
www.sunridgenurseries.com

Wonderful Nurseries
661-758-4777
www.wonderfulnurseries.com

GRAPE PESTS AND DISEASES

Pest-Related Damage to Foliage

Symptoms: At first, a scattering of small whitish spots on the leaves. Then yellow and whitish blotches on severely damaged leaves. Eventually the leaves turn brown and fall off.

Cause: Grape leaf hopper.

Habit: A ubiquitous pest in California, the adults are about ⅛-inch (3 mm) long, slender, and light yellow with red and brown marks. The white leaf spots are from feeding episodes by adults. With a severe infestation, leaves are destroyed. Such defoliation badly damages grape quality.

Treatment: A parasitic wasp, *Anagrus epos*, is a grower's best friend, as it keeps the hopper populations down to acceptable levels. Populations of young leaf hoppers of up to 10 per leaf are considered acceptable. Allow refuges of wild blackberries to grow nearby, as the parasitic wasp overwinters in them. French prune orchards also harbor the *Anagrus* wasp. The parasites can be purchased for release in the vineyard. Leaf hoppers can do considerable feeding before the damage is worth taking action against. Releases of lacewings can help. Sprays of pyrethrum and soap, soap and nicotine sulfate, or soap and sulfur are all effective.

Symptoms: One side of a leaf is rolled up, and there's frass (larval excrement) and, usually, a worm inside.

Cause: Leaf roller.

Habit: The worms are green. They attach wet lines of silk from the leaf edge to points near the center. When these dry, they roll the leaf right up. No treatment is necessary unless the damage is defoliating vines. Usually parasites keep this pest within bounds. If the pest's populations increase, the parasites will soon follow.

Treatment: *Bacillus thuringiensis* gives excellent control. Make sure your spray reaches inside the rolled leaves by spraying from all sides.

Symptoms: Larvae that are about ½-inch (1 cm) long and straw-colored — or sometimes greenish, gray, or smoky-colored — are seen in or on swollen buds, developing leaves, or shoot tips, then on leaves that are webbed together, and later in the clusters, where their webs are found. Fruit is punctured and decays, then shrivels.

Cause: Orange tortrix.

Habit: The adult moth is brown or beige, with a darker saddle of color across folded wings. It's found in the vineyard through most of the year in California. Another sign of this pest is oval, flat, cream-colored eggs deposited in overlapping layers.

Treatment: *Bacillus thuringiensis* gives positive control if vines are sprayed thoroughly from bud burst, and resprayed after each rain or every two months.

Symptoms: In early to midsummer, the leaves of red and black grape varieties begin to turn red, especially between the largest veins. This red color advances until only the main veins and a little tissue alongside is green.

Cause: Pacific mite.

Habit: It has a yellow to amber body and black spots on its back. It's barely visible to the naked eye. Prefers hot, dry positions on the vines.

Treatment: Predatory mites and ladybird beetles will keep the mites in check, but if the mites affect more than eight leaves per vine, release *Metaseiulus occidentalis*, the predatory mite proven capable of controlling Pacific mite. Lime-sulfur or flowable sulfur sprays used for fungus control will help control this West Coast pest.

Symptoms: Leaves shrivel shortly after opening. The lower and earliest leaf may turn black and die before it's half grown. Lower leaves are misshapen and mottled with a bronze-glazed appearance.

Cause: Willamette mite.

Habit: Barely visible, it appears pale yellow with very small black dots on its body. Prefers shaded, moist positions on the vines.

Treatment: The same predatory mite that controls Pacific mite uses Willamette mite as an alternative prey. Sulfur dust will also control this mite.

Symptoms: Leaves are stunted and start to curl. Older leaves turn a bronzy green. Little red mites are seen on leaves, canes, and trunk.

Cause: European red mite.

Habit: This familiar red mite attacks more and more American grapes in the East. It prefers high, central positions on older wood.

Treatment: Ladybird beetles and predatory mites, especially the black ladybird beetle, *Stethorus punctum*, offer the best control. If the mites are found more than three to a leaf, they'll need further treatment with sulfur dust, flowable sulfur, or lime-sulfur. If little spraying is done with insecticides, mites will seldom be seen.

Symptoms: Leaf tissue is eaten away, except for the veins and, in the early stages, the upper epidermis of the leaves.

Cause: Western grapeleaf skeletonizer or Japanese beetle.

Habit: The western grapeleaf skeletonizer is a yellow caterpillar with purple and black bands across its body. The Japanese beetle is metallic bronze and green and ¼ to ⅓ inch (6–8 mm) long.

Treatment: *Apanteles harrisinae* (a parasitic wasp), *Sturmia harrisinae* (a parasitic fly), a viral disease, and *Bacillus thuringiensis* have all been used to control the skeletonizer. A sex pheromone has been isolated from female skeletonizers that's being used to confuse males.

For Japanese beetles, use pheromone traps that lure males by a sex scent and food odor. This gives excellent long-term protection. Handpick until populations are reduced to acceptable levels by the traps. These beetles break out in regular 4- or 5-year cycles.

Symptoms: Large leaf areas and even whole vines come under attack by large, 2- to 4-inch (5–10 cm) caterpillars with a conspicuous horn, later replaced by an eye-spot, on the next-to-last segment of their bodies.

Cause: Sphinx (or hawk) moth larvae.

Habit: The color of these large worms is light green when young, with a dull red to black horn. Later they are yellow-green to red-brown marked with yellow, and they lose the horn in favor of an eye-spot.

Treatment: *Bacillus thuringiensis.*

Symptoms: Leaves and young shoots are eaten. You see lots of grasshoppers.

Cause: Grasshoppers.

Habit: These voracious insects are hard to kill, as they are so mobile.

Treatment: Poison grasshopper bait is available from agricultural outlets. One grower in Nebraska had success using a spray made from grasshoppers ground in a blender with water, then strained, diluted, and sprayed with a spray tank.

Symptoms: Buckshot-size, bristly green galls on the undersides of grape leaves and on young shoots.

Cause: Phylloxera.

Habit: This root louse has an aerial stage during which it produces characteristic galls on the leaves. Nick a gall apart with a fingernail and there's a darker orange area with a tiny whitish larva, louse, or eggs inside.

Treatment: Pinch off any galls you see and squash them. If there are too many, releases of green lacewing can help. Endolsulfan, the recommended chemical control, damages Baco Noir, Chancellor, Colobel, and Cascade varieties. Dusting with rotenone from pre-bloom to four weeks later should also help.

Varietal Susceptibility to Leaf-Damaging Phylloxera

MOST SUSCEPTIBLE	MODERATELY SUSCEPTIBLE	LEAST SUSCEPTIBLE
Seyval Blanc	Delaware	Niagara
Aurora	Ravat 51	Florental
Rayon d'Or	Léon Millot	Catawba
Cascade	Vidal 256	Maréchal Foch
Villard Blanc	Baco Noir	Steuben
Chancellor	Chelois	Cabernet Sauvignon
	Dutchess	Chardonnay
		Riesling

Pest-Related Damage to Buds or Young Shoots

Symptoms: Buds are eaten out and young shoots are cut off and fall over.

Cause: Cutworms.

Habit: Colors vary according to species, but the damage will be done at night. The worms are 1 to 1½ inches (3–4 cm) long and smooth-bodied.

Treatment: Rotenone dust worked into the soil around the base of the trunk will help, as that's where the worm goes during the day. Handpick any you see.

Symptoms: Swollen or just-breaking buds in the spring are eaten out, with a conspicuous hole in the center. Later, small larvae eat the emerging leaves, so leaves are misshapen. Emerging fruit clusters may be eaten.

Cause: Grape flea beetle or grape bud beetle.

Habit: The grape flea beetle is a small metallic blue or purple beetle that can jump like its namesake. Larvae that grow from eggs deposited in the buds grow to ⅓ inch (8 mm) and are yellowish brown with black markings.

The grape bud beetle is found primarily in the central valleys of California. It's similar to the flea beetle, except that it is gray.

Treatment: Rotenone dust effectively controls emerging larvae. Keep plants dusted from the swollen bud stage until shoots are 6 inches (15 cm) long. Adult beetles may survive rotenone, and if the infestation is bad, you may want to use pyrethroids. Sticky traps made from 1-gallon (3.8 L) jugs (see page 103) also help keep populations down.

Symptoms: Dwarfing and stunting of new shoots for the first five or six nodes. The growing tip of the shoot may be killed, causing a profusion of laterals that give a witch's broom effect.

Cause: Grape bud mite.

Habit: They live in the buds and are carried out the shoot as it elongates. Found mostly in California.

Treatment: There's no known chemical treatment, but a healthy vineyard ecology, with predatory mites and ladybird beetles, should help keep populations to a minimum. As a last resort, cut off infested shoots and burn them in a regular sanitation program.

Symptoms: Masses of brownish aphids are seen on young tips, leaves, shoots, and occasionally clusters. Usually accompanied by ants.

Cause: Brown grape aphid.

Habit: The ants lap up honeydew excreted by the aphids and protect them from predators. Usually the aphid damage isn't worrisome, but if an outbreak is severe, some shoot tips and fruit may be lost.

Treatment: A jet spray of soapy water (½ cup of liquid dish soap in a gallon of water, or 31 mL per liter) directed right on the aphids will rid the vines of most of them very efficiently. Aphids, by the way, really attract beneficial insects, so don't bother them unless damage is heavy.

Pest-Related Damage to Grape Flowers or Fruit

Symptoms: When the young shoots are 10 to 15 inches (25–38 cm) long, flower clusters, young leaves, and young fruit are eaten.

Cause: Hoplia beetles.

Habit: The beetles are found feeding in groups. They're broad, ¼ to ⅓ inch (6–8 mm) long, and grayish to reddish brown in mottles on the backs with silvery, shiny undersides. When disturbed, the beetles drop to the ground. Found mainly in the West.

Treatment: First try rotenone-ryania-pyrethrum dust. If the problem persists, try pyrethroids.

Symptoms: Grape clusters look sooty and sticky, and there are cottony, waxy masses down in the clusters.

Cause: Grape mealybug.

Habit: These are fine food for predators, and an outbreak usually means ants are keeping the mealybugs' natural enemies at bay.

Treatment: Ant traps. Pour boiling water down any anthills nearby. Pesticides are not recommended for control, as they kill natural controls.

Symptoms: Silvering, bleaching, or russeting of berries, stems, and leaves. "Halo spot" on berries where an insect's eggs were deposited. Later, scarred and scabby patches appear on the berries.

Cause: Thrips.

Habit: Thrips are small — ⅟₅₀ to ⅟₂₅ of an inch (0.5–1.0 mm) in length. They are winged insects, elongated, narrow-bodied, and can fly, run quickly, and hop.

Treatment: Much the same as for leaf hoppers (see page 222).

Symptoms: Berries are punctured, and juice exudes to form a brown, sticky, ugly mess. Occurs just before harvest. Berries soon shrivel and rot.

Cause: Consperse stinkbug.

Habit: Look for large — ⅜ inch (1 cm) long and ¼ inch (0.6 cm) wide — shield-shaped stinkbugs, brown on their backs and pale green underneath. Their amber legs have small black spots.

Treatment: This is a hard one, since damage occurs just before harvest and sprays of any kind aren't possible. Remove weedy, grassy patches near affected areas of the vineyard, if they exist, to destroy the bugs' habitat. If your vineyard is small enough, handpick and drop bugs into a can with kerosene in the bottom.

Symptoms: Flower clusters are eaten, blossoms first, then young fruit and leaves.

Cause: Rose chafer.

Habit: These insects are ubiquitous in the Midwest at grape blossoming time and sometimes show up in large numbers. They also damage ornamental bushes. The beetle is about ¼ to ⅓ inch (6–8 mm) long, light brown, and covered with light hairs. Its long, spiny legs give it a clumsy motion.

Treatment: If sandy areas near the vineyard are grassy with perennial weeds, cultivate them, because that's where the rose chafers pupate. Rotenone or other botanical dusts can be used on severe infestations.

Symptoms: Small whitish maggots feeding on flower parts in vineyards along Lake Erie.

Cause: Grape-blossom midge.

Habit: Mostly a minor pest, it can sometimes cause unacceptable damage in the Lake Erie area.

Treatment: Rotenone dusted on flowers, if the crop is threatened.

Symptoms: Blossoms and small berries are eaten and webby. Later in the season, berries show a purplish ringed spot with a hole in the center. Splitting the berry open reveals a larva. Damaged berries then decay in humid weather, or dry out in hot and dry weather.

Cause: Grape berry moth.

Habit: This pest — found throughout the eastern states from Maine to the Gulf and west to the Rockies — is a dark green to dark purple larva with a light brown head and black spots on the chest when seen on flower clusters and young leaves. It will cut a piece of leaf on three sides and fold it into a tent to construct a cocoon.

Treatment: Don't cultivate soil after August 1, so that the cocoons remain exposed after they fall to the ground. Cultivate in spring to bury remaining cocoons 3 inches (8 cm) deep, and don't disturb the soil until two weeks after bloom. If you spot the larvae on flowers or leaves, *Bacillus thuringiensis* provides excellent control without harming beneficial insects.

Symptoms: Small, squat beetles, about ⅒ inch (2.5 mm) long and similarly wide, appear on the leaves at about the time the grapes bloom. They leave short, curved groups of lines on the upper surface of the leaves. White grubs with no legs are discovered inside the berries in late July, and the beetles reappear to feed in the fall.

Cause: Grape curculio.

Habit: Their presence is best detected by the curved feeding marks they leave on the leaves. Check berries for worms later in the season.

Treatment: Rotenone dust on infested vines should curb them. Clean cultivation, as with the grape berry moth, will also help.

Pest-Related Damage to the Arms, Canes, or Trunk

Symptoms: In California and Oregon, shoots droop, wilt, or break off when 6–10 inches (15–25 cm) long. An inspection of the crotch of the spur from which the shoot arose reveals brown or black beetles, cylindrical, about ½ inch (1 cm) long, feeding in a burrow.

Cause: Branch and twig borer.

Habit: As these beetles eat their way through the wood, they plug the holes behind them with grass and chewed wood. They can cause extensive damage.

Treatment: Prune off the weakened shoots and the burrowed wood. Burn it and all other prunings that may be left around. As a preventive, burn spring prunings. Spraying usually doesn't help control this insect, but good vineyard sanitation does.

Symptoms: Canes are bored into by small beetles, although none are found in crotches near the base of the shoot and spur, in areas east of the Rockies.

Cause: Grape cane borer.

Habit: Most common in states bordering the Mississippi.

Treatment: Its control is the same as for branch and twig borer.

Symptoms: Sticky masses of dirty white or brownish spots appear on one- and two-year-old wood and sometimes older wood. A hand lens reveals masses of tiny insects, usually hemispheric in shape.

Cause: Scale insects.

Habit: These tiny insects live in colonies and exude a sweet and sticky honeydew. They make excellent food for ladybird beetles. There are many types of scale.

Treatment: Dormant oil spray.

Stunted, Dying Vines

Symptoms: The symptoms are indefinite, but the vine looks weak and sick, and is stunted in its growth. Pulling up some roots, you see roughened, knotted areas as if something is eating or colonizing the roots.

Cause: Phylloxera or nematodes.

Habit: Phylloxera lice are very destructive; once infested, the vine is best pulled. Nematodes, the other possible culprit, may cause root knots or other types of galls on grape roots.

Treatment: Planting vines on phylloxera-resistant rootstock is the only realistic control for phylloxera. Own-rooted susceptible vines are possible in sandy soils where the insect doesn't do well, and possibly in other kinds of soils that aren't in established vineyard areas. American vine roots resist the phylloxera because the insects don't chew far enough into the root to reach the cambium. In vinifera, the cambium is closer to the root surface, and the root lice eventually reach it and kill the roots. Own-rooted vinifera yield well for about five years, then suddenly crash when the phylloxera damage reaches the root cambiums. A phylloxera saliva constituent also stunts and kills grapevines.

Ordinary marigolds planted under the vines offer a degree of protection against nematodes. Turn them under in the fall and replant after frost danger is over. If the infestation is very bad, replanting on nematode-resistant rootstocks may be indicated. This pest is most frequently found in sandy soils. Maintain a ground cover that's as free of broadleaf weeds as possible (stick to grasses), as these are thought to be an alternate host for some nematodes.

Symptoms: Foliage discolors and wilts. Vigor decreases, production falls off, and eventually the vine dies. Occurs primarily in the southern Midwest and southeastern United States and affects all grapes, including muscadines. Inspection of the roots shows damage or insects feeding. The larvae penetrate the root bark, then eat an irregular furrow that may spiral around the root or run with the grain. The passageway is packed behind the insect with reddish brown frass.

Cause: Grape root borer.

Habit: In the destructive, larval stage, the borers are about 1¾ inch (4.5 cm) long. They're whitish, with brown heads, and are sparsely covered with stiff hairs.

Treatment: Female moths — which resemble large wasps, except that the rear pair of wings are clear and vibrate more slowly — are often found around the base of vines, laying eggs, in August and September, and can be easily killed by hand. The most effective control is to mound about 8 inches (20 cm) of dirt around the base of the vine around July 1, making it impossible for emerging mothers to reach the soil surface. The dirt can be removed safely after August 21.

Grape Diseases

Powdery Mildew

Also called *oidium*, it's the only fungus found in California vineyards. In the rest of the country, it's often joined by other types. Powdery mildew likes cool weather for germination and temperatures from 70 to 90°F (21–32°C) for rapid development. Although it grows best on leaves in the shade, it isn't dependent on moisture the way most other grape leaf and berry fungi are, which is why it's found in the dry California climate and the others aren't.

Powdery mildew attacks both leaves and fruit, but you'll notice it first on leaves, where it appears as whitish patches of cobweb-like growth on the upper surface. It will also attack flowers, which fail to set and fall off, and small berries, which will take on irregular shapes, crack, and dry. Ripe or ripening berries aren't affected. Later, the whitish patches turn gray as spore stalks are formed. The leaves eventually turn brown, then black. A badly infected vine smells like mildew.

Treatment involves several mechanisms. First, be aware that a temperature of 100°F (38°C) or more will effectively stop powdery mildew, but sulfur sprays will harm the heated leaves, so don't spray if it's that hot. Second, good sanitation under the vines — that is, cleaning up twigs, dead leaves, and fallen or dried berries in the fall and/or spring, then cultivating — is essential. Third, elemental sulfur dust is an excellent preventive. A pump-action duster will work well in a small vineyard. Keep a fine dust of sulfur on shoots, flowers or fruit, and leaves, making sure you get the leaves that are shaded.

Dust when the shoots are 6 inches (15 cm) long. This is most important, for that is the time when temperatures are right for spore germination. Dust when shoots reach 12, 18, and 24 inches (30, 45, and 60 cm), and every two weeks thereafter until mid-August. Also, reapply the dust right after every rain — don't put it off. Check leaves after mid-August. Even after the fruit is harvested, leaves are building the vine's food reserves and strength, so spraying protects them if powdery mildew shows up.

A lot of commercial growers are using Bayleton fungicide, because it protects against both powdery mildew and black rot. It's a systemic fungicide, working in the vascular tissues of the vine. I believe that if it's flowing around in the sap, it will flow into the grapes as well, and I don't want Bayleton in my wine.

Sulfur dust only *prevents* powdery mildew. Once it starts on the plants, the dust is no longer effective. Then turn to liquid lime-sulfur spray, available in most garden shops, or wettable sulfur powder. Apply them at the rates recommended on the labels after every rain, and at least every two weeks through July.

Vinifera are all susceptible to powdery mildew in varying degrees. The most susceptible are Carignane, Muscat of Alexandria, and Sylvaner. American grapes are less susceptible, but under cool, wet conditions conducive to the fungus's growth. Concord can be badly damaged. Concord is reputed to be damaged by sulfur sprays or dusts, especially in hot weather, but growers I've talked to said they had no problems with rates on the order of 1.5 pounds (0.6 kg) of wettable sulfur to 100 gallons (380 L) of water.

Downy Mildew

When it's raining and the vines are covered with a light film of water, downy mildew spores germinate, moving about by means of a flagellum — a whip-like tail as seen on spermatozoa. Early in the year it infects leaves, tendrils, pea-sized berry clusters, petioles, and succulent shoots. Lower leaves are often infected when rain splashes soil containing the free-swimming spores onto their surfaces. I tried an experiment once at a large vineyard near Harrisburg, Pennsylvania. We selected a few rows of susceptible vines and put reflective mulch under one row of vines just before bloom, leaving it there for a month. The reflective material was aluminum foil on cardboard, laid under the vines with the shiny side up. Not only did the mulch prevent soil from splashing up onto leaves, but it bounced sunlight up under the leaves, helping to keep them dry. We noticed no mildew on the mulched vines. I'm not necessarily recommending this as a treatment, as such a mulch is expensive, but rather pointing to the etiology of the disease. It's found everywhere east of the Rockies but has not been found in California.

Look for downy mildew early in the morning at about the time the grapes are blooming, especially after a wet or humid night. Later in the day, when the vineyard dries out, it's much harder to spot in its early forms. You'll see oily-looking spots on the upper surface of the leaves, and a swollen, water-logged appearance of the shoot tips, tendrils, and petioles if the fungus is present. The translucent oily spots on the leaves will, if left unchecked, produce a fuzzy whitish growth on the underside of the leaves, appearing a few days after the spots show up.

All varieties of vinifera are susceptible to downy mildew. French-American hybrids vary in their tolerance. Most American varieties aren't very susceptible.

The very susceptible varieties are Catawba, Chancellor, chardonnay, Ives, and riesling. Concord, seyval blanc, and De Chaunac are susceptible. Of all these, Chancellor is the most susceptible. Since this variety is so suited to the eastern climate and makes such fine wine, it's important for growers of this cultivar to follow the spray schedule. Chancellor may become systemically infected — that is, the fungus penetrates to inner tissues and spreads through the plants' vascular system. In such cases, your choices are to tear out the vines or to use a systemic fungicide like Maneb.

The spores overwinter in dead grape leaves on the ground. Good sanitation is important. That means all leaves should be raked up and burned, then the soil should be cultivated under the vines before bud break, and kept cultivated in the top 2 inches (5 cm).

Bordeaux mixture is the most effective treatment for downy mildew. Sulfur alone isn't nearly as effective. Sometimes Bordeaux mixture is found in garden shops ready-mixed. The old French formula is 2 kg (4 pounds) of copper sulfate, 0.75 kg (1.6 pounds) of slaked lime, and 2 kg (4 pounds) of salt per 100 liters (26 gallons) of water. Both the copper and the salt can harm leaf tissue at those rates, so I've adapted the formula to a lower — yet still effective — level.

Light Bordeaux Mixture

Copper sulfate	7 ounces (196 g)
Slaked lime	2 ounces (56 g)
Table salt	9 ounces (252 g)
Water	25 gallons (95 L)

Some vines don't tolerate Bordeaux mixture well, and you may have to substitute captan or Maneb, which are not as phytotoxic, if you have trouble.

Apply Bordeaux mixture just before bloom, seven days later, two weeks after that, and three weeks after that. Captan is applied on a similar schedule. It would be wise to spray routinely for downy mildew in humid areas if you're growing the above-named susceptible and very susceptible varieties. With other varieties keep a close eye on the vines, but don't spray unless you have to.

Black Rot

Black rot is probably the worst disease of grapes east of the Rockies. Californians can be thankful it doesn't affect vines there. I lost four successive crops of grapes to black rot before I finally said, "Let us spray." The fungus germinates in warm, humid weather, such as found east of the Mississippi in June. It attacks leaves, forming small, reddish brown, irregularly shaped spots that soon show black fruiting bodies. On the shoots, tendrils, and young stems, it makes small, dark elliptical cankers. Berries show its effects between the time they're half grown and véraison. At first, the berry has a little blanched area, which soon turns whitish with a brown ring around the edges. This grows quickly and becomes sunken. Within two days, the black fruiting bodies appear, and the whole spot turns reddish brown to black. The berries soon after shrivel to mummies firmly attached to the clusters.

These mummies contain the spores for the next infection, so vineyard sanitation is essential. The mummies must be removed and burned, and the soil under the vines should be raked and well cultivated.

Bordeaux mixture is effective. On vines that show toxic effects from Bordeaux mixtures, captan and ferbam are often used by commercial and home growers. It's important to spray at the right time, when the shoots are 18 and 24 inches (45 and 60 cm) long, just before bloom, just after bloom, and about two weeks after that. The sprays at blooming are the most important.

Anthracnose

Although common in the East where summer rains are frequent, anthracnose is not found in California. It attacks all new parts of the vine, producing grayish brown cankers with raised edges and a sunken center. These cankers will destroy the wood or tissue under them. On leaves, the spots are pale gray with reddish brown or purple borders, and they may accumulate and fall away, leaving holes in the leaves. They resemble black rot on the berries, except that there is a red or purple ring. These berries also shrivel into mummies full of spores, and they must be removed and burned. If you find anthracnose in your vineyard, prunings should also be burned. Good sanitation and cultivation are imperative.

American grapes range from moderately tolerant to moderately susceptible. French-American hybrids are usually more susceptible, and almost all vinifera varieties are highly susceptible. Muscadines are resistant.

For control, spray the vines during the dormant season with a liquid lime-sulfur mix, diluted one part in eight parts of water. Garlic oil in a 200 ppm solution pre- and post-bloom also works against this disease. Bordeaux mixture (see page 233) is commonly used during the growing season, applied when the shoots are 7 inches (18 cm) long, just before bloom, just after bloom, 10 days after that, and when the berries are about half grown. Captan is also effective. Repeat a spray if heavy rains come just after you've sprayed.

Noble Rot (*Botrytis cinerea*)

This fungal disease is only noble if you *want* it to develop in order to make the rare Sauternes-type wine. The rot develops late in the season on ripe grapes, usually right after a September rain. The grape skins crack or shrivel, and the cluster turns into a brownish, soft, moist mass of grapes with low acid and very high sugar — up to 40 percent sugar. The mold absorbs water from inside the grapes but doesn't harm the sugars or spoil the taste of the resultant wines, which are enormously rich and sweet. Some botrytized wines are made in California, mostly by wetting the grapes at the right time and purposely infecting them with botrytis. Such wines are also beginning to be made in the East, especially with varieties like Ravat 51 in the Finger Lakes region.

Botrytis is usually *not* wanted. It appears in warm, dry spells after cool, wet weather late in the season. It grows best between 65 and 75°F (18–24°C), needing only 15 hours of wetness for spore germination. Round, faint clear spots are seen on the berries at first. If pressed with the thumb, the skin cracks, and if rubbed, the skin slips away from the pulp underneath. After a few more days, large masses of gray- to buff-colored spores protrude through cracks in the skin, and the bunches look rotten.

Botrytis overwinters on decaying vegetation and in mummies, so good sanitation is important. Mummies and prunings from infected vines should be cleaned up and burned. Make sure the vine growth is open and airy. As far as I know, none of the less toxic fungicides work very well against botrytis. Even captan only protects 60 percent of berries in the bunches. This should be applied just before bloom, and every two weeks thereafter until August. Or work with it and start making botrytized wine.

Dead-Arm (Eutypa Dieback)

Other fungal diseases include dead-arm disease in California, called Eutypa dieback in the East and in Canada. In California, it's a problem in the cool, foggy coastal regions. In the East, it's a growing problem in the Finger Lakes. Badly affected buds will be dead in the spring, and spots will develop on both sides of leaves about three weeks after a rain. These spots are light green with brown to black pinpoint centers and yellow borders. Similar spots develop on the shoots, which eventually can split the stems and form blackened areas. During the winter, the affected parts of the canes turn whitish, with small black points. All types of grapes are susceptible to this disease.

Prune off all diseased parts as soon after leaf fall as you can and burn them. Cultivate thoroughly under the vines during the growing season. Try lime-sulfur or Bordeaux mixture when the shoots are just 1 inch (2.5 cm) long and again at 7 to 8 inches (18–20 cm). Growers in California often spray routinely with captan when the shoots are an inch long, and that seems to give good control. New research shows that infection risk is greatest in winter when pruning creates open wounds. One good recommendation is to leave 1- to 2-inch (3–5 cm) stubs when pruning trunks or canes, then go back after growth starts and the weather is warm to prune off the stubs. Infection is unlikely at this time, and any winter infection is cut off with the stubs. Burn the stubs.

Black-Mold Rot

Black-mold rot is a problem in some areas where tight-clustered varieties are grown. Sometimes the berries squeeze each other to the point that some rupture, spilling sugary juice over themselves and nearby berries. The black to purplish sooty mold soon develops and ruins the berries for winemaking. There is no known control for black-mold rot. Make sure the clusters are well separated. In very tight-clustered varieties, thinning of berries from the clusters would help, but this is enormously time-consuming. Some growers use gibberellic acid, a plant hormone, to cause the clusters to grow more loosely. Rhizopus rot is similar to black-mold rot, and berry-thinning the clusters with gibberellic acid is also the remedy.

Crown Gall

Any puncture in the vine trunk, such as from freezing, can be invaded by the bacterium, *Agrobacterium tumefaciens*, that causes crown gall. It's a problem in many temperate wine-growing areas of the world, such as in plantings of vinifera in the East. The galls are seen in cracks in the trunk, creamy to green in color in the spring. As they grow, they turn dark and rough. Often the galls will disappear after a few years, but a bad infection will stunt and kill the trunk. There's no commercial product registered in the United States for crown gall, and it's not much of a problem in California, so it doesn't get much attention there. Here's where some experimentation could pay off.

Since crown gall is caused by bacteria, prevent further infection by not cutting through galls when pruning. Sterilize your blade by dipping it in alcohol after each cut on a badly infected vine. If there's very serious damage to the trunk, bring up a new trunk and plan to bring more new ones up regularly over the years, as the gall will most likely stay with you. Keep the area under the vines cultivated, and possibly covered with paper (if you use plastic, cover it with something opaque or the sun will bake the soil) to keep the organisms from splashing up onto the trunk during rains.

Good soil care under the vines and trunk renewal can be supplemented with your attempts to rid the vines of the bacteria by experimenting. Garlic has natural antibiotic properties, and agrobacteria probably wouldn't like it any more than your friends do after you've eaten a garlicky salad. Garlic oil at only 200 ppm kills pathogenic fungi, including anthracnose. I'd make a garlic solution by whizzing cloves in the blender, then drenching the root area with it. You could plaster the galls with rich compost and wrap it on with tape as a kind of bandage — possibly replacing the monopoly of agrobacteria with a panoply of soil organisms. After a season, unwrap, wash, and take a look. This has worked with blight cankers on American chestnut.

I haven't tried those things because I've never had to deal with crown gall on my grapes. I'm just suggesting the kind of homemade gee-whiz tactics you can use.

There's an old saying that a farmer's footsteps are the best fertilizer. While making those footsteps, a farmer is observing, thinking, and mapping out the next move. And so do we all have to get smart when confronted with intractable problems. I know one farmer who got so smart he realized the question wasn't "What do I do next?" but "What don't I do next?" Now hardly making a move, he gets some of the best rice yields in Japan.

Pierce's Disease

Originally thought to be a virus, this disease is now known to be caused by a rickettsia-like organism. Nevertheless, its symptoms are virus-like. It first appears in late summer as a scaling and burning of the leaves along the margins and tips of the large veins. The scalded area turns brown. If the whole leaf is involved, it will drop away, leaving the petiole attached to the shoot. It starts with one shoot, then gets progressively worse. The fruit may be poorly formed and wither, or ripen prematurely, turn soft, and then wither. In the following year, growth is slow and the first leaves are deformed and mottled. Scalding will show up on the later leaves, and the canes will fail to mature properly: some green patches will remain among the matured cane's normal brown.

Diseased vines should be uprooted and replaced with varieties resistant to Pierce's disease, or with certified disease-free stock. In the latter case, be prepared to replant again, for the disease will probably return. It's sometimes a problem in California, except in the hottest regions, but doesn't usually take whole vineyards. In the past, however, it has done just that. The disease is native to the Gulf Coast, where resistant varieties of wild and cultivated grapes are found.

Schedule for Controlling Fungal Diseases

Powdery mildew (preventive)	Dust with sulfur when shoots are 6, 12, and 18 inches (15, 30, and 45 cm), and every two weeks thereafter until August. Reapply after every rain.
Powdery mildew (control)	Apply wettable sulfur or lime-sulfur when shoots are 6 inches (15 cm), then every two weeks until August.
Downy mildew	Apply Bordeaux mixture just before bloom, just after bloom, then seven days later, two weeks after that, and three weeks after that.
Black rot	Apply Bordeaux mixture when shoots are 18 and 24 inches (45 and 60 cm), just before bloom, just after bloom, and two weeks after that.
Anthracnose	Apply lime-sulfur when vines are dormant. Apply Bordeaux mixture when vines are 7 inches (18 cm), just before bloom, just after bloom, 10 days after that, and when berries are half grown.
Botrytis (bunch rot)	Apply Bordeaux mixture just before bloom, then every two weeks until August. Often the spray at bloom will be enough.
Dead-arm or Eutypa dieback	Apply lime-sulfur or Bordeaux mixture when shoots are 1 inch (3 cm) long and when they reach 7 to 8 inches (18–20 cm).

Spraying for one of these with Bordeaux mixture or lime-sulfur will control most of the other diseases simultaneously. While it's never wise to spray unless there's a problem, fine wine grapes in the East will become infected with one or another disease, and preventive sprays in that region are necessary.

Grape Viruses

Many viruses affect grapevines. Rather than name them all, be aware that they all mottle or yellow the leaves or cause them to be badly misshapen. One virus causes the leaves to roll downward at the margins. They can be spread by insects and by soil nematodes, but most often they are the result of planting infected wood.

Dr. Joseph Foster of the Animal and Plant Health Inspection Service, the USDA agency that quarantines plants before release, says that Europe is a reservoir of grape virus and cautions all of us not to bring home cuttings from our friends' châteaux in Bordeaux. "Europe has a yellows virus that isn't found here," he told me. "The North American leaf hopper is the vector in Europe. If the disease got over here, it would undoubtedly be spread by leaf hoppers." He said that many European varieties are infected with stem pitting, corky bark, leaf roll, and other viruses, and so grape plants and cuttings are prohibited from entering this country. But they do enter Canada. Some Canadian nurseries sell grapes grafted with European scion wood to U.S. buyers, and Dr. Foster says there's a good chance that these vines are infected with one or more of the virus diseases.

The recommendation, therefore, is to make sure you're buying certified virus-free stock from a vineyard in the United States. If a virus even then shows up in your plants, replant with certified stock from some other source.

Soil-borne viruses that are transmitted by nematodes may be controlled by plantings of marigolds under the vines as a preventive measure. In some areas, commercial growers fumigate the soil.

Keep in mind that there are other conditions that can mimic disease. Spring frost injury to young leaves can look at first like a mottling virus, but subsequent leaves are healthy. Soil nutrient deficiencies, which we covered in our discussion of fertilization (see page 105), can cause yellowing and poor performance, which could be mistaken for a virus. In areas where air pollution is heavy, such as southern California, or near the New York area, small brown to black stippled spots on the leaves may be ozone damage rather than disease.

Large Vineyard Pests

Deer are a very serious pest in the vineyard, nibbling tender parts, setting back the vines, delaying maturity, and reducing yields. The last thing I read about deer was that the only thing a grower can do is fence in the vineyard. But take heart. I know other remedies that may preclude that enormous expense.

Illinois orchardist Ray Grammer has found a deer remedy he claims is "99 and 44/100ths percent effective." He hangs bars of soap from his trees. He's tried several brands, including deodorant soaps, and found they all worked the same — better than any repellent he's used in the past. You could sprinkle soap shavings along the tops of some leaves so they melt down over the lower areas, or hang bars near the top wire every 8 to 10 feet (2.4–3.1 m). Just make sure the soap doesn't drip onto the grapes or your wine may be "bubbly" in the wrong way. Probably the smell, so perfumedly human, as well as a soapy taste on the leaves, repels the deer.

Also, you can ask your barber for a day's worth of hair clippings. Bag these in old nylon stockings or any netting that lets air through. Hang them every 10 feet (3.1 m) or so all around the vineyard's perimeter. Men's hair is more repellent simply because it's not usually coated with hair setting or holding chemicals and has a more human smell.

In Glenora, New York, Roger and Sayre Fulkerson erected a klapotetz in their vineyard and found it effective in keeping birds away. This device is a windmill that causes wooden flaps to revolve and hit a striker, making a clapping sound. A similar device is used to keep moles from gardens and lawns. The ancestor of the klapotetz was introduced into Lower Styria (Austria) by Roman legionnaires at around 100 B.C. to help keep birds out of their vineyards.

What about windless days? "Perhaps the klapotetz simply stares down would-be raiders. After all, who's going to question two thousand years of active duty in Austria?" commented an eastern wine writer.

Bees, yellowjackets, and sugar-loving wasps attack ripening and ripe fruit. They are trouble, and I've been stung several times on the hand reaching to pick bunches, and once above the eye by what must have been a lookout bee. They seldom if ever puncture the fruit themselves but come in after birds have slashed open the berries to suck up the sugary innards, or after berries cracked or split for other reasons. Some growers spray Sevin, a toxic chemical. To be of any use, it has to be sprayed too close to harvest, so I'd never use it. The home vineyardist can erect a trap for these insects — one per row, spaced toward alternate ends of the rows. A fish carcass or piece of meat is hung from the bottom trellis wire 4 to 6 inches (10–15 cm) above a pan of water with some oil floating on its surface. The wasps will prefer this to the grapes, gorge themselves, then try to take off. Just like overloaded planes, they'll fall into the water and be killed

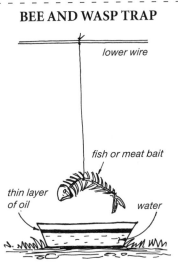

BEE AND WASP TRAP

lower wire

fish or meat bait

thin layer of oil

water

by the oily water. One grower reported reducing the bee and wasp problem in his vineyard by 90 percent using these traps. They'll only be needed just before harvest.

In a few areas of the country, woodchucks, porcupines, mice, and voles can be a problem. Woodchucks and porcupines have been successfully kept out of vineyards by electric fence wire suspended about 2 to 3 inches (5–8 cm) above the ground around the vineyard. Make sure no grass grows to touch the wire by weighting down newspapers under the wire. A .22 rifle is another effective weapon. Mice and voles are best baited, or you can march some of your lazy cats to the vineyard and tell them to get to work.

A very effective sway to produce quality grapes and protect them from birds, bees, and many diseases and fungi is to bag the bunches. This is very time-consuming, but it's sure and effective if you've got a small-enough vineyard to do it. The bags are placed over the developing clusters when the berries are about half grown, or even earlier if you want to ward off fungal diseases. Cut off the lower corners to allow moisture to drip out, and attach them as shown below.

BAGGING GRAPE CLUSTERS

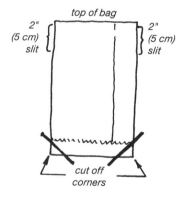

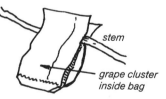

one flap folded over stem, then
second flap folded over first,
secured with tape

INDEX

Page numbers in *italic* indicate illustrations; page numbers in **bold** indicate charts.

A

accoutrements, 205–6
acetic acid (vinegar), 121, 137
acetobacter
    fruit flies and, 121
    topping up and, 167
    wine disorders and, 170–71
acid(s)
    acetic (vinegar), 121, 137
    amino, 191
    citric, 137, 166
    fatty, 190, 191
    grapes and, 184
    lactic, 138, 151
    malic, 137, 138, 151
    nucleic, 191
    reduction of, 138
    tartaric, 137–38
acid blend, 137
acidity
    adjustment of/pH, 137–140
    blending and, 173
    first few days and, 123
    reduction of, 160
    titratable (TA), 112–13
acid levels, orientation and, 42
adjuvants. *See* riddling aids
after-dinner wines, 176
aging. *See also* barrels; vintage(s)
    bottle size and, 169–170
    California and French reds, 16
    considerations, 168–170
    disgorgement, sparkling wine and, 193–95
    en tirage - sparkling wine and, 189–193
    overview, 8
    peak maturity and, 8

racking and, 122
storage conditions for, 170
airlocks
    foam and, 156, *156*
    reattachment of, 168
    types of, *154*
    using, 154, *154*
    winemaking and, 155–57
air security, 170–71
aisles. *See* rows and aisles
alcohol content
    of finished wine, 175
    of natural wine, 135
    "potential alcohol," 136
    sugar and, 134–37
Alden grapes, 93
Alicante Boushet, 173
alkalinity, 139
allelopathic effect, 47
Alley, C. J., 93
American varieties
    Brix readings and, 110
    fruitfulness and, 78
    pruning and, **83**
    training systems for, 77
    wine appreciation and, 17
American Viticultural Areas (AVAs), 23–25
American Wine Society, 12, 214
amino acids, 191
anthocyanins, 174
anthracnose, 234–35
aroma(s)
    off aromas, 184, 185
    retronasal, 209–10
    varietal, 209
aroma compounds, 191
Assmanshausen wine yeast, 145
Aurora

cluster thinning and, 95
training systems and, 101, *101*
Auslese, 176
autolysis, 190–93

B

Bacillus thuringiensis (Bt), 102
bacteria. *See also* acetobacter
    cleanliness and, 126
    corks and, 171
    Leuconostoc, 151, 152
    Oenococcus oeni, 151
    punching down cap and, 147
Bailey, L. H., 14
balanced pruning, 80–81, **83**
Balling, degrees, 109
bare-rooted grapestock, 61–62
    handling of, 60–61
    trimming roots of, 61–62, *61*
barrels, 160–68
    bung and, 164, 165, *165*
    conversion to planters, 163, *163*
    filling, 165
    frame for holding, *162*, 163
    leaching new, 164, **164**
    leaks and, 164
    mold and, 167
    oak flavors and, 153, 160–61
    sanitization and, **166**
    size of, 162, 163
    storage of empty, 166
    toast/charring and, 162
    topping up, 167
    whiskey, 128

basal buds, 85, *85*

base wine, sparkling wine and, 184–87
  browning and adding sulfites, 185–86
  charging with sugar and yeast, 195–96
  fining and cold stabilization, 187
  malolactic culture, adding, 186
  pressing grapes for, 185
  yeast, adding, 186

basket press, 142, *142*

batonnage, 169

Beaulieu Rutherford, 167

Beaulieu Vineyard, 161

beds. *See* rows and aisles

bees, 143

bee trap, 241–42, *241*

bellows effect, 203

beneficials, 67, 102

bentonite, 172, 187

berries, sample, 109, *109*

bidules, 188, 193, *193*, 197

bilateral three-wire training, 101, *101*

bitartrate, 159

bitter principles, 124, 143

black-mold rot, 236–37

black rot, 234

"bleeding," at ends of canes, 92

blending, 173–74

body of wine
  blending and, 174
  sensory evaluation and, 211

Bollingers, 194

Bordeaux
  blending and, 173
  city of, 12, 13, 149
  "controlled appellation" and, 21
  growing regions for, 18
  oaking and, 168
  soil and, 43, 66
  tannic, 174

Bordeaux mixture, downy mildew and, 233–34

botrytis, 117, 191. *See also* noble rot (*Botrytis cinerea*)

botrytized grapes
  harvesting, 117
  SO$_2$ and, 132

bottles, *sur pointe*, 198, *198*

"bottle sickness," 171

bottling, 176–78
  bottle types and, *177*
  filling bottles and, 178
  indentation/punt and, 176
  measurements before, 177–78
  overview, 8
  pre-cleaning bottles and, 177
  second cleaning and, 178
  sparkling wine and, 187–88, *188*, 197

bouquet, 209

brettanomyces, 171

Brix, 109–11
  about, 109–10
  high, 176
  hydrometers and, 109–10, **111**
  must and, 134
  natural wine and, 135
  sampling berries and, 109, *109*
  TA ratio measures ripeness, 114–15

browning, 185–86

bud(s)
  basal, 85, *85*
  fruitfulness and, 78–79, *78*
  pest-related damage to, 225–26
  sucker, 85, *85*, 87

bud break, 77

bung, 165, *165*

Burgundy
  bottling of, 176–77
  city of, 149
  wine quality and, 15

C

Cabernet, California, 15

Cabernet franc, 169, 173

Cabernet Sauvignon
  blending and, 173
  extended macerations and, 150
  "nose" of wine and, 208
  skin contact times and, 148
  trellises and, 51

California. *See also* Napa Valley; UC Davis
  brettanomyces and, 171
  Cabernet, 15
  fruitfulness and, 78–79
  grapes shipped from, 120
  heat summations, **31–32**
  hot regions, grapes for, **34**
  phylloxera and, 35
  pruning and, 89
  training systems in, 96, *96*, 97, *97*, 99, *99*, 101, *101*
  trellises and, 50, 53, 54
  vinifera in, **33–34**
  weather and, 16
  wild yeasts and, 130

California Champagne (*Saccharomyces bayanus*), 145

California reds, 16

Campden tablets, 133, 134, 157, 185, 186

cane(s)
  fruiting, 84, *84*, 85, *85*
  pest-related damage to, 229–231

cane-and-spur renewal system, 89, *89*

cane-length pruning recommendations, eastern regions, **82**, *82*

cane pruning, 97, *97*

caps, sparkling wine and, 187–88, *188*

carboys
  airlocks and, 155–57, *156*
  cleaning, 157
  oak chips in, 167

pressing whites and, 142, 143
primary fermentation and, 128
racking and, 158–59
transfer to, 122
Carignane vines, 51, 96
Cascade, 173
Catawba, 124
Cayuga vines, 37, 38
cellaring wine, 202–4
insulated storage area, 203–4, *204*
temperature of cellar, 202–3
Chambourcin, 174
Champagne
serving temperature, optimum, 210
soil and, 39
sparkling wine and, 182
vintage, 194
wine quality and, 15
Chancellor, 11, 22, 64, 93, 173, 225, 233
chaptalizing, 134
Chardonnay
aging and, 161, 169, 170
downy mildew and, 233
fermentation temperature, 148
growing regions for, 11, 18, 19
malolactic fermentation and, 152
must and, 123
oaking and, 167
pruning and, 78, 80, 81
sparkling wine and, 183, 184, 194
stemming and crushing grapes, 125, 149
sulfites and, 130
trellis systems and, 51
vineyard size and, 38
Château Ducru-Beaucaillou, 43
Château d'Yquem, 12
Chateau Esperanza Chancellor, 22

Château Lafite Rothschild, 35
Château le Puy, 66
Château Mouton-Rothschild, 181
Chenin Blanc
cluster thinning and, 94
trellises and, 55
citric acid, 137, 166
clarity, 207
cleanliness. *See* sanitization, 124
clearing wine. *See* fining
cloudiness
fining and, 172
racking and, 168
settling out, 169
spent yeast and, 149, 168
cluster thinning, 93–96, *94*
benefits of, other, 94–95
cluster-thinned shoots, positioning of, 94
timing of, 93–94
which clusters to remove, 95–96, *95*
Clyde Robin Seed Company, 66
cold stabilization
about, 159–160
sparkling wine and, 187
Colobel vines, 22, 173, 225
color
clarity and, 207
correction of, 173
wine connoisseurs and, 140
"complete dryness," 175
compost, making, 106
Concord grapes, 57, 209
construction, of trellis, 56–60
controlled appellations, 21
cordon-cane system, 88–89, *88, 89*
cordon-spur/cordon-cane pruning, 98, *98*
"corked" wine, 171
corking, 179–180, *179*
corkscrews, 204–5, *205*
Côte des Blancs, 145

Côte d'Or Burgundy, 16
Cottrell, Tom, 119, 123, 131, 148, 149
courses. *See* education
cover crops for beds, 64, 92–93
Crane, Eileen, 193, 195
crops, tending of, 108
crown gall, 237–38
crushing grapes. *See* stemming and crushing grapes
crystals, tablets vs., 134

D

dead-arm (Eutypa dieback), 236
decay microorganisms, 125. *See also* bacteria
De Chaunac, 78, 95, 125, 145
deer, 49, 240–41
degrees Balling, 109
delayed and double pruning, 91–92
dessert wines, 176
disease(s)
pruned canes and, 81
weeds and, 65
disgorgement, sparkling wine and, 193–95, 200–202
disorders, wine, 170–72
Domaine Chandon, 183
dosage, calculation of, 199–200
double trunking, 74
downy mildew, 232–34
drainage, 47
drip irrigation, 68
drought, spring, 68
drought-prone areas, 63
"dryness, complete," 175
DV_{10}, 195–96

E

earth anchors, 57, 58, *59*, 60
eastern regions
cane-length pruning and, **82**, *82*
training systems in, 98, *98*, 100, *100*

eastern seaboard, vinifera on, 19–20
education, 15–19
    wine appreciation courses, 17, 19
    wine quality and, 15–17
Émile Peynaud, 12
end point, 113
end posts, 56–57
en tirage - aging on the yeast, 189–193
enzymes
    en tirage and, 190–91
    extended maceration and, 150
Epernay 2 (*Saccharomyces cerevisiae*), 145
equipment. See winemaking equipment
"estate bottled" designation, 21
esters, 190
Eutypa dieback, 81, 236
extended maceration, 150–51

F

fatty acids, 190, 191
fermentation. *See also* in-bottle fermentation; primary fermentation; secondary fermentation
    malolactic, 151–52
    pressing whites for, 141–43, *142*
    of sparkling wine, 197
    stuck, 146, 175
ferric *casse*, 44
fertilization, 105–6
filtering, 172
fine lees, 169
Finger Lakes region
    botrytized grapes and, 117
    Chardonnay, 11
    climate and, 19
    Eutypa Dieback and, 236
    soil and, 41, 47
    wine grapes for, **26**, 183

fining
    about, 172–73
    sparkling wine and, 187
finished wine, alcohol content of, 175
finishing, 122
first racking, 157–59, *158*
"first-run" juice, 126
flavor(s). *See also* off-flavors; sensory evaluation of wine
    "buttery," 184
    oak, 160–61
Flor Sherry (*Saccharomyces fermentati*), 145
flower(s). See also cluster thinning
    first years and, 75
    pest-related damage to, 226–29
foliage damage, 222–25. *See also* phylloxera
forested land, proximity of, 49
Foster, Joseph, 239–240
four-arm Kniffen training, 98, *98*
France
    Bordeaux, 12, 13, 149
    Burgundy, 149
    Champagne region of, 182, 195
    chaptalizing and, 134–35
    Cognac region of, 44
    nonvintage wine in, 117
    soil types in, **44**
    vine spacing in, 39
Frank, Konstantin, 47–48, 183
free-run juice, 183–84
freeze danger
    mulch and, 65
    pruning and, 81, 91
    slope and, 41, *41*
French-American hybrids
    Brix readings and, 110
    cluster thinning and, 95
    fruitfulness and, 78
    grapestock and, 19, 22

Hudson River umbrella and, 99, *99*
    overcropping and, 105
    pruning and, **83**
    training systems for, 77
    trellising systems and, 53
    vineyard size and, 37
    wine appreciation and, 17
French reds, 16–17
frost. *See* freeze danger
fruit flies (*Drosophila melanogaster*), 120–21, 123
fruitiness, 140, 148
fruiting cane, 84, *84*, 85, *85*
fungal diseases, schedule for controlling, **239**

G

Geneva double curtain trellis, 55, *55*, 100, *100*
Gewürztraminer, 124
glass containers. *See* bottling; carboys
glasses. *See* wineglasses
glossary, 1–5
glucans, 191
grape(s). *See* wine grapes
grape growers, spirit of, 15
grapestock. *See also* vine(s)
    bare-rooted, handling of, 60–61, *61*
    ordering and planting, 60–64
    trimming roots of, 61–62
grape sugar, 135
grapevine. *See* vine(s)
Graves, 15, 43
gravity. *See specific gravity*
Grgich, Mike, 80, 144
gross lees, 149, 153
growing seasons, 52
Gusmer Enterprises, 144, 151

H

"hang time," 115

harvest. *See also* ripeness,
determination of
of botrytized grapes, 117
day of, tasks and, 7, 141
as function of sugar/acid
ratio, **116**
procedures for, 118
titratable acidity (TA)
and, 112
Haut-Brion, 16
"Haut-Médoc," 21
haze, fining and, 172, 173,
187, 207
head training, 51, *51*, 96, *96*
heat summations, for
California, **31–32**
herbaceousness, 124
history, classic wine grapes
and, 12–15
Hudson River region
grapes for, **26**
soil and, 43
Hudson River umbrella,
99, *99*
hybrids. See French-
American hybrids
hydrogen sulfide (H$_2$S), 106,
144, 170, 171. *See also* rotten-egg smell
hydrometer(s), *110*
Brix and, 109–11
correcting readings
based on temperature,
111
readings/Brix equiva-
lents, **111**

I

in-bottle fermentation
(*methodé champenoise*)
additives and, 196
bottling and, 187
sparkling wine and, 189,
196
yeast for, 195
insects. *See also* beneficials;
pest control; pest(s)
cover crops and, 67
fruit flies, 120–21
pruned canes and, 81

"sweet toothed," 143
weeds and, 65
Iron Horse Vineyards, 192
irrigation, 63, 68
isinglass, 172

J

J. W. Burmester Vintage
Port, 181

K

klapotetz, 241
Kloeckera apiculata, 143
Knapp, Doug, 12
Kniffen system, 89, *89*
four-arm Kniffen train-
ing, 98, *98*
umbrella Kniffen, 100,
100
Krug, 194

L

label(s)
information on, 176
removal of, 178
labeling, 180–82, *181*
attaching labels, 181–82
faking labels, 181
foil capsules and, 182
lactic acid, 138, 151
land. *See* site
Laurent-Perrier, 194
leaf deficiency symptoms,
trace elements and, **107**
lees
cold stabilization and,
159–160
fine, 169
fining and, 172–73
gross, 149, 153
racking and, 169
L'Ermitage, 189
Leuconostoc bacteria, 151,
152
light, 170. *See also* sunlight
Long Island, 19
low acid wines, 137
low-alcohol wines, 134
lyre or moveable trellis,
99, *99*

lyre trellis, 54, *54*

M

maceration, extended,
150–51
maderization, 202
Malbec, 173
malic acid, 137, 138, 151,
184
malolactic culture, spar-
kling wine and, 186
malolactic fermentation
about, 151–52
potassium metabisulfite
and, 132
soil types and, 44
sparkling wine and, 184
mannoproteins, 191
manures, 106
marc, 143
Maréchal Foch, 149, 173
McGrew, John, 65, 77, 112,
144, 148, 167
measurements, before bot-
tling, 177–78
Médoc, 15, 21
Merlot, 173
methodé champenoise, 195
microorganisms. *See*
bacteria; mold(s); spoil-
age microorganisms;
virus(es)
mid-Atlantic regions, balanced pruning and, **83**
Mission vines, 37, 57
Mitchell, Jim, 11
modified Keuka renewal
training, 101, *101*
mold(s). *See also* black-
mold rot; noble rot
(*Botrytis cinerea*)
aging and, 170
airlocks and, 155
barrels and, 163, 167
cleanliness and, 126,
127, 143
corks and, 171
crushing grapes and,
120, 124
harvesting and, 118

mold(s), *continued*
    punching down cap and, 147
    in the South, 20
    trellising systems and, 51
Montrachet, 17
Montrachet (*Saccharomyces cerevisiae*), 144, 145
Mosel, 15
mouthfeel, 191, 211
Mouton, 181
movable wire trellis, 54, *54*
mulch
    stone, 67, *67*
    whether or not to, 64–65
Munksgard, David, 192, 193
muscadines (*Muscadinia rotundifolia*)
    growing regions for, 30
    musts and, 145
    pruning mature vines, 91
    vineyard size and, 37
Muscat of Alexandria, 39
must
    adding sugar to, 134–37
    adding sulfite to, 129–134
    pH of, 140
    preparation of, 121
    pressing the, 152–53
    resting of, 129
    specific gravity of, 135, 136–37

N

Napa Valley
    aisle management and, 65
    pruning in, 78
    real estate in, 35
    vine spacing in, 39
natural wine, 135
new wine, 152, 155
New York. *See* Hudson River region; Long Island
nitrogen, 92, 105–6
noble rot (*Botrytis cinerea*), 191, 235–36
nonvintage wines, 117, 195

northern-tier regions, balanced pruning and, **83**
"nose" of wine, 209
"nouveau," 149
nucleic acids, 191

O

oak flavor/oaking
    barrels and, 153, 160–61
    carboys and, 153
    importance of, 167–68
    oak chips and, 167
    reduction of, 174
Oenococcus oeni bacteria, 151
oenophile, 176
off aromas, 184, 185. *See also* rotten-egg smell
off-flavors, 108, 153, 168, 185, 189
official viticultural areas, 21. *See also* American Viticultural Areas (AVAs)
off smells, 209
oiliness, 171
overcropping, 79, 105
overoxidation, 128
overpressing grapes, 185
overview, 6–9
oxidation
    bellows effect and, 203
    botrytized grapes and, 117
    disgorgement and, 194
    high-pH wines and, 140
    maderization and, 202
    overoxidation and, 128
    potassium metabisulfite and, 130
    sparkling wines and, 194
    white wines and, 123, 142
    yeast and, 129, 191, 193

P

Pasteur Champagne (*Saccharomyces bayanus*), 144
Pasteur Institute, 144
Pauillac, 16

pest(s)
    foliage damage and, 222–25
    forested land and, 49
    large vineyard, 240–42
pest control, 102–5
    applied biological controls, 102–3
    botanical insecticides, 104
    chemical insecticides, 104–5
    dormant sprays, 104
    naturally occurring, 102
    repellants and, 103
    traps and, 103
Petite Sirah, 51, 209
Petit Verdot, 173
pH
    acid adjustment and, 139–140, *139*
    ripeness and, 113–14
    soil testing, 45
    sulfite additions and, 133
phenolic compounds, 123, 124, 185, 194
phenolphthalein solution, 112
phylloxera, 35, 47, 225, 230
Pichon Lalande, 16
Pierce's disease, 20, 238
pink grapes, stemming and crushing, 125–26
pink wines
    carboys and, 122
    must, preparation of, 121
Pinot Noir
    fertilization and, 105
    growing regions for, 18
    pruning and, 81
    soil and, 47–48
    sparkling wine and, 183, 184
    training systems and, 101, *101*
    yeast for, 145
planting
    replant status and, 47

vines, 62–63, *62*
polysaccharides, 190, 191
pomac cakes, 143
pomace, 142
Port, 176, 181
potassium bitartrate, 187
potassium metabisulfite, 130, 131–32, 134, 140. *See also* sulfite(s)
"potential alcohol," 136
powdery mildew, 231–32
pressing grapes, 185. *See also* stemming and crushing grapes
primary fermentation, 146–153
    extended maceration, 150–51
    fermentation temperature, 147–48
    malolactic fermentation, 151–52
    overview, 7
    pressing the must, 152–53
    punching down cap, 146–47
    skin contact time, 148–49
    steps in, 121
    vat for, 127–29, *128*
Prise de Mousse (*Saccharomyces bayanus*), 184
Prohibition, 22
pruning in first two years, 69–75
    allowing no fruit in first years, 75
    back to one bud, 72, *72*
    back to one cane, 71, *71*
    for established main cane, *74*
    growth of vine, explained, 70
    to maintain multiple trunks, *75*
    single vs. multiple trunks, 74

training vines to trellis and, 71–75
tying canes to trellis wires, 72, *72*
unpruned vine and, 69, *69*
pruning mature vines, 77–93
    balanced pruning, 80–81, **83**
    "bleeding" and, 92
    cane length, eastern regions and, **82**
    cordon-cane system, 88–89, *88, 89*
    delayed and double pruning, 91–92
    fruitful buds and, 78–79, *78*
    how much to prune, 79–80
    how-to guidelines, 84–87, *84, 85, 86, 87*
    Kniffen system, 89, *89*
    muscadines, 91
    overcropping and, 79
    reasons behind pruning, 77
    spur pruning system, 90, *90*
    vine vigor, management of, 92
    when to prune, 77–78
punt, 176

R

racking
    carboys and, 158–59
    early, 148
    first, 157–59, *158*
    further, aging and, 168–170
    schedule for, 122, 169
Ramey, Bern, 15
Ravat 51, 117, 139, 235
reagents, 112
recordkeeping, 212–13
red Bordeaux. *See* Bordeaux
red grapes, stemming and crushing, 124–25

Red Rhône varieties, growing regions for, 18
red wines
    aging and, 169–170
    barrel aging and, 161
    bottling and, 176–77
    California and French, 16
    carboys and, 122
    fermentation temperature, 148
    must and, 121, 153
    tannic, 8
    regions. *See* wine-growing areas
renewal canes, 86, *86*
renewal spur, 84, 85, *85, 87*
replant status, 47
residual sugar, testing, 175–76
retronasal aroma, 209–10
Rheingau, 15
"Rhine of America," 22
rhizopus rot, 237
riddling, sparkling wine and, 197–99, *198*
riddling aids, 196
riddling box, homemade, 198, *198*
Riesling
    crushing grapes and, 125
    growing regions for, 18
    sparkling wine and, 183
rim, looking at the, 207–8, *208*
ripeness, determination of, 108–16
    better measure of ripeness, 115
    Brix, 109–11, *110*, **111**, 114–15
    harvest as function of sugar/acid ratio, **116**
    pH and, 113–14
    sampling berries, 109, *109*
    titratable acidity, 112–13
ripening process, beginning of, 108
Roederer Estate, 189, 192

root(s), trimming, 61–62,
  61
rootstocks
  handling bare-rooted,
    60–61
  for problem soils, 47
ropiness, 171
Rosenbrand, Theo, 144
rotten-egg smell, 130, 171,
  209. *See also* hydrogen sulfide (H$_2$S)
rows and aisles, 64–67
  aisle management tech-
    niques, 65–67
  cover crops for beds, 64
  mulch and, 64–65, 67, *67*
  weeds in beds, handling
    of, 65

S

Sabrevois, 12
Saccharomyces bayanus, 144,
  145, 184
Saccharomyces cerevisiae,
  143, 144, 145
Saccharomyces fermentati,
  145
sampling berries, 109
sampling wine, topping up
  and, 167
Sangiovese, growing regions
  for, 18
sanitization
  of barrels, for storage,
    166
  carboys and, 157
  cleanliness and, 126
  of grapes, 124
  leaching new barrels,
    164, **164**
  sterilizing solution and,
    127
Sauternes, 12, 176
Sauvignon Blanc
  growing regions for, 18
  sulfite and, 131
seasons, growing, 52
secondary fermentation,
  153–57
  about, 153

airlocks, use of, 155–57
  overview, 8
  steps in, 122
self-education. *See*
  education
sensory evaluation of wine,
  207–11. *See also* aroma(s);
  flavor(s)
  body of wine, 211
  clarity and color, 207
  legs and, 208, *208*
  nose, education of, 210
  "nose" of wine, 209
  retronasal aroma,
    209–10
  rim of wineglass and,
    207–8, *208*
  taste of wine, 210
serving temperature, optimum, 210, **210**
Seyval Blanc, 125, 145
shoot(s)
  growth of, 70, *70*
  pest-related damage to,
    225–26
site, 41–49
  about, 35
  drainage, 47
  forested land, proximity
    of, 49
  orientation and, 42
  prevailing winds and, 49
  slope and, 41–42, *41*, **42**
  soil and, 43–46, **44**
  soil preparation, 47–49
  sunlight and, 41–42, *41*,
    42, 43
skin contact time, 126,
  148–49, 150
smelling wine. *See* sensory
  evaluation of wine
soda ash. *See* washing soda
soil
  amendments to, 48–49
  depth, determining, 46
  grape quality and,
    43–46
  hardpans and, 46, 48
  moistness and, 63
  pH testing, 45

preparation of, 47–49
problem, rootstocks
  for, 47
stone color and, 46
trenching and, 48, 49
type, determining, 45
types, in France, 44, **44**
southern U.S., vinifera
  problems in, 20
sparkling wine, 182–202
  aging of, 193–95
  base wine for, 184–87
  bidules for, 193, *193*
  bottles and caps for,
    187–88
  bottling of, 197
  disgorgement and,
    193–95, 200–202
  en tirage - aging on the
    yeast, 189–193
  fermentation, in-bottle,
    189
  fermentation and tirage
    of, 197
  grapes for, 183–84
  putting sparkle in,
    188–195
  riddling and, 197–99
  styles and, 183
  sugar dosage, calcula-
    tion of, 199–200
  yeast for, 183–84
specific gravity
  alcohol content and, 175
  Brix and, 109, 110
  of must, 135, 136–37
  of pure ethyl alcohol,
    175
spoilage microorganisms,
  117, 124, 163. *See also*
  bacteria
spring spritzing, 152
spur pruning system, 90, *90*
stakes, 57
staples, 57
stemming and crushing
  grapes, 124–26. *See also*
  pressing grapes
  immediately after pick-
    ing, 120–21, 123

red grapes, 124–25
white and pink grapes, 125–26
sterilizing solution, 127
"St. Julien," 21
stock. *See* grapestock
stone color, soil and, 46
stuck fermentation, 146, 175
sucker buds, 85, *85*, 87
sugar
    adding to must, 134–37
    adjustment, figuring, **136**
    "complete dryness" and, 175
    dosage, calculation of, 199–200
    grapes and, 184
    testing residual, 175–76
sugar/acid ratio, harvest as function of, **116**
sulfite(s), 129–134
    how much to add, 130–32
    pH effect and, 133
    sparkling wine and, 185–86
    tablets vs. crystals, 134
    wine yeasts and, 130
sulfur dioxide (SO_2), 130, 131–32
sunlight
    cane pruning and, 97
    cluster thinning and, 94
    flower bud formation and, 79
    fruitfulness and, 78
    grape ripening and, 108
    latitudes and, **43**
    mulch and, 232
    slope and, 41–42, *42*
    trellises and, 54, 55
    wine quality and, 170
sur lie, 169

T

tablets, Campden, 133, 134, 157, 185, 186
Tanglefoot, 103
tannic reds, 8

tannins
    blending and, 173–74
    en tirage and, 191
    extended maceration and, 150
    fining and, 172, 173
    overpressing and, 185
    SO_2 and, 131
    stemming and, 124
tartaric acid
    acid adjustment and, 139–140
    sparkling wine and, 184
    titratable acidity (TA) and, 113
tasting wine. *See* sensory evaluation of wine
Taylor Wine Company, 145
teinturier grape varieties, 22, 123, 173
temperature
    cold stabilization and, 159
    optimum serving, 210, **210**
    primary fermentation and, 147–48
    yeast and, 149
tensioners, Wirevise, 57–58
thinning. *See* cluster thinning
Thompson Seedless, 37
Tiburzi, Tom, 183, 184, 190, 191, 193, 194, 199
tirage, sparkling wine and, 197
titratable acidity (TA)
    about, 112–13
    acid adjustment and, 139–140
    sparkling wine and, 184
tools, trellis construction and, 58
topping up
    defined, 161
    sampling and, 167
trace elements
    compost and, 106
    leaf deficiency symptoms and, **107**

training systems, 96–101
    bilateral three-wire training, 101, *101*
    cane pruning, 97, *97*
    cordon-spur/cordon-cane pruning, 98, *98*
    four-arm Kniffen training, 98, *98*
    Geneva double curtain, 100, *100*
    head training, 96, *96*
    Hudson River umbrella, 99, *99*
    lyre or moveable trellis, *99*
    modified Keuka renewal training, 101, *101*
    umbrella Kniffen, 100, *100*
    varieties and, 56
    vertical cordon, 97, *97*
    vine spacing and, 39
training vines
    establishing system for, 75, 77
    overview, 6
    trellising systems and, **56**
    tying canes to trellis wires, *72*
trellises, 50–56
    construction of, 56–60
    Geneva double curtain, 55, *55*
    lyre or movable wire, 54, *54*
    one-wire, 53, *53*
    selection of system, 55, **56**
    single stakes, 50–51
    systems, types of, 50–55
    three-wire, 53, *53*
    training vines to, 71–75, *71*
    two-wire, 53, *53*, 59
    tying canes to wires of, *73*
trenching, 48, 49

trunk, pest-related damage to, 229–231
TTB (Alcohol and Tobacco Tax and Trade Bureau)
    about, 21
    regional designations and, 21
    viticultural areas, 22
Tudal, Arnold, 144, 148
Turkington, Ross, 91–92

U

UC Davis, 12, 39, 51, 81, 93, 114, 144, 145, 151, 192
umbrella Kniffen, 100, *100*
United States. *See also* California
    vinifera in, 19–21
    wine grapes for regions of, **26–30**
USDA, 65, 77, 144
USDA plant hardiness zones, 183

V

varietal aromas, 209
vats, primary fermentation and, 127–29
véraison
    Brix and, 114–15
    ripening process and, 108, 109
vertical cordon training, 51, *51*, 97, *97*
Vidals, 125, 145
vinegar (acetic acid), 121, 137
vinegarization, 170
vinegar-producing organisms, 152–53
vine(s). *See also* grapestock; pruning in first two years; pruning mature vines; training vines
    biblical references to, 14
    first-year growth and, 63–64
    grafted, 63
    growth of, explained, 70

number of, calculating, 38
parts of, 36, *36*
planting, 62–63, *62*
spacing of, 39–40, **40**
struggling, 11, 12
training to trellis, 71–75
on two-wire trellis, *59*
unpruned, growth of, 69, *69*
vigor and, 92–93
watering and protecting, 63
winterkill and, 76
vineyard. *See also* rows and aisles
    drainage, 47
    size of, computing, 37–38
vineyard management, overview or, 7
vineyard preparation, overview of, 6
vinifera. See *Vitis vinifera* (wine grape, classic)
vin nouveau. See new wine
vin parfait, 79
vintage(s). *See also* aging
    auspicious years and, 11
    exceptional, 17
    irrigation and, 68
    nonvintage wines and, 117, 195
    poor wines and, 117
virus(es)
    about, 239–240
    weeds and, 65
"viticultural areas," 21
Vitis labrusca, 13
Vitis rotundifolia (muscadine grape), 145. *See also muscadines* (*Muscadinia rotundifolia*)
Vitis vinifera (wine grape, classic)
    about, 12–13
    Brix readings and, 110
    in California, **33–34**
    on eastern seaboard, 19–21

pruning and, **83**
    in the South, 20
    training system for, 77
    in the United States, 19–21
    varieties, sampler of, 18
    on west coast, 20

W

Wagner, Bill, 11
Walthari method, 130
washing soda, 164, **164**
wasp trap, 241–42, *241*
watering vines. *See* irrigation
weather, 117. *See also* freeze danger; sunlight
Weaver, Robert, 12
weeds in beds, handling of, 65
west coast, vinifera on, 20
Weyrich, Arnaud, 189, 192
whiskey barrels, 128
white grapes
    pressing for fermentation, 141–43, *142*
    stemming and crushing, 125–26
white wines
    aging and, 170
    bottling of, 176
    carboys and, 122
    fruitiness and, 148
    must and, 121, 152, 153
    oxidation and, 123
    potassium metabisulfite and, 132
    sulfite and, 132
winds, prevailing, 49
wine appreciation courses, 17, 19
Wine Appreciation Guild, 214
wine cellar, 202–4
wine connoisseurs, 17, 114, 140
wine disorders, 170–72
wineglasses, *206*
    about, 206

rim of, wine evaluation and, 207–8, *208*

wine grapes. *See also Vitis vinifera* (wine grape, classic); *specific variety*
  allowing no fruit in first years, 75
  bagging clusters of, 242, *242*
  diseases of, 231–39
  evolution of modern, 13
  high-acid, 138
  most important decision and, 22
  origin of classic, 12–15
  pest-related damage to, 226–29
  ripeness and, 184
  sample berries and, 109, *109*
  soil and, 43–46
  for sparkling wine, 183–84
  tending crops, 108
  for U.S. regions, **26–30**
  varieties, sampler of, 18

wine-growing areas, 21–34. *See also* California; France; *specific region*
  American Viticultural Areas (AVAs), 23–25
  most important decision and, 22
  regional designations and, 21
  TTB viticultural areas, 22
  wine grapes for, U.S., **26–30**

Wine Institute, 131

winemaking. *See also* barrels; primary fermentation; secondary fermentation; sparkling wine
  about, 119–120, 123–24
  acidity, adjustment of/pH, 137–140
  airlocks and, 154, *154*, 155–57, *156*
  blending and, 173–74

cleanliness and, 126, 127
  cold stabilization, 159–160
  filtering and, 172
  fining and, 172–73
  first racking, 157–59
  harvest day summary, 141
  measurements before bottling, 177–78
  new wine and, 155
  primary fermentation vat and, 127–29, *128*
  stemming and crushing grapes, 120–21, 124–26
  sugar, adding to must, 134–37
  sulfite, adding to must, 129–134
  whites, pressing for fermentation, 141–43
  yeast, adding, 143–46

winemaking equipment. *See also* barrels; bottling; carboys; labeling
  corking and, 179–180, *179*
  pressing whites and, 141–42
  sterilizing solution for, 127

wine(s). *See also* sensory evaluation of wine; *specific type*
  dessert, 176
  natural, 135
  new, 152, 155
  nonvintage, 117, 195
  "nouveau," 149
  quality of, recognizing, 15–17
  quantity to make, 37–40
  resting of, 129
  secrets of good, 11–12
  "travel sick," 170

wine yeasts. *See* yeast(s)

winterkill, 76

wire, 57

Wirevise tensioners, 57–58

Y

yeast(s), 143–44
  adding, 143–46
  autolysis of, 190–93
  in-bottle fermentation and, 196
  cloudiness and, 149, 168
  encapsulated, 198
  en tirage and, 189–193
  off-flavored, 120
  oxidation and, 129, 191, 193
  sparkling wine and, 183–84, 186, 189–193, 195–96
  strains of, 143–44
  stuck fermentation and, 146
  temperatures and, 149
  types of, 144–46
  white table sugar and, 135
  wild, 129–130, 131

yeast extract, 196

Yquem, 12

Z

Zinfandel
  growing regions for, 18
  head training and, 96, *96*
  pruning and, 80
  skin contact times and, 148
  trellises and, 51

BROADEN YOUR BEVERAGE-MAKING TALENTS
with More Books from Storey

- -

Drink the Harvest by Nan K. Chase & DeNeice C. Guest
Make and preserve your own fresh juices, wines, teas, and more from fruit, vegetables, and herbs. From strawberry juice to dandelion wine, citrus peel tea, or watermelon mint syrup, this guide teaches you how to make nutritious drinks year-round.

The Homebrewer's Garden, 2nd Edition
by Joe Fisher & Dennis Fisher
From seed to suds, you can do it all with these easy instructions for growing your own hops, malt grains, and brewing herbs. The 29 specialty homebrew recipes will showcase your homegrown ingredients.

The Homebuilt Winery by Steve Hughes
Home winemakers will find everything they need to set up a home winery and construct their own equipment. Building plans and step-by-step instructions for 43 winemaking projects put the perfect setup within reach for everyone, regardless of skill level or budget.

Making Wild Wines & Meads by Pattie Vargas & Rich Gulling
Herbs, fruits, and flowers take center stage in these 125 unique recipes. Simple step-by-step instructions will guide you through the process of making exquisite elixirs with fresh ingredients from your local farm stand or backyard.

The Winemaker's Answer Book by Alison Crowe
From choosing grapes and macerating red varieties to sanitizing bottles, serving, and storing, this reassuring reference explains the entire winemaking process and offers proven solutions to every potential mishap.

- -

Join the conversation. Share your experience with this book, learn more about Storey Publishing's authors, and read original essays and book excerpts at storey.com. Look for our books wherever quality books are sold or by calling 800-441-5700.